Fictions of Well-Being

Fictions of Well-Being

Sickly Readers
and Vernacular Medical Writing
in Late Medieval
and Early Modern Spain

Michael Solomon

PENN

UNIVERSITY OF PENNSYLVANIA PRESS

PHILADELPHIA . OXFORD

Published by
University of Pennsylvania Press
Philadelphia, Pennsylvania 19104-4112

Printed in the United States of America
on acid-free paper
10 9 8 7 6 5 4 3 2 1

Library of Congress Cataloging-in-Publication Data

Solomon, Michael (Michael Ray)
Fictions of well-being : sickly readers and vernacular
medical writing in late medieval and early modern Spain /
Michael Solomon.
p.   cm.
Includes bibliographical references and index.
ISBN 978-0-8122-4255-3 (hardcover: alk. paper)
1. Medicine, Popular—History. 2. Medicine, Medieval—
Spain—History. 3. Medical literature—Spain—History.
I. Title.
[DNLM: 1. Consumer Health Information—history—
Spain. 2. History, 17th Century—Spain. 3. History, Early
Modern 1451–1600—Spain. 4. History, Medieval—Spain.
5. Literature, Medieval—history—Spain. 6. Literature,
Modern—history—Spain. 7. Writing—history—Spain.
WA 11 GS6 S689f 2010]
RC81. S665   2010
808'.06661—dc22   2010009048

for Victoria

CONTENTS

ILLUSTRATIONS

The idea for this book emerged on a cold winter day while I was researching vernacular medical works in Salamanca, Spain. As an academic and scholarly reader, my goal was to examine manuscripts and printed treatises that would offer clues about popular notions on health and illness. After several days, as often happens during the winter months, I developed a painful sore throat, a stuffy nose, and a relentless headache, the stubborn symptoms of a common cold. Curiously, with my minor illness came a shift in the way I was reading. I caught myself thumbing through the folia of large fifteenth-century compendiums on pharmaceuticals, not with the idea of documenting these medieval concoctions for my study, but rather with an eye toward finding a quick and effective cure for my disruptive illness. I was reading as a patient. Perhaps, I reasoned, some efficacious yet forgotten remedy lurked in these late medieval medical writings. The authors, compilers, and translators of these works were encouraging: "You will find in this work everything you need," wrote one author. Others offered enthusiastic and heartening comments about cures and recipes: "this one works marvelously," "this is a proven remedy," "I have given this cure to a thousand patients and all have been instantly cured." As I read these recipes and imagined their benefits for my aching throat and throbbing head, I myself suddenly became the immediate and final object of my study. I began to create what Bruno Latour calls a "technological project," a type of fiction—in this case, a fiction of my own imminent well-being based on the information gleaned from a medieval text.[1]

This book is about sickly readers, readers like myself who when confronted with the painful, disruptive, and often alienating conditions of physical disorder looked for relief in written sources. This book is also about the way certain physicians and medical writers attempted to refashion medical information so as to appeal to these readers. My hope is to explore a medical imaginary of well-being as kindled in the tropology of over three hundred vernacular sources. These include treatises, compendiums, manuals, plague tracts, summaries, dialogues, encyclopedias, and recipes—some discrete, occupying a single volume, others forming parts of larger treatises, and still others consisting of nothing more than a few lines inserted in the margins of diverse manuscripts.

My chronological point of departure is the beginning of the fourteenth century when the curricular changes at Montpellier and the subsequent rise of New Galenism began to filter into the Kingdom of Aragon by way of the renowned physician Arnau de Vilanova. More specifically, I begin around 1305 when Jaume II convinced Arnau to write him a simplified medical handbook, the *Regimen sanitatis ad inclitum regem Aragonum*, a work that would become one of the most popular medical guides for nonprofessionals in the Iberian Peninsula and throughout Europe. I have set the modern limits of the study at 1650. These dates roughly correspond with Nancy Siraisi's suggestion that historians of medicine treat the years between 1300 and 1600 as a distinct historical period; pointing to factors such as the Black Death, the revival of Greek learning, and the invention of the printing press, she argues that "by the early fourteenth century, important aspects of medicine had already acquired a shape they would retain until at least the late sixteenth century, and in some respects and some areas well beyond" ("Some Current Trends" 586–87). Forms of medical writing for nonprofessionals existed in Europe prior to the translation of Arnau's *Regimen*, and the desire to create health guides for the general public certainly did not end in the middle of the seventeenth century. Nevertheless, the three-hundred-fifty-year span of these texts offers me the opportunity to examine vernacular medical writing during several pivotal moments in the social history of western medicine, including the rise of medical licensing, the development of the modern hospital, the evolution of ontological notions of disease, the identification of new botanical materials from the New World, and the legitimization of medical subprofessions such as surgery and anatomy. This broad chronological space also allows me the opportunity to observe changes in the way medical information was disseminated from the limited realm of manuscript culture to a society characterized by the abundant circulation of printed material related to health and hygiene.

Given the dearth of general studies and critical bibliographies on the production of vernacular medical writing in late medieval and early modern Spain, my study necessarily and somewhat awkwardly serves the double purpose of conveying an informal inventory of vernacular medical writing while attempting to set forth a theory of reader response to this body of writing. Because of this, I have generally avoided lengthy close readings of individual works in favor of documenting broad tendencies and trends as they appear in a variety of texts over the period covered in the study. I recognize that this may leave some readers with the legitimate desire for more detailed readings of individual works. My hope is that this study will serve as a catalyst and paradigm for future work on the production, dissemination, and reception of medical writing for the lay reader.

A word about proper names, titles, translations, cited sources, and bibliographies is in order. For Castilian and Catalan authors, I have used the names as they appear in their medical treatises, adding only accent marks and regularizing the capitalization according to modern standards. The same is true for the titles of vernacular medical treatises. To reach a wider public, I have translated all sources into English, providing the original in the notes. Unless otherwise indicated, all transcriptions of vernacular medical works are my own. I have not attempted to regularize inconsistencies or to modernize the late medieval and early modern orthographic conventions with the exception of adding punctuation and capitalization, and regularizing the use of "u," "v," and "b" ("provecho" rather than "prouecho") according to modern standards. Although I bear full responsibility for these transcriptions, I have relied heavily on the extensive and ground-breaking corpus of medical texts published by the Hispanic Seminary of Medieval Studies to help me resolve paleographic difficulties. These electronic editions, given their machine-readable, and hence searchable format, have also provided invaluable assistance in my research.[2] I have embedded the bibliographic information for these transcriptions in the comprehensive bibliography of vernacular medical works (1300–1650) that appears in the end material of this study. I have also provided separate bibliographies for nonvernacular medical treatises and for secondary works.

As a final note, I want to insist that the following study serves as an introduction to a highly overlooked genre of vernacular writing from Spain. I have posited the singular claim that vernacular medical writing employed certain conventions and tropes that gratified a reader who, due to the compelling nature of biological disorder, was prone to highly self-reflective reading. I also recognize that it is difficult to speak with certainty about the practices of reading in the medieval and early modern period, practices that, according to Roger Chartier, "only rarely leave traces" and are scattered among innumerable singular acts (*The Order of Books* 1–2). How does one document those moments of pain, anxiety, and alienation that punctuate the experience of illness and send the patient to the pages of a medical book? This study, necessarily, emerges cautiously from my limited ability to imagine sickly readers of the past imagining their own well-being in the vernacular medical text.

Physicians, Sickly Readers, and Vernacular Medical Writing

During the later part of the Middle Ages, educated laypeople throughout Europe began turning to written sources to address their physical and hygienic needs. General medical compendiums, such as Bernard of Gordon's *Lilio de medicina*, and more specialized treatises, such as the gynecological work known as the *Trotula*, appeared in all the major European languages including English, French, German, Hebrew, Dutch, Castilian, and Catalan. As Pahta and Taavitsainen summarize, "Medical texts originating in learned contexts found their way into several vernaculars and gradually spread through society as they demonstrated their usefulness to all" ("Vernacularisation" 10). By the end of the sixteenth century, vernacular readers could find hundreds of printed translations, even many original works describing the basics of health and hygiene as well as complex procedures related to surgery and pharmacology. Whether caught in a life-threatening illness, troubled by a painful but minor condition, or uncertain as to the efficacy of their hygienic practices, these readers increasingly believed that information bound in manuscripts or books could provide remedies, relief, and some sense of control over the bewildering conditions of their bodies.

Such a reader was Queen Blanca d'Anjou (1280–1310), wife of Jaume II (1262–1327), ruler of the crown of Aragon. Having suffered extensively from five pregnancies and possessing an overall delicate health, she approached her husband's royal surgeon with an unusual request. Jaume had convinced his distinguished personal physician, Arnau de Vilanova, to write a simplified health guide for his personal use. Unfortunately for Blanca, Arnau had composed the *Regimen sanitatis ad inclitum regem Aragonum* in Latin, a language, we gather, that was difficult for the queen to read. She thus pleaded with the court surgeon, Berenguer Sarriera (ça Riera), to provide her with a vernacular translation.[1]

Berenguer appeared to be reluctant. "There are many words and ideas," he writes, "that cannot be put into romance."[2] His initial hesitation may have originated in more than the linguistic difficulties related to translating Latin medical writing into a vernacular tongue. As a highly trained surgeon, Berenguer would have been familiar with one of the basic principles that emerged from the rediscovery and rereading of Galen during the later part of the thirteenth century. New Galenism or Medieval Galenism, as it has been called, posited a form of radical individualism in which the preservation of the body was linked to the intrinsic nature, daily activities, and particular circumstances surrounding the individual (García-Ballester, "On the Origin" 115). As the title of Arnau's treatise suggests, the *Regimen sanitatis ad inclitum regem Aragonum* was written specifically with King Jaume's sanguine complexion in mind, not necessarily as an outline for universal hygiene. Berenguer would have acknowledged that, given the diversity among human beings, individual medical prescriptions for maintaining a specific patient's health could be useless or even dangerous when applied universally. But the Catalan surgeon was a practicing healer who understood that his livelihood and reputation depended on his ability to please his patients. He also knew that helping the patient to develop an optimistic disposition was an essential part of the art of healing according to the prevailing rules of medical deontology. A patient was more likely to benefit from a particular treatment if she believed it could be effective. Hence, Berenguer not only took to translating the little work, as his patient desired, he also modified the treatise by writing a prologue, inserting rubrics, and adding some marginal notes so as to make the treatise more useful for his patient. Perhaps caught up in the same enthusiasm that motivated Queen Blanca to ask for a translation, Berenguer also imagined that the work would be useful for a more extended public. Expanding on Hippocrates' first aphorism, he prefaced his translation with the following explanation:

> Given that the art of medicine is very long, and that wise and learned physicians have written about it extensively (such that the noble lords engaged in great affairs, not to mention the common people, cannot adequately understand it), the aforementioned master Arnau, in honor of the very noble lord Jaume the second, king of Aragon, has created this book to provide a rule for living in health and for arriving

at natural old age for those who desire to understand it and put it to use.[3]

The case of Queen Blanca and the surgeon Berenguer points to a social, medical, and literary phenomenon that I shall call "sickly reading." On one hand, we have a reader who, while anticipating or suffering from physical maladies, has envisioned that a particular book of medical information could restore her health and help her avoid future illnesses. On the other hand, we have a medical professional who responded to this need by offering to transform this information into a legible, abbreviated, ordered, and easy-to-use form. For the ailing reader, a vernacular medical treatise is more than just a collection of technical information; such a work implies that there is a degree to which the reader/patient can do "in text" or "with a text" what the physician normally would do "in person" or at the bedside. In the imagination of this reader, the vernacular medical treatise becomes a type of palpable instrument that, like all technological objects, encourages her to envision its possible use and benefits. Likewise, for the practicing physician, the creation of a vernacular treatise is more than just a way to serve his patients in absentia. The creation of such a work offers him a mechanism to promote his medical knowledge and skills while permitting him to imagine that the general public will continue to acknowledge the value of his most effective cures and useful advice, perhaps even beyond his professional or natural life. As I will argue in this study, vernacular medical writing from late medieval and early modern Spain emerged from the interrelated imperatives to address the immediate or future hygienic and pathological needs of the patient while promoting the reputation and learned credentials of the physician.

Vernacular Medical Writing in Late Medieval and Early Modern Spain

In traditional scholarship, vernacular medical writing has fallen into a disciplinary hinterland. Medical historians, concerned with describing breakthroughs in theory and therapeutics, have found little of interest in vernacular renderings of longstanding and often elementary medical knowledge. Literary historians, preoccupied with the singular genius of writers such as Rojas, Garcilaso, Quevedo, and Góngora, have resisted examining the rhetorical and narrative elements in works primarily identified as guidebooks and instruction manuals. Meanwhile, philologists, while often noting the lexical

innovations of these works, have seldom extended their research to the social and literary aspects of vernacular medical writing. And finally, medical
anthropologists, those who are perhaps best prepared to deal with the way
a patient would respond to medical information transmitted through texts,
have traditionally limited their attention to contemporary cultures and living
subjects, applying their theories and methods very infrequently to historical
contexts.[4]

Although scholars have produced several bibliographies of vernacular
medical and scientific writing in medieval and early modern Spain, there
have been no rigorous attempts to categorize these works and to identify their
common and diverging features.[5] Such a study is indeed necessary, and as a
preliminary step I have identified three broad categories of vernacular medical writing: (1) health guides and plague treatises that were theoretically based
on the Galenic system of non-natural hygiene and were explicitly designed
for use by patients; (2) professional or paraprofessional treatises designed for
surgeons, apothecaries, and less-educated medical practitioners such as bo-
nesetters and midwives, who could not read Latin; and (3) recipes (remedies,
experiments, secrets, and medicinal prayers) that circulated individually or
were incorporated into larger medical works. Although a more detailed description and enumeration of specific features—both formal and thematic—
is necessary to establish a coherent generic foundation for these works, two
overarching and interrelated traits characterize the various manifestations of
vernacular medical writing from plague tracts and *regimina* (health guides)
to treatises on pathology, surgical guides, and collections of recipes. First,
medical writers clearly envisioned that their works could be used by all readers regardless of their medical training; and second, they claimed that Christian charity and a deep concern for the public good motivated them in their
production of vernacular medical works.

Overwhelmingly, the implied reader of most vernacular medical treatises
is an ambiguous and all-encompassing everyman, a "tot hom," "qualquier
home," "cada uno," and "hombre común."[6] Authors fancied that their treatises would be used by "todos," "aquels qui ho volran" [those who so desire],
"qual quien lo leyere" [whoever might read it], and "cada vno que quiera"
[each one who desires].[7] Admittedly, not all vernacular medical treatises lend
themselves equally to a nonprofessional reading. Although we would think
that works designed for the exclusive use of patients, such as many health
guides and plague treatises, would best engage lay readers, even works designed for surgeons and paraprofessionals explicitly invited nonprofessionals

to read them. For example, Bernardino Montaña de Monserrate claims that his book on human anatomy will be "very useful and necessary for physicians and surgeons who want to perfect their skills, and pleasing for other discreet men who so desire to know the secrets of nature."[8] Likewise, López de Villalobos, whose *Sumario* was written specifically for the instruction of physicians, explains that this summary of Avicenna's *Canon* will be "useful and beneficial for the nobility and learned men in other disciplines."[9]

Some authors sensed concern that the distribution of medical information in the vernacular might be misused by the uneducated. Any opposition, however, quickly dissipated under the long-standing theological imperative to assist the poor. We see this attitude in early works such as Petrus Hispanus's enormously popular *Thesaurus pauperum* (1277), a medical handbook directed toward poor clergymen and scholars. Likewise, the translator of Bernard of Gordon's *Lilio de medicina* claims that the author will treat common problems and that the work can easily be used by the poor and humble.[10] With the outbreak of the plague in the middle of the fourteenth century, the dissemination of medical information came to be seen as an act of Christian charity. Jacme d'Agramont, for example, explains that he wrote his treatise on the plague out of "true love and charity" [verdadera amor e karitat] (*Regiment de preservació de pestilència* fol. 1r). In 1506, a bout of the plague in Seville motivated Diego Alvarez Chanca to write his *Tratado nuevo*, in which he pleads with God to help him write a treatise that will be useful for restoring health to the countless sufferers in his native city.[11] Physicians perceived the act of composing, compiling, simplifying, and translating medical information as a pious act. Citing Saint Gregory ("probatio dilectonis exhibitio en operis"), El Licenciado Forés claims that his plague tract, directed to the rich and poor of Seville, provides testimony of his love and charity (*Tratado útil* Salamanca fol. 1r). By the middle of the sixteenth century, with an increased preoccupation with social welfare, any author could easily justify the disclosure of medical information on the grounds that it would serve the needs of the poor.[12] Damián Carbón claimed that he was moved by charity ("movido de caridad") to write his treatise on obstetrics.[13] Likewise, Luis de Toro explains that he was inspired to write his little treatise on the merits and dangers of drinking chilled water by "the charity and obligation that I owe to my fellow man as a Christian."[14]

During the sixteenth century, the notion of one's responsibility to his or her country arose alongside charitable obligation as an additional motive for writing about medicine in the vernacular. "Experience that is communicated is nobler," Ruy Díaz de Ysla tells us in the beginning of his treatise on the pox, "and those instructed in science and the medical arts are obligated to serve their friends and countrymen through their writing."[15] By the sixteenth century, promoters of public health argued frequently with a nod toward the Aristotelian notion of *republica* that the written dissemination of information was necessary for the *utilitatem communem*. Such is the explicit motive behind the creation of Francisco Martínez de Castrillo's treatise on dentistry; persuaded by some of his friends, he was passionately moved to provide "some benefit for the republic."[16]

Sickly Reading and the Vernacular Medical Treatise

How did readers respond to these benevolent attempts to secure their physical well-being? What benefits could readers expect to obtain by engaging with a vernacular medical treatise? We may assume that readers of such works believed that the information contained in them, when properly applied, could remedy illness. This study, however, focuses on those moments prior to applying or using medical advice, when patients began to imagine that the recuperation or preservation of their well-being was to be found in the text itself. I acknowledge, as have many medical anthropologists, that every type of interaction between a healing professional and a patient may have therapeutic as well as hygienic and prophylactic value. For late medieval and early modern physicians and patients, even the acquisition of a medical treatise or the intention to read one factors into this extended concept of therapy. In its most exemplary form, nonprofessional medical reading consists of more than a routine appropriation (and subsequent application) of the information in the text; it begins with a rhetorical manipulation of the afflicted reader's imagination.

Medieval and early modern medical theorists deeply embraced the belief that the patient's health could improve or deteriorate based solely on the faculty of the imagination. In one of the earliest vernacular treatises on the plague, Jacme d'Agramont directly warned that "the imagination alone causes some diseases." Jacme offers a simple and frequently described experiment to prove his point: lay a wooden beam on the ground and a man will walk along it without any problem; place the beam high above the ground and the same man will fall, imagining that he will fall (*Regiment* fol. 12r). Medical deontologists warned that people often die simply because they imagine that their death is imminent. Physicians should thus avoid talking about death in the presence of the patient. Conversely, the physician's ability to compel the patient to acknowledge or imagine the physician's virtuous moral and professional character as well as the efficacy of his therapies was the most powerful instrument at his disposal. According to Alfonso Chirino, it is the patient's "ymaginaçión buena" [good imagination] that cures more patients than the physician himself (*Replicación Espejo de medicina* fol. 42v). So important was this "good imagination" in the healing process that venerable physicians even recommended that practicing physicians learn to lie if necessary to preserve it, or at least modify their manner of speaking to the patient so as not to produce the ill effects of pessimistic or alarming thoughts.[17]

With the idea of preserving or creating a salutary disposition in the patient, the most characteristic authors of vernacular medical treatises flood their works with claims of usefulness, insisting that what they have created will be easy to read, straightforward, and purged of medical jargon and longwinded discussions. They argue that the material in these works will be divided into chapters and indexed, making it easy to find the desired information. The authors assure readers that the medical advice and remedies have been developed following extensive book study and in collaboration with other celebrated physicians. The authors often detail their medical training and years of successful practice, and offer the reader abundant claims of proven efficacy, including frequent anecdotes, stories, and case studies of patients (frequently in the hundreds) whom they have successfully cured. Although I will not evaluate the potency or performance of any of the drugs or therapies described in medieval and early modern medical writings, the rhetorical framing of these medicines clearly attempted to please readers and capture their imagination. In this sense, a vernacular medical work gained an undeniable placebo function, suggesting to readers that the very possession of a piece of medical writing could be the key to their enduring well-being.

The abundant tropes of usefulness, professional competence, and efficacy fell upon the ears and eyes of a highly motivated implied reader, one deeply moved by the compelling and often overwhelming conditions of illness. At the heart of this study is the notion that late medieval and early modern vernacular medical texts appealed to readers who were experiencing or anticipating those unwanted bodily conditions that we have come to characterize as disease.[18] These "sickly readers," as I shall call them, approached medical texts with an eye (and other ailing parts) toward restoring or preserving the body. Unlike members of other interpretive communities, sickly readers crossed geographical, religious, class, and gender boundaries, gaining membership

not on the basis of literary competence, or past experience, but rather on
account of certain bodily conditions that were compelling enough to divert
the object of interpretation from the text and its direct references toward the
readers and the immediate condition of their bodies.

Although reception theory—from Eco, Jauss, and Fish to Bennett and
Malarox—has developed extensively over the past thirty years, to my knowledge there have been no general considerations of the way a reader's physical
condition may determine the interpretation of a text.[19] I argue that a reader
who is ill or suffering from bodily pain has the tendency to approach a text
differently from a healthy reader. Although it is dangerous to posit a single
and transhistorical response to bodily affliction, we can generalize that the
onset of illness powerfully encourages the ailing subject to engage in inten-
sive moments of self-reflection.[20] Sickness or the threat of illness encourages
the afflicted to consider the social significance of their disorders and seek
answers to questions related to the "hows" and the "whys" of their conditions.
Such self-reflection necessarily forms part of the ailing subject's struggle for
meaning and recuperation. As Michael Taussig pointed out in his seminal
article, "Reification and Consciousness of the Patient," the "sick person is one
who is plunged into a vortex of the most fundamental questions concerning
life and death. The everyday routine of more or less uncritical acceptance of
the meaning of life is sharply interrupted by serious illness which has its own
pointed way of turning all of us into metaphysicians and philosophers" (3).
When the sick approach a text, they do so enveloped in the conditions of the
body and with a heightened desire to restore order, eradicate the disconcert-
ing phantoms of despair, and above all to eliminate those symptoms—pain
and diminishing physical and mental capacities—that relentlessly tell them
that life is out of whack. These readers are anxious, impetuous, and eager to
assimilate information that would help them understand and remedy their
unwanted physical status. In this study, the phenomenon of sickly reading
manifests itself fully when the ailing subject approaches a textual object with
the purpose of initiating a therapeutic or hygienic strategy. In its most fundamental sense, it is not the medical content (hygienic advice, recipes, and
etiologies) or even the form of exposition (organization and rhetorical conventions) that distinguish popular from professional medical writing, but
rather the utility that the ailing or hygienically conscious reader imagines the
text will offer. Sickly reading emerges as such when the afflicted either invents
or accepts the text's explicit claims that the work in hand will serve his or her
immediate medical needs. The value of the vernacular medical treatise lies in

the ability to help this sickly reader develop a healing strategy, a technological project of returning from a state of illness, and a fiction of his or her imminent well-being.

Sickly reading, therefore, is highly self-referential. It operates similar to the consumption of myth, on what Roland Barthes in *Mythologies* identifies as a second level of signification. For the sickly reader, words, advice, and instructions in a medical text are immediately incorporated into an extended reading of the patient's body. Any medical information gleaned from a text is destined to assist in the projection of a particular strategy that is specific to the reader's bodily condition. Take for example the following text from Alfonso Chirino's *Menor daño de la medicina* [The least damage from medicine]:

> The flowers, roots, and leaves of white lilies are beneficial for all disorders of the nerves. [Çuçenas flores y raizes y fojas provechan para todo mal de nervjos.] (fol. 93r)

As a simple exchange of medical information, the text is remarkably straightforward; lilies aid nervous disorders. Sickly reading, however, only begins with the reception of medical instructions. It appropriates the idea of the salutary benefits of the lily and incorporates this idea, often embellished with belief in its efficacy, into a projection or plan for the ailing subject's physical recovery or defense from future ailments.

Sickly reading is best described as a stance or approach to a text in which the ailing subject uses the reading process to create a healing strategy. Bear in mind that I am referring to a provisional or temporary reading posture rather than a habitual practice of reading. Likewise, sickly reading is not necessarily restricted to a particular type of text. Any kind of work could plausibly be the object of a sickly reading if the patient approached the text seeking comfort or a solution for his or her pathological condition. In fact, it is possible for a reader to carry out a sickly reading and a nonsickly reading of the same text.

Although I have confined my examination to texts written in the vernacular (Spanish, Catalan, and Portuguese), I recognize that there is no reason why a treatise written in Latin, Arabic, or Greek could not have produced various sickly reading responses, especially if such a work encouraged the reader to envision a utility in reading the text. Without question, there were many learned nonprofessionals, such as the aforementioned Jaume II, who, relying on their knowledge of a learned language, could have read a nonvernacular text with the desire to remedy a personal health matter. Nevertheless,

I argue that, by employing the vernacular language, medical writers created a unique textual space for a clinical encounter between patient and physician. The very presence of the vernacular forcefully told readers and patients that they belonged in the text and that this space had been designed for them. It constituted the textual equivalent of an over-the-counter drug—an entity that has been developed by doctors yet requires no secondary professional intervention to justify its use.

The idea that a medical treatise, even in a simplified form in the vernacular, could be used by the general public might appear to be nothing more than a pious (or patriotic) fiction. Indeed, one of the criticisms modern scholars have leveled against the notion of a "popular" medical treatise is that relatively few individuals could actually read such a text. Studies on literacy in sixteenth-century Spain point to a society that was still largely molded by orality. In spite of increased availability of written works, the explosion of *cartillas* and *catecismos* designed to teach people to read, and the growth of new grammar schools such as those founded by the Jesuits, the level of literacy in Spain was limited (Viñao Frago 41). It is in this state of "semialfabetación," marked by various levels of literacy and diverse reading abilities, that the medical treatise flourished, in large part because reading in the fifteenth and sixteenth centuries never ceased to be collaborative and collective. Our modern concept of the solitary bookworm turning pages in the isolation of his or her study does not sufficiently describe the situations in which the popular medical treatise was used in early modern Spain. More importantly, the reading of a medical treatise in this semiliterate society operated on the interplay between a system of signs (the medical text) and a system of objects (the physical book).

The phenomenon of sickly reading begins on the level of the textual object itself as patients grant an element of functionality to the medical codex, book, or folio. For the sickly reader, a medical treatise is a tool or instrument designed to assist the user, as would any quotidian object, such as a knife or sewing needle. Every instrument has the potential to suggest an idea (myth or fiction) of its implied function. Through its form, weight, and physical morphology, an object simultaneously informs the user of its intended or possible application and provokes the user to project a potential use. Take the drawings of the surgical instruments featured in Giovanni Andrea Della Croce's Latin surgical treatise published in Venice in 1573 (see Figure 1). Although we may ignore the more specific functions of these tools, only the least perceptive observer would fail to recognize that these are devices for sawing or cutting: on

10 apud prifcos ad rimas oblongas tollendas ufum fuiffe, quæ præfertim tranf-
uerfim feruntur , & fano ofsi conterminant . de quibus Auicenna dicebat,
quandoque abfoluitur opus fubtili ferra , quam eam effe arbitramur cuius
imaginem inferius delineauimus;quanquàm per fubtilem ferram, cum Hippocra
te,ferratum modiolum intelligere aliqui uideantur,dum dicit . At fi inter initia
ad ægrum non accefferis,fed homo alteri priustraditus,minus tempeftiuè tibi cō
mittatur,acutiori ferra os protinus excidere,ufque ad menibranas conuenit.fub
inde autem tollendum ferramentum eft, & demiffo fpecillo , eiuscircuitus confi
derari debet;circuitus uerò non nifi a tereti inftrumento prouenire folet, ut illud
eft,quod Græci chinycidam,aut cænitium,& Latini modiolum uocant; dè quo in
20 frà multa fumus dicturi. Igitur diuerfa eft fubtilis ferra Auicennæ, à tereti ferra
Hippocratis; & quia Auicenna terebrorumdiftinctè hiftoriam commemorauit,
ideò perfubtilem ferram hic inftrumenta fimilia intellexiffe credendum eft, quæ
in aliquibus fracturis utilisfima , ac apud chirurgos peritos obferuatisfima funt ;
faciunt adhuc in leuioribus,ac profundioribus fedibus ac rimis ad offa lenienda,
fi inæqualitates contineant,afperitatesdelendas, & fruftula conterenda ; fiqui-
dem,ut offe detecto caro coalefcat, circumhæreatque omni parti , illud nitidum
effe debet. id inde maxime eueniet,fi neque fordes,neque oleofa fubftantia ade-
rit,atque quælibet uitiati,ac detecti ofsis pars planè pura,ac ficca fuerit. Serrula-
rum imagines uariæ funt,nam aliquæ breues,aliquæ longiores,aliquæ planæ, ali
30 quæ afperæ & limatæ,aliquæ rectæ,aliquæ conuexæ & curæ:fubtiles tamen omnes effe debent,dentibus benè acuminatis,& proprio manubrio firmiter infertæ;
ualent in amplo offe quod tundendum uenit, interdum acuto fcalpro prius fulci
parandi funt nè huc,aut illuc ferra delabatur;fæpe pedetentim,fecura manu, fola
ferra opus perfici poteft.Sed danda opera erit,cum in primis in omnibus,tum vero maximè in his,quæ circa cranij partes fiunt operationibus , vt breui tempore,
& citra dolorem,tum denique,ut tutisfime cures. Tutisfimè autem curabis, vbi
quod aggredieris omnino abfolues,uel fin minus,cubantem faltem non læ das. ci
tò vero iucude & commode rem expedies,cum tui habita ratione,tum illius , qui
curatur,inftrumentorū,ac luminis.Serrularum formæ hæ funt, quas paratas plu-
40 es habere tenemur.

SERRVLÆ.

DE

Figure 1. Surgical saws. Giovanni Andrea Della Croce, *Chirurgiae* (Venetiis 1573).
Biblioteca Universidad Complutense, Madrid (fol. 34r).

one end we have a space used for gripping, and on the other a serrated metal edge. The exact function of blades' particular form (serration and curvature) eludes the nonprofessional. We can only imagine, only project, how we might employ these instruments in a surgical procedure. If our level of competence, or user literacy, were greater, if we could read the Latin text above illustrations, we would learn that each tool has a specific application. Our inability to accertain the prescribed use for these tools would not undermine our ability to develop a use for these instruments. The use (performance) of any object is not dependent on a high or "proper" level of user competency. Everyone is free to invent a purpose for an object and, if the need arises, to enact an imagined task for it.

Sixteenth-century inquisitorial records describe such an imagined use. An illiterate woman healer (*metgessa*) from Valencia developed a treatment in which she projected the pages of the medical text through a mirror and onto the patient's body.[21] Clearly, this is not the way the author of this treatise envisioned that his work would be used. The arguments, descriptions, remedies, and recipes were to be read and, once understood, applied to the ailing body. But as Michel de Certeau reminds us, the "reader takes neither the position of the author nor an author's position. He invents in texts something different from what they 'intended.' He detaches them from their (lost or accessory) origins. . . . He combines their fragments and creates something un-known in the space organized by their capacity for allowing an indefinite plurality of meanings" (*Practice of Everyday Life* 169).

What Certeau attributes to the reading of a text can also apply to the use of a textual object in its tangible and palpable form. Who has not occasionally used a book as a paperweight, as a step to reach objects, or as a doorstop? Every philologist is familiar with anecdotes and legends of needy monks who used medieval manuscripts as heating fuel or to fulfill their hygienic needs. The truth is that one does not have to know how to read to be able to use a book. Hence, in the most extreme cases, the user of a medical treatise does not need to read the information transmitted through the text to create a mode of utility for the textual object. The *metgessa*'s ingenuity lies in her ability to construct a use—any use—out of an object at once material and discursive. It is my contention that sickly readers, highly motivated by the onset or threat of illness and its characteristic conditions of dysfunction, alienation, and pain, embraced the physical textual artifact and its encouraging rhetoric, and began to posit therapeutic or hygienic uses for this object.

Such "fictions of well-being," fashioned on the verge of illness or in the throes of infirmity, emerged directly from late medieval and early modern popular medical writing whose rhetorical and discursive mechanisms predisposed and oriented readers toward reading postures in which the afflicted addressed their immediate or imminent biological conditions in the form of technological projections of well-being. In this study I hope to draw attention to the rhetorical, discursive, narrative, and material conventions that medical authors exploited to help stimulate readers' imaginations and encourage them to believe that the work in hand, be it an entire treatise or nothing more than a brief note in the margins of a single folio, could cure their ailments and serve as a prophylactic resource against future ailments. To this end, I will examine in detail three general technological projects, or "fictions of well-being," that vernacular medical writers encouraged the reader to develop.

In the first chapter, I examine the way vernacular medical writers reformulate and structure medical information so as to convince readers of its therapeutic and prophylactic usefulness, encouraging these readers to believe that they can effectively and easily apply the contents of the work to their particular biological conditions regardless of previous training in medicine. Writers promote the idea of utility by emphatically claiming that their treatises are brief, ordered, indexed, and cast in simplified prose and succinct explanations that allow anyone to find with ease useful information. I argue that the practice of summarizing, modifying, reducing, extracting, and in general managing medical information was a habitual function of learned medical authors who struggled to reformulate the extensive work of Galen and its reemergence in Avicenna's *Canon* for pedagogical ends. Although such a practice was originally developed to aid student physicians, the simplification of medical information became increasingly directed toward the general public. With great confidence, authors exploited this praxis in their creation of vernacular medical treatises, claiming loudly that their works were extremely accessible, easy to use, and effective. At the heart of these arguments, authors frequently offered a passionate defense of Romance as a legitimate vehicle for medical instruction, arguing that for the transmitting of efficacious knowledge the vernacular was as capable as Latin or Greek.

Perhaps the most stunning claim of utility that these authors make is that their treatises can be used independently of practicing physicians, suggesting that with the book in hand, the patient can do what was otherwise accomplished with the physician at the patient's bedside. They stress that many times patients find themselves in places where no professional medical attention is available; in such times, these authors argue, the vernacular treatises will prove to be a priceless artifact, capable of providing the necessary information to remedy the reader's maladies. In this regard, the author often reminds readers of the deplorable diseased status of humankind. According to these writers, pain, suffering, ailments, afflictions, and threats to well-being greet readers at every turn. There is nothing more valuable than good health, these authors claim, and it is imperative that readers take steps to preserve good health as if it were a priceless jewel. The most expedient way to accomplish this is to pay heed to the counsel and precepts embedded in the useful organization of a vernacular treatise.

I dedicate the final part of this chapter of fictions of utility to an analysis of Nicolás Monardes's sixteenth-century reformulation of Juan de Aviñón's fourteenth-century professional treatise, *Sevillana medicina*. Monardes's adaptation offers us a unique opportunity to see the way an author, zealously engaged in promoting health to the public, reformulated for a lay reader a treatise originally designed for use by medical students.

In the second chapter of this study, I confront the ethical and therapeutic problems that were thought to arise when a written work served as a surrogate for a bedside medical professional. I show how authors avoided anonymous expositions of strictly medical information, seeking vigorously to establish a clear authorial persona for the reader. Packing their works with autobiographical details, stories of successful cures, and the details surrounding the invention of innovating therapies, authors attempted to establish a clear presence in the text that compensated for their absence at the bedside. Many authors enthusiastically garnished their own opinions with extensive comments from reputable physicians and medical theorists. In this way, these authors complied with a deontological principle that promoted medical practice as a collaborative activity among medical professionals.

Justified by the belief that making the patient trust the practitioner was an essential element in the healing process, authors exploited the vernacular treatise to promote themselves and solidify their reputation. A vision of heroic medical practice emerges in many vernacular works in which dedicated practitioners described themselves as fearless warriors defending the general public against the bellicose onslaught of disease. They often represented themselves as solitary heroes, struggling tirelessly against incompetent healers and stubborn maladies, only to emerge triumphant with an extraordinary cure. In this sense, I will argue that writing physicians used the vernacular treatises as a device to reinforce their often tenuous reputation as effective healers. There was no profession wrought with more uncertainty than that of a practicing physician whose successful cures could instantly be forgotten in the wake of an unsuccessful encounter with an ailing patient. The vernacular medical treatise gave these physicians the opportunity to document their credentials while broadcasting their most triumphant acts of healing.

In the third chapter, I examine the rise of a new pharmaceutical imaginary in which material medicaments become the preferred form of medical therapy among patients. I explore the rhetoric of the medical recipe and its ability to encourage patients with claims of proven efficacy and multiple uses. In opposition to the tenets of Galenism and its therapeutic imperative to treat each patient individually, many new drugs and concoctions promised universal effectiveness. Patients eagerly responded to these claims and found comfort in the tangible nature of pharmaceutical therapy. I argue along with anthropologists that the charm of medicines lies in their ability to be warehoused, bartered, and redistributed, offering patients freedom from physicians and immediate access to therapy. In this sense, I argue that vernacular medical writing, in the form of an entire treatise or a few lines written on a scrap of paper, acquired the same appeal as the very medications described therein.

By way of conclusion, I dedicate the final chapter to a reflection on the vernacular medical treatise's participation in an emerging culture of pathology, one plagued increasingly with the anxiety of disease and perceived threat of latent bodily disorders. Specific names for what once had been ambiguous or imprecisely defined ailments merged with the dreaded names of new epidemic diseases such as syphilis, forming fictions of ill-being in the minds of patients. Vernacular works, especially treatises on pathology, in effect, began to look like a hypochondriac's handbook, detailing innumerable infirmities ready to develop at any moment from the top of the head to the tip of the reader's toes.

CHAPTER ONE

Fictions of Utility

Near the end of the fourteenth century, a physician from the Kingdom of Aragon compiled an extraordinary little treatise on the health benefits and physical dangers related to sexual intercourse. The author advertises the special utility of his work:

> The works that treat fucking are many, but I have never come across a complete treatment of the subject. Rather I have found that most works are so rambling and digressive that they cause more harm than good. I want, therefore, to speak on this question completely and clearly so that all men who so desire can profit from it.[1]

It is not the focused subject matter that makes the *Speculum al foderi* unique. Galen, Avicenna, Constantine the African, and even Maimonides recognized that coitus served a hygienic function within the paradigm of the non-naturals (or the humoral balancing of physical properties) and wrote extensively on the benefits and dangers related to sexual intercourse.[2] The *Speculum al foderi*, or "A Guide for Fuckers," as some critics have suggested it might be literally translated (Jacquart and Thomasset 135), is an astounding treatise in its explicit attempt to adapt medical information for the general public. The author compiled information from various sources, summarized it, translated it into Catalan/Valencian, and organized it into chapters for easy consultation.[3]

On the level of content, the author of the *Speculum* fulfilled his promise, providing the reader with information on the benefits and dangers of sexual intercourse, remedies for impotence, recipes for aphrodisiacs, and descriptions of coital positions (twenty-five in all). It is not, however, the medical information that would have initiated a sickly reading of this treatise. Before the reader could imagine how the regular expulsion of semen, according to his age and temperament, would clear his mind and calm his anxious and angry moods, before he could consider fully the dangers such as fatigue, blindness, and baldness that were related to excessive coitus, and before he could envision himself achieving a healthy erection by applying one of the concoctions described in the final chapter, the reader would have already convinced himself that the little treatise might provide some benefit. What makes the *Speculum* a remarkable treatise is its explicit attempt to encourage nonprofessionals to take advantage of its medical information. Unlike the anonymous *Liber minor de coitu*, the work's major Latin source, or Constantine the African's *Liber de coitu*, the author of the *Speculum* provided a compelling preface designed to convince the reader that the work in its vernacular form would be accessible for all.[4] He also translated the titular and key word "coitus" as "foder," a popular and perhaps vulgar rendering of the clinical Latin term for sexual intercourse, thus clearly alerting readers that the work was directed toward the layman.[5]

One of the fictions that first emerge from an encounter between a sickly reader and a medical treatise is the idea that the text in the sickly reader's hand can be useful, beneficial, and even necessary for recovering or preserving one's health. The introduction to the *Speculum al foderi* clearly signals a trend, and subsequent authors of vernacular medical treatises would thus be preoccupied with convincing the public that their treatises were useful. Exploiting various rhetorical tropes and highly self-referential comments on their works, these authors encouraged the sickly reader to believe that their treatises were accessible, succinct, focused, ordered, indexed, and, above all, easy to use.

Making Utility

The medical writer's process of refashioning information for nonprofessionals began by embedding various tropes of usefulness into the titles and prefaces of vernacular works. The sickly reader who approached one of these texts would immediately find titles bearing terms such as *útil* "useful," *utilidad* "utility," and *utilísimo* "very useful," or *provecho* "benefit," *provechoso* "beneficial," and *provechosísimo* "very beneficial." The title of Alvarez Chanca's plague treatise informed the reader that the work was "no less useful than necessary" (*Tratado nuevo, no menos útil que necessario* [1506]). El Licenciado

Forés straightforwardly referred to his work as a "useful and very beneficial treatise" (*Tratado útil y muy provechoso . . .* [1507]). In the title of his health guide for nobles, Luis Lobera de Avila identified subject matter covered in the book as "very useful things" (*Libro de las quatro enfermedades cortesanas que son catarro, gota arthetica, sciatica, mal de piedra y de otras cosas utilísimas* [1544]). Likewise, the title of Girolamo Manfredi's book on medicine and natural philosophy told readers forthrightly that the work contains "many things that are very beneficial for the preservation of one's health" (*El porque libro de problemas en que se da razones naturales de muchas cosas provechosissimo para conservación de la salud . . .* [1581]). The title of Antonio Girualt's plague treatise is more directly described as "a very useful, speedy, and easy remedy for preventing and curing the plague" (*Utilissim, promte y fecil remey e memorial per preservarse y curar de la peste* [1587]).

Throughout their prologues and prefatory material, authors of vernacular medical texts emphasize that the work will be of great benefit and utility for the reader. Reiterating the intention of the author of the *Speculum al foderi* that all men "can profit" from his work (e que es pusque[n] aprofitar d'ell), Francisco Núñez de Coria, in his *Tractado del uso de las mugeres* (1586), explains that the application of the subject matter in the treatises will produce "no small utility, using it as one should for the health of the body."[6] Arias de Benavides tells us he will reveal things that he has discovered and proven to be "valuable and beneficial for my patients."[7] In the early sixteenth century, the house of Andrés Burgos in Granada published a *regimen*, which Maestre Gil, a physician from Spain who served in the French court, had translated into Spanish. With the idea that such a work would provide some "benefit and utility" [provecho y utilidad] for the people of Granada, the publisher divided the work into chapters, added some additional recipes, and included the *Virtudes del romero* [The virtues of rosemary] (attributed to Arnau de Vilanova). To make the work even more accessible, he modernized the treatise, which he claimed was originally written in poor and "archaic romance" [romançe viejo].[8] And the Portuguese translator of Johannes Jacobi's *Regimento proueytoso contra ha pestenença* (1476) told his readers that "Here begins a good regiment, very necessary and very beneficial for the living and for the preservation of their health" (fol. 2r). Indeed, given the immediate and universal threat of epidemics and communicable diseases in general, authors of plague treatises were particularly keen on having their readers recognize the utilitarian value of their work.

We find the same idea expressed in the prefatory material of sixteenth-century medical texts such as in the mandatory *aprobaciones, privilegios,* and *licencias.* Philip II, for example, explains that Martinez de Castrillo's work on dental hygiene, *Tratado breve y compendioso sobre la maravillosa obra de la boca y dentadura* (1570), contains "many cures and many tested and necessary things that will result in very great benefit and utility" for those who want to use them.[9] The *privilegio* at the beginning of Díaz de Ysla's *Tractado llamado fructo de todos los auctos: contra el mal serpentino* (1542) announces emphatically that the work is for treating the pox and "is beneficial and very necessary and should be published."[10]

Medieval and early modern authors emphasized that the utility of a vernacular medical treatise lay in its simplicity; readers could easily understand their written advice and quickly apply their remedies without needless complication. "I intend to treat things that are common, simple and beneficial," Bernard of Gordon tells his readers in the introduction of his *Lilio de medicina* (1495).[11] Not only are the matters described in these works simple to understand, they are also easy to apply. Cristóbal Méndez, author of the *Libro del ejercicio corporal* (1553), claims that he has sought out "the simplest thing that one can do to achieve bodily health."[12] When discussing diagnostics, remedies, and hygienic strategies, authors frequently employ adverbs and adjectives such as *fácilmente* [easily] and *fácil* [easy]. Jerónimo Soriano, in his *Libro de experimentos médicos, fáciles y verdaderos* (1599), says that he will only include remedies that are "easy to make": "I do not trouble myself with including those that are difficult and laborious to create."[13] Similarly, Juan Cornejo explains that his clear and straightforward style of writing will allow anyone to "easily and surely" understand and take advantage of his work.[14] And Nicolás Monardes reassures prospective readers of the *Sevillana medicina* (1545) that, if they take a closer look at seemingly unintelligible words, they will "easily" be able to understand them.[15]

The author of the *Speculum al foderi* decried what he perceived as the dangerous ramblingly and divergent nature of many medical treatises: "los trobe desviats e escampats en manera que era major lo dany que havien que lo profit" (47). He suggested that a popular medical treatise would be easier to use if it were brief and focused.[16] Later authors frequently explained that they reduced and summarized larger discussions and eliminated superfluous material. The nonprofessional reader was thereby spared getting lost in long-winded discussions, complicated arguments, tiresome debates, and what Bernardino Montaña de Monserrate refers to as a "prolixity of doctrine" (*Libro de anathomía del hombre* [1551] fol. 9v). The concern that detailed and extensive writing might undermine the nonprofessional's ability to understand the text appears frequently in the prologues of many vernacular medical works. Juan Cornejo, in organizing his treatise, limited his advice to the control of two hygienic principles: diet and bowel movements.

> Being a physician and being in great need of health, seeing myself sur-
> rounded by diseases and enemies and burdened with so many apho-
> risms, so many medical precepts, so many recipes for medication, so
> many apothecary apparatuses, so many empirical and rational cures,
> so much juice and smoke from tobacco, so many poisonous concoc-
> tions, oils to induce vomiting, mineral powders, potable gold, and the
> alchemists' fifth essence in a perpetual battle of fearful confusion, and
> considering the brevity and simplicity of the two parts, definition and
> demonstration—the truth doesn't require many words, for it consists
> of one indivisible point—I resolved to understand them, comprehend
> them, perfect them, and modify them in a style and form so clear and
> plain that any mind can easily understand them; and with an exposi-
> tion so easy and certain that a prudent man, without fear, can use and
> benefit from them.[17]

References to brevity also greet the sickly reader prominently in the titles of many vernacular treatises. Andrés de Laguna titled his plague treatise a "brief discourse"; Agustín Farfán succinctly named his work a "brief treatise on medicine"; Francisco Ximénez de Carmona offers his readers a "brief treatise" on the virtues of water; Pedro Barba identified his plague treatise as a "brief and clear summary."[18] In their prologues and prefatory material, au-thors emphasized the abbreviated nature of their work by referring to their treatises as a "little work" (*obrezilla, librito, pequeñuelo trabajo*) or directly as "this brief treatise."[19] For example, Bernardino Montaña de Monserrate insists in his work on anatomy that he will speak as briefly as he can "with-out allowing the brevity to obscure the doctrine."[20] The Castilian translator of Marsilio Ficino's treatise on the plague tells us that the author will "leave out long-winded and taxing disputes" [disputas agudas y prolixas] and, re-specting the norms of brevity, will limit himself to supporting his cures and preventative strategies with a few sound arguments.[21] Alfonso Chirino an-nounces that he created the *Menor daño de la medicina* as a "brief compen-dium of medicine."[22] And Luis Mercado states that his intention was to write a treatise on orthopedics with "few and clear words" [con breves y claras palabras] (*Instituciones para el aprovechamiento y examen de los algebristas* [1539] fol. 3v).

These claims of brevity are often supported by the physical size of the treatises. Some are as few as one or two folios, such as the anonymous *Remedios para la pestilencia* [Remedies for the plague] (1515). Plague treatises are notably small, most containing from two to fifteen folios.[23] Although usually more extensive than plague treatises, *regimina*, or health guides, also appeared in abbreviated formats. The Vatican manuscript of Arnau's *Regiment de sanitat* consists of nine folios, while the Catalan translation of Johannes de Toleto's *Regiment de sanitat* occupies only four.[24] Although the number of folios is relative to the size of the codex, a vernacular health guide of even eighty or so folios, such as Lobera de Avila's *Banquete de nobles caballeros e modo de vivir desde que se levantan hasta que se acuestan . . .* (1530), is a far cry from compendious works such as Avicenna's *Canon*, whose typical Latin translation consisted of over one million words on more than 250 folios in forebodingly small print.[25]

Declarations of brevity combined with the small physical size of these treatises no doubt fostered the assumption that one could acquire medical knowledge quickly through a highly condensed text. This idea would have stood in opposition to the well-known notion that professional medical competency is obtained only after dedicated study of the canonical, and often extremely large, compendiums of medicine. "Art is long," according to medieval readings of Hippocrates' first aphorism, not only because it is capable of determining truth beyond the limitations of personal experience, but because it requires a long time to learn. Juan de Aviñón explains:

> Hippocrates said that life is short, art is long, judgment grave, time brief, and proof doubtful. The reason that this art [the art of medicine] is long, according to Boethius, is because it is divided into seven parts, and each part requires a long time to acquire.[26]

For some writers of vernacular medical treatises, the unwieldiness of large medical works had the effect of discouraging their use. Bernardino Montaña de Monserrate complains passionately that many errors are made because the treatises of ancient and contemporary authors on anatomy are so "frightfully long" that even if readers were to study them during the course of a lifetime, they would not be capable of knowing all that is contained in them; as a result, many physicians simply stop reading them.[27] An examination of medical instruction in the late middle ages and Renaissance reveals that medical pedagogues had struggled with this very dilemma for centuries. This was particularly true of attempts to assimilate into medical training what has been called New Galenism, the incorporation of Galen's technically complex, repetitive, opinionated, and often rambling medical writings. Even a work such as Avicenna's *Canon*, which provided a much-needed framework for Galen's theory, was so large that it became virtually unmanageable (McVaugh, ed., *Tractatus de intentione medicorum* 131). The history of medical training from the thirteenth century can be plotted as an ongoing attempt to reduce, summarize, organize, and clarify medical information and, in general, make it more useful and easier to acquire. As Nancy Siraisi has shown, by the sixteenth century, Avicenna's *Canon* had gone through drastic abbreviations and rearrangements, which often reduced the original text and full Latin translation to a highly compact list of aphorisms that could easily be committed to memory ("Changing Fortunes" 21).[28] This is the organizing principle behind López de Villalobos's *Sumario de la medicina* (1498), an early vernacular attempt not only to abbreviate the *Canon*, but also to render it in verse to facilitate its memorization.

Already convinced of the value of an abbreviated format for disseminating medical information for students, medical writers took matters a step further by creating truncated instructions on medicine and health expressly for use by nonprofessionals. These authors recognized, however, that there was an inherent danger in such reduced presentation: lay people might attempt to make a diagnosis or prescribe a therapy based on extremely limited knowledge gleaned from treatises. A solution was to be found in the distinction between knowledge that pertained to a "regiment of preservation" (hygiene) and knowledge that pertained to a "regiment of cure" (therapeutics). Nonprofessionals could be entrusted with the former but were advised against pursuing the latter. Jacme d'Agramont makes this clear at the beginning of his plague treatise:

> Without any danger, all men can use this treatise without a physician
> as a regiment for preserving their health. But the regiment for curing
> is reserved for the physician, because anyone who does not know the
> art of medicine could easily err.[29]

Physicians, therefore, could justify a succinct textual dissemination of basic principles related to preserving the reader's health as long as they avoided discussion of matters treating therapy. Indeed, many of the treatises that fall under the category I am defining as a popular medical treatise deal extensively with instructing patients on how to establish control of their diet, sleep, exercise, bathing, and bowel movements. But limiting medical information to the realm of non-natural hygiene, or the daily regulation of the body, proved to be more an ideal than a reality. There are very few vernacular medical treatises that do not contain at least a handful of pharmaceutical and practical therapies for various ailments. In fact, as writers soon discovered, much of the appeal of a popular work was its ability to disseminate information previously limited to physicians and other learned men.

As a stylistic ideal, the trope of brevity had been employed frequently from antiquity, and medieval and Renaissance authors made extensive use of it in their prose and poetry (Curtius 487–94). Furthermore, pedagogues in various fields made use of the idea that one could learn a skill or an art quickly by means of an abbreviated treatise. Jerónimo Cortés, for example, titled his little treatise on accounting techniques *Tratado del computo por la mano, muy breve y necessario para los eclesiasticos* (1591), and Juan de Robles called his treatise on reading and writing *Arte para enseñar muy breve y perfectamente a leer y escrebir* (1565). The claim that one could learn something quickly no doubt served as a powerful device for luring potential readers, especially sickly readers, whose condition compelled them to take action immediately. Much like the "fast relief" promises used to advertise modern-day pain relievers, claims of brevity conveyed in the physical size of a work, in its title, or in the author's prefatory statements tell the highly motivated sickly reader that the text in hand will provide quick access to health information that can be used to find a speedy remedy for health problems.

Frequently authors claim to provide "all the information needed," or "everything necessary," and that they will treat the matter at hand fully. The author of the *Speculum al foderi* announces that he will not only speak clearly but also completely [complir e bé declarar]. Damián Carbón explains that his treatise on midwifery will contain "everything necessary" for matters related to obstetrics (*Libro del arte de las comadres* fol. 2v). Likewise, Francisco López de Villalobos introduces his metrical version of Avicenna's *Canon* by saying that he has made a summary that includes "all the universal and particular diseases" (*Sumario de la medicina* fol. 1v). Many authors insinuate that their writing is the result of years of experience and a consideration of all sources and authoritative opinions. For example, Ruy Díaz de Ysla titled his earlier-mentioned treatise on syphilis a "treatise called the fruit of all works"

(*Tractado llamado fructo de todos los auctos: contra el mal serpentino*) and explains in his introductory statement, "I have seen and have passed through my hands all the cures and experiments that can be made for this disease, from which I have learned the origin, cause, definition, and effects [of this malady]."[30]

For many authors, the notion that a vernacular medical treatise meant conciseness threatened the perception that it was also complete, implying that useful information on diseases and ailments that threatened or afflicted the reader had been omitted. It is not uncommon, therefore, to see writers qualifying their declarations of brevity with various and sometimes contradictory claims of completeness and comprehensiveness. Martínez de Castrillo, for example, titled his work on dentistry a "brief and compendious treatise" (*Tratado breve y compendioso sobre la maravillosa obra de la boca y dentadura*). The editor of Marsilio Ficino's vernacular compilation on surgery, the plague, and other health matters explains that, with "great brevity and diligence" [summa breuedad y diligencia], he will discuss "extensively" [largamente] all that is necessary (*Libro compuesto por Marsilio Ficino* [1598] fol. 5r). Likewise, Agustín Farfán tells us that, although he has treated his subject "with brevity" [con breuedad], he has included all the most necessary remedies in his treatise (*Tractado breve de anathomía y chirugía* [1579] fol. 134r). Jerónimo Soriano explains that he has decided to make his "little book" [librito] public so as to allow readers to use his proven remedies in the treatment of an "infinite number of diseases" [infinitas enfermedades] (*Libro de experimentos médicos* fol. 7v). Cristóbal Acosta, anticipating that some might criticize him for his straightforward description of medicinal plants from Asia, tells his readers not to look at the small size of his work, "for although it appear small in quantity, its quality is great" (*Tractado de las drogas* [1578] fol. 2r). Gregorio Méndez expresses an almost identical claim, saying that his versified health guide is "small in quantity" but "great in its benefits"; he reminds readers that, in many cases, there is great value in small things, such as pearls and precious stones (*Regimiento de salud* [1562] fol. 2r).

That a reader could have all he or she needed in a device small enough to fit into a hand was, of course, a long-standing medieval codicological fantasy. For medical practitioners, such an idea inspired the creation of a *vade mecum*, a small reference work that medical practitioners could attach to their belts or easily carry in their bags (Siraisi, *Medieval and Early Renaissance Medicine* 32–33). The advent of small, portable books contributed to the rise of vernacular medical treatises, especially those designed primarily for professional subalterns such as surgeons. Fernando de Córdoba explains in his *Suma* of basic surgery: "I have chosen among all the books of this aforementioned art of surgery to relieve surgeons from the burden of carrying enormous volumes of books from one land to another when they have to travel."[31]

Acknowledging that readers would be using their works in the hopes of addressing their individual needs, medical writers promoted personal access to their treatises, suggesting that the reader could jump around the text in search of particular discussions, advice, or remedies that addressed specific conditions. Assuring readers that they would "effortlessly" be able to find useful information, authors incorporated various indexing devices, from simple rubrics or chapter headings to tables, indices, and other ordering schema. The author of the *Speculum al foderi* informs his readers that he will divide his work into chapters so that it "will be easy to find the sought after information."[32] As we have seen, Berenguer Sariera claims to have modified Arnau de Vilanova's *Regimen* by adding what he calls "some marginal notes" so that readers will be able to "easily find" hygienic principles in the *Regimen de sanitat*.[33] And López de Villalobos explains, "It will be beneficial to insert rubrics at the beginning of the treatises and chapters in this book, so that the material that is treated therein can be more easily found" (*Sumario de la medicina* fol. 1v).[34]

In larger and more compendious treatises, notably those dedicated to pathology, surgery, and pharmaceuticals, vernacular authors informed their readers that the text had been carefully ordered and indexed to allow for quick consultation. Frequently, a head-to-toe schema was used to order bodily ailments, beginning with neurological disorders such as loss of memory, epilepsy, and lethargy and continuing down the body to include kidney stones, gynecological disorders, and urinary problems. Here again, popular medical writing benefited from a longstanding tradition in medical education that sought to provide ordered and indexed treatises for medical students. Around 1285 and in the wake of renewed interest in the works of Galen, John of St. Armand developed what Michael McVaugh has called an "original and ambitious technique for rendering the new Galen manageable" (*Tractatus de intentione medicorum* 131). St. Armand states that his *Revocativum memorie* "was designed so that students who pass sleepless nights looking for information among the works of Galen may be relieved of their struggles and worry and may more quickly find what their thirsty, exhausted intelligence is seeking."[35] Works with similar intentions appeared throughout the medical faculties in Europe during the late middle ages; in 1433, for instance,

Magister Alfonsus produced for the medical faculty in Salamanca his *Collectiones doctorum in arte medicina ad facilem inventionem capitulorum et memoriam confortandam et recordationem* [Fragments and summaries of the learned men in the art of medicine for the easy location and memorization of these concepts] (García-Ballester, "Galenismo" 216).

By the end of the sixteenth century, publishers regularly included various tables and indices to aid their readers. Mathias Gast, for example, expanded the 1570 version of Andrés de Laguna's *Acerca de la materia medicinal* to include "a table for finding remedies for all kinds of illness and other curious things never before published." An extensive index, which included concepts, names, and anecdotes in alphabetical order with the corresponding location in the treatise, occupies the several folios of Cristóbal Méndez's *Libro del ejercicio corporal*; an additional table of contents follows the prologue (fols. 2v–3r, ed. Alvarez del Palacio 246–48). To his *Tractado llamado fructo de todos los auctos*, Ruy Díaz de Ysla appended a final chapter [capítulo XIII] dedicated to a list of clarifications that the reader could "quickly find" [brevemente hallar] and use to resolve any doubt by referring to the alphabetical ordering indicated in the margins.

During the sixteenth century, lengthy indices and tables of content became common, often occupying ten folios or more. The 1597 edition of Alvarez de Miravall's general health guide, *Libro intitulado la conservación de la salud del cuerpo y del alma* [Book titled the preservation of health for the body and soul] contains an indexed table of "notable things" that is over forty folios long (see Figure 2). These indexing devices clearly show that vernacular medical literature was designed to be accessed in medias res as well as linearly and to allow readers to address the diversity of bodily ailments while quickly finding proper cures and preventative measures.

Autonomous Use

When the author of the *Speculum al foderi* claims that "all men" can use his treatise, he edges towards one of the boldest claims made by vernacular medical writers; the idea that a treatise could be used independently of or with a certain degree of autonomy from a practicing physician. Antonio Pérez explains, "It has occurred to me to write this brief treatise so that all who so desire can learn about the said plague, can avoid it, and can cure themselves with very little help from physicians."[36] Almost invariably, Castilian editions of the enormously popular *Tesoro de los pobres* (see Figure 3) begin with the

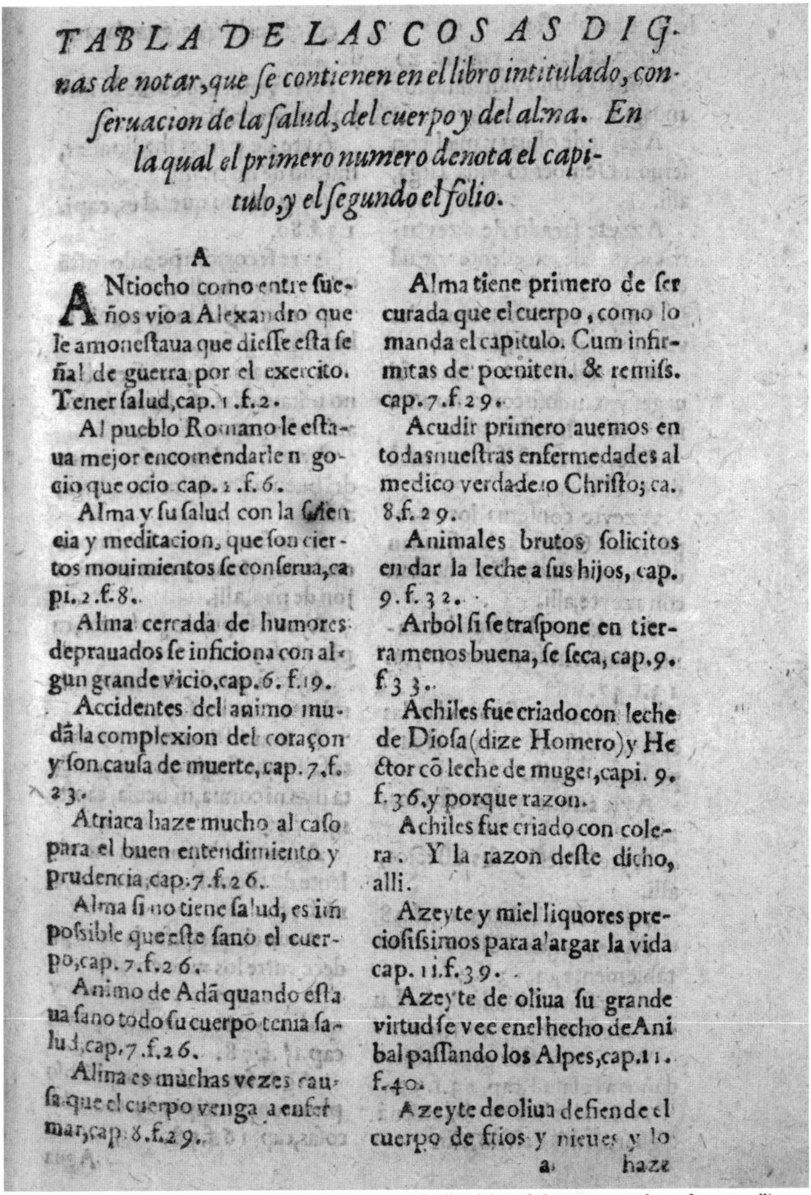

TABLA DE LAS COSAS DIGnas de notar, que se contienen en el libro intitulado, conseruacion de la salud, del cuerpo y del alma. En la qual el primero numero denota el capitulo, y el segundo el folio.

A

ANtiocho como entre sueños vio a Alexandro que le amonestaua que diesse esta señal de guerra por el exercito. Tener salud, cap. 1. f. 2.

Al pueblo Romano le estaua mejor encomendarle negocio que ocio. cap. 1. f. 6.

Alma y su salud con la sciencia y meditacion, que son ciertos mouimientos se conserua, capi. 2. f. 8.

Alma cercada de humores deprauados se inficiona con algun grande vicio, cap. 6. f. 19.

Accidentes del animo mudã la complexion del coraçon y son causa de muerte, cap. 7. f. 23.

Atriaca haze mucho al caso para el buen entendimiento y prudencia, cap. 7. f. 26.

Alma si no tiene salud, es impossible que este sano el cuerpo, cap. 7. f. 26.

Animo de Adã quando estaua sano todo su cuerpo tenia salud, cap. 7. f. 26.

Alma es muchas vezes causa que el cuerpo venga a enfermar, cap. 8. f. 29.

Alma tiene primero de ser curada que el cuerpo, como lo manda el capitulo. Cum infirmitas de pœniten. & remiss. cap. 7. f. 29.

Acudir primero auemos en todas nuestras enfermedades al medico verdadero Christo; ca. 8. f. 29.

Animales brutos solicitos en dar la leche a sus hijos, cap. 9. f. 32.

Arbol si se traspone en tierra menos buena, se seca, cap. 9. f. 33.

Achiles fue criado con leche de Diosa (dize Homero) y Hector cõ leche de muger, capi. 9. f. 36. y porque razon.

Achiles fue criado con colera. Y la razon deste dicho, alli.

Azeyte y miel liquores preciosissimos para alargar la vida cap. 11. f. 39.

Azeyte de oliua su grande virtud se vee en el hecho de Anibal passando los Alpes, cap. 11. f. 40.

Azeyte de oliua defiende el cuerpo de frios y nieues y lo

a haze

Figure 2. "Tabla de las cosas dignas de notar" ("Table of things worthy of noting"). Blas Alvarez Miravall, *Libro intitulado La conservación de la salud del cuerpo y del alma* (Medina de Campo 1597). Biblioteca Universidad Complutense, Madrid.

¶ Aqui comiẽça vn libro muy prouechoſo en me
dicina llamado teſoro delos pobres. El qual mãdo hazer el papa Juan avn medico ſuyo
llamado maeſtre Juliano hõbre muy ſabio y eſperimẽtado en medecina. El ql por ſer
uir a ſu ſãtidad: y por ſeruicio de dios y por bien delos proximos buſco quantos doctores
y maeſtros auia en medecina en aquel tiempo: en que ouo cincuenta y ſeys doctores, que a
llego para eſta obra: muy ſabios, para que los hombres ſe ſepan curar ſin medico dõde no
lo ouiere y ouiere mucha neceſſidad.

Eln nom
bre õ dios padre
y hijo y ſpũ ſctõ
t res pſonas cõ vna
eſſencia diuinal q
biue ſin comiẽço
y reyna ſin fin. El
ql crio todas las
coſas q enel mun
do ſõ. E a cada v
na dellas dio ſu ppia vtud para obrar e to
das las coſas q ſon para ſu ſctõ ſeruicio y a
prouecho õl hõbre. El ql dio al põbre ſabidu
ria y ciẽcia pa obrar de cada vna dellas ſe
gũ ſu ppia virtud. E por ede yo maeſtre ju
liano creyẽdo firme y verdaderamẽte: y cõ
fiado ẽla merced õl mi ſeñor dios y cõ ſu ſã
ta ayuda ẽtiẽdo fazer y acabar eſte libro: y
poner enl la doctrina medecinal q los ſabios
y maeſtros e medecina fallarõ y prouarõ y
eſperimẽtarõ y derã alos biuiẽtes q la q
ſiere vſar y aprẽder e dotrina: la ql ſe llama
ra teſoro delos pobres. Por la ql todas las
enfermedades q puede ſer e cuerpos õlos hõ
bres y delas mugeres pueda auer remedio
de ſalud: tãbie pa las ſias como pa los cu
erpos cõ ayuda õ aquel ſeñor glorioſo que
los crio: y todas las coſas a ſeruicio del hõ
bre. Por ede enel nõbre de nro redemptor
jeſu xpo: el ql es verdadera ſalud pa los cu
erpos y animas medeciar quiero eſta obra
començar: y enel comiẽço y enla fin le ſupli
co me õ ayuda y ſocorro para q le pueda a
cabar: porq los pobres q õlla vſarẽ pueda
las enfermedades guarecer y ſanar. Y por
q la cabeça del hõbre es mas noble q los
otros miembros: porende primeramẽte q
ro hablar della: y como guareſceran las po
ſtillas dela cabeça: y deſpues dẽde adelãte

¶ Capitulo primero pa
ra ſanar las poſtillas o la ſarna.

Si quiſieres guarecer las poſti
llas õla cabeça: dize maeſtre ma
cedo que te laues muchas vezes
cõel caldo õlos gamones maja
dos y cozidos y ſanaras. E otroſi dize eſte
miſmo maeſtre, que el maſtuerço majado
con vnto de anadon, vnta las poſtillas y ſa
naras. Item dize el miſmo maeſtro, que
tomes las hojas õlas violetas majadas cõ
miel y vnta las poſtillas y ſanaras. Jtẽ di
ze maeſtre Ricardo q tomes el caldo dela
gallina: y vntes las poſtillas õla cabeça y ſa
naras. Eſto miſmo haze ala ſarna del cuer
po. Otroſi dize maeſtre Diatico q tomes
los grumos nucuos q naſcen al pie dela hi
guera y las hojas dellos: majalas: y deſte
plalas con agua fria: y ſi fuere vieja deſtẽ
pla las con vinagre fuerte y haz dellas co
mo maſſa y vnta las poſtillas, o la ſarna
y ſanaras. Item dize Auicena que tomes
las almendras amargas y limpia las con a
gua caliente y maja las y pon las en vn po
co de azeyte roſado y haz dello vnguento
y rapa la cabeça y vnta la conello y ſana
ras. Jtẽ dize el Eſpimetador q tomes las
rayzes del eneldo y los grumos õlas higue
ras con ſus hojas y las almẽdras amargas
y buelue lo todo con vinagre fuerte y con
azeyte. E deſpues toma los tallos õlas co
les y las riſtras delos ajos y quema los y
haz los poluos y toma deſpues el azogue
y la ſal y muele lo todo envno y laua la ca
beça con orines y cõ vinagre y vntala cõ eſ
te vnguento y ſanaras. Jtem dize maeſtre
Diaſcorides que tomes la corteza dela hi
guera cabrahigo y quemala y haz poluos

a iij

explicit affirmation that this text was written "so that where there is great necessity and no physicians, men will know how to cure themselves without a physician."[37] Maestre Gil tells us that, in the absence of a physician, men can use his book on foods and medicines every day, guided only by their own good sense and resorting to physicians only at times when they are afflicted by ailments that do not appear in his work.[38] Even physicians such as López de Villalobos, who were reluctant to have nonprofessionals use their vernacular treatises, recognized that their works could effectively assist readers when professional care was not available:

> Moreover, it will be useful and valuable for the nobility and the learned in other fields who want to learn something about medicine so as to be able to speak with their physicians, ask them questions, and experiment; and if they also make an effort to understand this summary, they will learn a sufficient amount and will be able to use it for several days in time of need until a physician arrives.[39]

The autonomous use of a text in place of a physician often arose in response to a specific illness or vexing ailment. As I discussed in the introduction, the anxiety caused by Arnau's frequent visits to Montpellier compelled Jaume II to ask him to write a health guide that could be used in the physician's absence. The cost of medical care appears to have prompted the publisher Pedro de Castro to change the title of Gregorio Méndez's *Regimiento de salud* to *Arte para conservar el dinero en la bolsa con el qual en gran manera se remedia lo mucho que se gasta con el orinal* (1562) [The art of keeping your money in your pocket which in great way remedies much of what is wasted in the urine flask]. New World authors were concerned over the lack of professional care available to colonists in the Americas and suggested that their treatises would serve those who lived in remote areas. Ortiz de Hinososa's approbation of Agustín Farfán's *Tractado breve de anathoïia y chirugía* specifically states that he has examined the work and has "found it useful and valuable for all kinds of people in our New Spain, especially for those whose houses and dwellings are in cities and villages and places where there is a lack of physicians and pharmaceuticals."[40] Likewise, López de Hinojosos explains that his *Suma y recopilación de cirugía* (1578 and 1595) will serve those "outside the city, in the mines, on the estancias, in the villages and remote parts where medical treatment is not at hand."[41]

The desideratum of presenting medical information to those without access to physicians, often through texts qualified with an emphasis on preservation rather than cure, comes to full fruition in the *regimina* and other treatises in the later middle ages and early modern periods. In 1589, Bernardino Gómez Miedes, the bishop of the Aragonese town of Albarracín, wrote a little treatise on gout for Felipe II in which he recounts how Rey Jaume I of Aragon extracted an arrow from his uncle, who had been wounded in battle:

> Engaged in the conquest of the Kingdom of Valencia, having surrounded the town of Burriana, the king's beloved uncle, Don Guillen de Entença, was seriously wounded by an arrow shot from those inside. The king ordered that he be brought to his royal tent, where with his own hands he extracted the arrowhead that had penetrated his uncle's leg. In the presence of all the physicians and surgeons, he cleaned and bandaged the wound with great skill and happy results. For this he was praised by all.[42]

Gómez Miedes's anecdote about Jaume I implies that any literate layperson might learn and practice medicine. He claims that he has written the work in such a plain and clear way that any of his readers will be able to understand and use the work relying only on their good judgment and without any additional medical training or other scientific study. Gómez Miedes describes his treatise, *Enchiridion* (1589), as an instrument or manual arm that provides an immediate or direct use, without the presence of a physician: "there is nothing more at hand for man's use than his own hands" (fol. 8v). Ruy Díaz de Ysla extends this argument, claiming that humble and rustic shepherds are often more capable of healing their ailments than famous physicians. "I have seen many famous physicians die of this disease [syphilis]," he declares, claiming that, in the year 1542, he saw eight physicians and surgeons die of the pox, whereas a shepherd who had a very advanced case of the disease was able to cure himself, carefully treating each canker with a treatment derived without help of a learned physician. According to Díaz de Ysla, this example clearly manifests the Word of God as transmitted in the gospels: many things are hidden from the wise and prudent that are revealed to the small, to whom God reveals his secrets.[43]

For vernacular medical writers, humans are not only capable of caring for their bodies; they are, in fact, obligated to do so. Medieval and early modern authors regularly incorporated into their medical treatises various arguments supporting the idea that humans must do everything possible to preserve their health. Alfonso Chirino sees a failure to do so as an act tantamount to homicide:

> God has commanded us to love our neighbors as ourselves, and there-
> fore we are required to love our temporal health in such a way that if
> on account of our blame or negligence we should lose it, we would be
> guilty of killing ourselves. Such a homicide is worthy of greater pun-
> ishment than one against our neighbor according to Saint Augustine
> in the third book of the *City of God*.[44]

Authors frequently promoted their treatises by reminding the reader of the value of good health: "Everything ends with good health," Cristóbal Méndez tells us. "Oh priceless, oh generous, oh magnificent health, worthy of being loved as life itself, for without it we can call ourselves dead even though we are alive."[45] Along these same lines, Sorapán de Rieros begins his collection of vernacular proverbs on good health and long life by reminding his readers that "the most precious jewel that a man can possess in this world is health." Acknowledging that the ancients recognized this fact, he insists that "neither the rich nor the strong, the learned, or those who enjoy fame, nor those who have loyal friends, blessed children, and spouses can call themselves happy if they do not enjoy good health."[46] Some writers took a more negative approach, reminding their public that earthly existence is replete with illness and afflic-tion. Maestre Gil explains that "fire burns us, water drowns us, and the air kills us with cold, heat, pestilence, or some other harmful condition, and the firmness of the earth kills if we fall upon it." He tells the reader that the world is replete with things such as stones and herbs ready to injure and poison us; there are serpents to attack us with their poisonous bites, and beasts such as lions, bears, and bulls waiting rip our bodies in tiny pieces; even the foods we eat to sustain us can work against us, for "if we don't eat, we die, but by eating we risk all kinds of ailments."[47] Cristóbal Méndez would agree: "There is nothing in it [the world] big or small, perfect or imperfect that is not, has not been, or cannot be sick, and for this and with great justification we must greatly value our health."[48]

Arguments about the vulnerability of good health were used by physicians and theologians throughout the middle ages as an "explanatory model of ill-ness," a term employed by medical anthropologists to describe a belief or set of beliefs that account for the onset and persistence of bodily ailments (Klein-man, "Concepts and a Model"). In the popular medical treatise, however, this argument was used not to help readers resign themselves to their worldly conditions, but to remind them of the role medicine could play in ameliorating their condition. Hence, although Maestre Gil argues that sin and Adam's fall might have brought calamities upon the human race, he reminds his readers that "God has given us enlightened philosophers who in their wisdom have created the science of medicine so that men can preserve and maintain their health while they have it and know how to cure their diseases and remedy their pains when they arise."[49] By extension, the vernacular text that the sickly reader holds in hand proposes to offer him or her the necessary information for physical well-being.

The Vernacular and the Space of the Clinic

For the sickly reader, the presentation of medical information in Romance rather than in Latin constituted the single most powerful convention of usefulness; vernacular writing stood well above other rhetorical strategies designed to encourage readers to believe that written medical information could be instrumental in preserving one's health. Obviously, medical advice would have been of little value if its language were unintelligible to the majority of readers. But more significantly, in the highly arcane world of professional medicine, writing in the vernacular created a space in which patients could envision their place in a clinical encounter with a trained physician.

At the beginning of the sixteenth century, Latin and Romance were employed for distinct purposes: the vernacular was relegated to matters of poetry, preaching, pedagogy, and administration, while Latin was the preferred language of philosophy, theology, and the sciences, including medicine (Montero Cartelle, "El humanismo" 31). Although medical writers increasingly transgressed this norm, their decision to write in Romance remained highly charged and frequently required an explicit justification. The majority justified their use of the vernacular on the utilitarian grounds that I have already discussed, arguing that writing in Romance would make their treatises available to all. Alfonso Chirino announced forthrightly that "all that one will find written herein will not be in medical words or obscure words but rather in popular speech that any man can understand."[50] Francisco Franco resolved to write his book "in the Castilian language so that everyone in their own home can use it in times of need," while Francisco Díaz claimed he was "looking after the good of the republic," writing "in our vulgar language so that all can enjoy this work."[51]

Others saw their vernacular writings as a service to surgeons, apothecaries, and other non-university-trained practitioners who were not able to advance their knowledge of medicine due to their ignorance of Latin. Daza Chacón explains that he wrote his vernacular work on surgery having seen many "ciruganos romancistas" who, well-disposed to practice medicine, nevertheless fell behind for lack of good books in their language.[52] Some writers, such as Montaña de Monserrate, took this idea a step farther, complaining that the physician's fixation on Latin impeded or undermined a practical knowledge of medicine:

> I have been moved to write this book in Romance because many surgeons and other men of discretion do not know Latin and will want to benefit from reading it; also because I find that in these days many physicians are so obsessed with Latin that they dedicate all their thinking to the language. . . . And this is one of the strongest reasons why today we find few physicians who know anything about medicine and many who write about it.[53]

Miguel de Sabuco is more succinct: "Let us leave Latin and Greek and speak in our language, because there is sufficient damage in the world because the sciences (especially law) are in Latin."[54]

Certainly there were those who disagreed, arguing with humanistic zeal that a failure to understand Latin would hinder or diminish a true understanding of medicine. Others complained about the difficulty of finding appropriate words in Romance, while still others suggested that a vulgarization of medicine would present a danger for the patient. Physicians who wrote in Romance for paraprofessionals and subprofessionals were aware that, once medical information was redacted in the vernacular, the doors would be open for all to use such works. Villalobos expressed his concern that his versified summary of Avicenna's *Canon* would give the impression that anyone could practice medicine without first having received the proper training (*Sumario de la medicina* fol. 1r–v). Vernacular writers combated these reservations, arguing that by writing in Romance they provided a much-needed service for the Republic and that, just as the great writers of antiquity—Cicero, Hippocrates, Avicenna—wrote in their native languages, Spaniards should likewise write in theirs:

> To assure the common good of our Spanish nation, to which we are all obligated, I brought this book to light in vulgar Castilian. . . . And

because our language is called vulgar, there are those who imagine that we can only write vulgar and low things in it. This is a great error. Plato wrote things that were not vulgar in his vulgar language, and Cicero wrote in the language that was the vulgar language of his time things that were not minor or less elevated. What can we say about Saints Basil, Chrysostom, Gregory Nazianzus, and Cyril, with all the antiquity of the Greeks, who wrote the divine mysteries of our faith in their Greek mother tongue, which as children they drank it with their mother's milk, and even the vendors in the square spoke it. To bring this closer to what I do, Cornelio Celso, Roman knight and physician, wrote so exquisitely and elegantly about medicine and surgery that they called him the Latin Hippocrates. And Avicenna wrote in his Arabic a great volume of medicinal arts. . . . Hence, for these reasons and many others that I will not mention, I have dared to publish this book, as always, desiring that in this way the unlearned can take from it whatever pleases them.[55]

With respect to the selection of Romance over Latin, historians attribute the progressive rise of Castilian in medical writing during the sixteenth century to four phenomena: the belief that the mother tongue was "natural" and, therefore, the best way to express oneself; influence by Italian models; Erasmus' and the humanists' promotion of the vernacular, especially for the translation of scripture; and the increasing use of Castilian in Carlos V's administration. These factors, combined with the need to transmit medical information to medical subspecialists such as surgeons, offer a compelling explanation for the rise of the vernacular in medical writing. There was more, however, at stake here. Writing in the vernacular can be seen as an attempt to address one of the most difficult problems that confronts the professional practice of medicine: how to reconcile the scientific discourse of medicine by which arcane knowledge is transmitted with the compelling biological needs and limited knowledge of the patient. At the heart of this problem lie two very different approaches to and interpretations of bodily disorder, and two often-conflicting domains of experience: that of the physician and that of the patient.

No serious medical writer would have argued that practitioners, including surgeons and other subspecialists, would not benefit from knowing Latin. In fact, the knowledge and use of this language was formative in constituting the esoteric domain of the medical professional. As I will discuss in the following chapter, one of the distinguishing and often celebrated character-istics of a competent physician was his ability to manipulate texts written in classical languages; medical deontologists listed knowledge of Latin among the first skills that a competent physician must have. Even vernacular writers complained emphatically about professors' and students' faulty or minimal knowledge of Latin. Juan Méndez Nieto, for example, insinuated that his own success as a medical practitioner was, in part, due to his advanced knowledge of the language.[56]

If physicians' knowledge of Latin, combined with their training and ex-perience, placed them in opposition to the ignorant and untrained, it was the ability to understand an illness from the inside—manifested as pain and bodily dysfunction—that distinguished the patient. They cared little if their ailments were identified in Latin, Greek, Arabic, or Romance; they cared even less if an efficacious cure was the result of a concoction taken from the Ga-lenic corpus or from the unsystematic procedures of empirics. This antago-nism between physicians and patients, often defined by medical anthologists as the opposition between concepts of "disease" and "illness" respectively re-quired that the physician and the patient find a middle ground, a common place where they could communicate in a common discourse. In traditional medical practice, the physical spaces of the clinic—the bedside, the hospital room, the examination room—constituted such a middle ground, where phy-sician and patient could interact. In textual practice—that is, when a patient turned to a medical work as though it were a surrogate physician—it was the vernacular language that established this shared space and allowed the patient and physician to interact (on a metaphorical level if not in actuality). By converting their knowledge into simplified, ordered, and abbreviated re-dactions written in the vernacular, medical writers forcefully suggested that the writer and the reader could meet as physician and patient in the common ground provided by the vernacular text. And although patients remained subordinate to the more educated and more experienced minds, they found in the vernacular medical treatise a textual space that they were authorized to occupy. While it is true that learned patients could (and many times did) read professional medical treatises in Latin, they could not do so without at least vaguely sensing that in some way they were entering into material that was not written with the intention of directly helping the ailing patient find remedies for a disorder. On the contrary, the vernacular text functioned as a powerful signifier that suggested to the reader a nonprofessional use. Unlike the foreboding and impenetrable Latin compendium, often written in small letters and alien words, the vernacular treatise opened a familiar door for the layperson, inviting him or her to consider the possibility of using the text on his or her own terms.

Nicolás Monardes, the *Sevillana medicina*, and the Creation of a Popular Medical Treatise

In the mid-sixteenth century, a young Nicolás Monardes, the distinguished author of the celebrated *Historia medicinal de las cosas que se traen de nuestras Indias Occidentales que sirven en medicina*, came across a little medical treatise in his family library. The work, appropriately titled the *Sevillana medicina*, had been written almost two centuries earlier as a guide to preserving and restoring the health of Seville's inhabitants. Motivated by the same utilitarian zeal as the author of the *Speculum al foderi* and many other contemporary vernacular medical writers who claimed that their treatises provided brief, simple, and easy-to-use medical information, Monardes enthusiastically edited the work and in 1545 published it, believing that, despite its archaic language, all could benefit from its instructions. Curiously, Juan de Aviñón, the fourteenth-century author of the *Sevillana medicina*, suggested just the opposite.

In the original prologue, which Monardes published immediately following his own introduction, Aviñón provided an extensive outline of the nature of the medicinal arts. Beginning with an exposition on Hippocrates's first aphorism, "life is short, art is long . . . ," he explains that the art of medicine is protracted precisely because it has six parts, and "each part takes a long time to learn" (fol. 5r). According to Aviñón, a physician needs to know the human body and the complexion of each individual member. He must keep in mind that man has 248 bones, 580 muscles, 375 nerves, and 284 veins; he needs to understand all types of diseases and their causes, which ones are simple and which ones are complex (there are 690 simple diseases). The physician must also grasp how seasons and geographical location affect the various bodily compositions and how to cure each part of the body. Finally, he must know everything about the composition and nature of all foods and medicines. In addition to this extensive knowledge, physicians must be trained in the seven liberal arts and so must acquire a firm knowledge of grammar, logic, rhetoric, geometry, arithmetic, music, and astrology. For these reasons, Aviñón tells us, Hippocrates concluded that the art of medicine is the most complete in the world and, by comparison, the life of man is short (*Sevillana medicina* fol.

5r–v). Throughout his prologue, Aviñón reiterates this idea, insisting that one requires a great deal of time and dedication to learn all that is necessary about the human body and its pathologies and cures.

Clearly, Aviñón did not intend to write a popular medical text in the same vein as Chirino's *Menor daño de la medicina* or a treatise such as Lobera de Avila's *Vergel de sanidad* (1542), which provides instructions for the nobility on how to prepare a healthy banquet. Aviñón offers no references to brevity, accessibility, ease of use, or clarity of exposition, and there are no comments suggesting that the reader will effortlessly be able to use this treatise in the absence of a physician. Moreover, the original treatise was written in Latin, and thus would have discouraged all but the most desperate or persistent sickly readers from imagining that it might provide an immediate use in addressing their ailments. One may wonder, then, what it was that persuaded Monardes to edit and publish Aviñón's treatise as a useful instrument for the general public.

Perhaps it was the fact that the *Sevillana medicina* was organized around the familiar Galenic system of the non-naturals that encouraged Monardes to contemplate its benefits from a generic standpoint and to classify it among the *regimina* and plague tracts that made use of the same structure. Or perhaps he was caught up in what appears to have been a fervor of medical-related printing in Seville during the mid-sixteenth century.[57] It is more likely, however, that Monardes shared with his contemporaries an extraordinary interest in assigning medicinal utility to common things. Although contemporary and modern critics have long praised Monardes as one of the first Europeans to publicize the medicinal properties of New World plants (his *Historia medicinal* was an immediate success and led to various expanded reprintings, and translations, such as John Frampton's well-known *Joyfull newes out of the new-found worlde* [1577]), the majority of the plants referred to in Monardes's treatises had already been described, often with great detail, in the writings of Columbus, Oviedo, Cortés, and Acosta. Moreover, Monardes himself never traveled to the New World, and although he kept a small garden at his home in Seville, much of his experience with New World botanical species came secondhand from the reports of those who had already identified and announced publicly the news of their existence. Although Monardes was celebrated as a champion of rational methods promoted by humanistic Galenism, his modus operandi as a naturalist and researcher was based more on a keen ability to find a utility in recently discovered things. As I shall show in chapter 3, this ability was not limited, as might be expected, to ascertaining the value of new plants, animals, and minerals from the New World, but extended to a passionate search to find a medicinal value in substances that were already familiar.

Throughout his professional life, Monardes operated with the ethos of a scavenger—first he reexamined material that had been overlooked, underappreciated, or deemed useless, and then he envisioned a fiction for its utility. We see this clearly expressed in his dialogue on the benefits of iron, *Dialogo de las grandezas del hierro, y de sus virtudes medicinales* (1574), in which he defends the utilitarian value of iron over that of gold and silver. It is in this spirit that Monardes enthusiastically published the treatise that he happened to find on the shelves of his family library. Overlooking Aviñón's discouraging prologue and the fact that the treatise had been written specifically for the people of Seville, he took to crafting an introduction that would convince readers that the text afforded a universal medicinal value that could benefit the entire republic.

Monardes begins his prologue with a lengthy commentary that establishes the importance of living in good health. He starts with the question, "What is there that is more beautiful, more affable, even more prosperous than good health?" [Qué cosa ay más hermosa, más amable, ni qué más prospera sea que la salud] (fol. 1v). He reminds the reader of the tenuousness of the human condition:

> We see that man is fragile, born to toil, and that all that surrounds him is against him; the air corrupts him, water drowns him, fire consumes him, and the earth is the stepmother who gives him things that afflict him and seek to bring him to his end. If he receives some good, she compensates by giving him a hundred maladies.[58]

He goes on to argue that nothing is more valuable than good health, "because where health is lacking, all things in abundance, all wealth in excess, is small comfort" (fol. 2v). Hence, it is the responsibility of each human being to attend to the needs of the body and to learn that health is a balance of the humors that can be achieved by governing one's life properly.

Monardes explains that human beings, unlike animals, have the rational capacity to determine the needs of their bodies. He offers a lengthy list of historical figures who neglected their health, such as the emperor Septimus Severus, who ate and drank himself to death, and follows with a list of others who lived long lives through careful regiment, such as the emperor Flavius

Vespasianus who washed his body every day, fasted once a month, and never experienced an illness. "It is certain," Mondardes warns, "our bodies are not made of diamonds. Unlike animals, God has given man a rational capacity and the thus the purpose of books is to teach each person how he or she should order eating, drinking, and other matters related to health." For this reason, Monardes concludes, he has gone to the trouble of publishing the *Sevillana medicina* for the benefit of the city and for the conservation of everybody's health.[59]

Monardes's prologue converts Aviñón's professionally oriented treatise into a popular health guide for patients by mediating the difference between a professional approach and a popular one. His introduction is a tour de force in the rhetoric of popular utility, and like the author of the *Speculum al foderi* who refashioned the material in the *Liber minor de coitus*, Monades's efforts to disseminate the *Sevillana medicina* provide a vivid example of the way medical authors attempted to broadcast often complicated and difficult material to the general public by rhetorically predisposing the reader to believe that the work had a utilitarian value.

CHAPTER TWO

Fictions of the Physician

[D]esideramus fervencius presenciam vestram nobiscum
adesse . . . quia vos pro cura et conservatione salutis nostre
sentimus necessarium et utilem.
>—King Jaume II to Arnau de Vilanova while
>suffering from an illness in the spring of 1305[1]

In a vernacular translation of Ischaq Israeli's *Tratado de las fiebres* (Treatise on fevers), the author breaks from his general discussion on the choleric causes of syncope, and recounts an anecdote about Galen's treatment of a suffering man.

> Galen said there was a Roman noble who suffered from abscesses in his intestines, a malady that caused him to expel much blood and putrefaction. The noble physicians of Rome medicated him, but the more medicine they gave him, the more the putrefaction grew until the physicians secretly told the patient's friends that he would not recover from this ailment.

At this point, Israeli abandons his third-person account, allowing Galen to speak directly:

> The patient heard that I was in Rome and sent for me. I went to visit him, and when I entered I discovered that he had lost hope of living. First of all, I began comforting him with pleasing words. Then I asked him how he had come to develop this disorder. He described the cause

of the malady and the medicines that the physicians had prescribed for him. After considering the matter, I determined that there could be a remedy for his ailment.[2]

Galen's exemplary bedside manners point to a deontological imperative that prevailed in the ancient and medieval period and was subsequently developed and promoted during the sixteenth century: for a physician to successfully cure, he needed to act clinically, in the etymological sense of treating his patients at "the bedside" where, in addition to prescribing remedies and applying cures, he could listen to his patients describe their bodily complaints. Even if this encounter was nothing more than an exchange of pleasing words or a touch of the hand, physicians were taught to acknowledge that in times of failing health their patients desired and benefited from the healer's physical presence.[3]

Although writers of vernacular medical treatises justified the creation and dissemination of their works as a professional obligation and as an extension of their medical practice, the idea that a text might function as a surrogate medical practitioner would seem to ignore the patient's need to have direct contact with the physician. It would also appear to challenge the ethical principle that encouraged physicians to treat their patients at the bedside. It might even threaten to efface or diminish the role of the practicing physician, for if patients could cure themselves with a medical text in hand, as many writers suggested, they would have less of an incentive to pay for the services of a professional.[4] In response to these problems, vernacular medical writers attempted to create a quasi-clinical encounter between physician-author and patient-reader. Rather than eliminate the physician, these authors created a literary persona who effectively encouraged the sickly reader to imagine the presence of the physician while reading and consulting the text. In these works, the late medieval and early modern reader would find much more than an impersonal collection of medical information. Among the instructions, explanations, therapies, and recipes, most readers would have immediately sensed the presence of an attentive physician who was busily selecting his most valuable advice, copying down his most proven remedies, outlining his most effective methods, revealing some of his most guarded secrets, and detailing the most egregious mistakes of less experienced practitioners. Far from effacing their role as physicians, medical writers presented themselves as unwavering advocates, solitary heroes, and dauntless warriors in the fight against their patients' biological disorders. There is indeed a physician at the patient's side in the textual space of vernacular medical treatises; though sickly readers may not have felt the touch of his healing hand, they certainly heard his voice and imagined his presence.

The Physician in the Text

Very few Spanish vernacular medical treatises are anonymous. Most writers and publishers encouraged readers to note the personal and professional identity of the physician-author. As might be expected, this begins when the author introduces himself at the very beginning of his work: "It was my desire to work to produce the following treatise which I, Master Jacme d'Agramont, with humility and appropriate reverence, present to the distinguished men of Lerida"; "I, Master Alfonso Chirino among the professors of medicine . . . , have ordered for you this brief treatise on medicine"; "I, Saladino, doctor of arts and medicine and your lord's physician, propose to compose this treatise that I want to call *A compendium for pharmacists*."[5]

In *portadas, dedicatorias, privilegios, aprobaciones, licencias, tasa, poesías*, and other parts of the sixteenth-century vernacular medical book, the reader learns the physician's name and discovers details about his training and professional appointments. We read on the first page of *Regimiento contra la peste* (1501) that the treatise was written by "the excellent doctor Fernando Alvarez, your Lord's physician, head chair of medicine in this University of Salamanca" (fol. 1r); the opening page of *Libro del arte de las comadres o madrinas* (1541) [The book of the art of midwifery] identifies the author as "the very excellent doctor in arts and medicine, Master Damián Carbón of Mallorca" (fol. 1r); the first page of the *Orden para la cura y preservación de las secas y carbuncos* (1599) presents the author as "Doctor Andrés Zamudio de Alfaro, mayor and chief examiner, general *Protomedico*, chamber physician of His Majesty, and general advisor of the inquisition" (fol. 1r).

The description of the physician that greets the reader in the introductory material takes on a personal and more immediate tone in the exposition of the *materia medica*. Here we find the physician in the first-person voice commenting, deliberating, comparing, recommending, advising, and observing. The following phrases from Cristóbal Méndez's *Libro del ejercicio corporial* (1553) [Book of bodily exercise] are typical of the way an author presents himself throughout a medical treatise:

I usually say that . . . ; And as such I would give as advice . . . ; For this I say many times . . . ; And I said to him . . . ; I swear that . . . ; I was present . . . ; I thought that . . . ; I do it this way . . . ; To this I respond . . . ; I would not advise . . . ; I believe it well . . . ; I have determined . . . ; I didn't consider it a joke . . . ; I have been informed . . . ; I don't know what to say about it . . . ; I have not found a better medicine for it . . . ; When I see something . . . ; I asked . . . ; I am not speaking about these . . . ; I do not feel that . . . ; I cannot find written . . . ; I want to put it into practice . . . ; I saw . . . ; I met a man . . . ; I saw in Mexico . . . ; I ordered. . . .[6]

Throughout these treatises, personal information about the lives of the authors abounds. Ruy Díaz de Ysla mentions the city of Baeza among the urban areas affected by the early sixteenth-century syphilis epidemic and emphatically explains that this city "is in Spain, in Andalusia, where I was born" (*Tractado llamado fructo de todos los auctos* fol. 3v). Others tell of their success in using a particular medicine. Jerónimo Soriano writes, "I have used it [a nonsurgical remedy for removing a tooth] an infinite number of times in treating my patients and myself"; "I have experimented with this [a remedy for asthma] with felicitous results"; "I use it [a salve for hemorrhoids] and it mitigates the pain wonderfully" (*Libro de experimentos médicos* [1599] fols. 31r, 37v, 60v). In his discussion on diarrhea (*celica diarrhea*), he recounts his own bout with this intestinal disorder:

> I only want to recount what happened to me in the year 1587. I developed a case of diarrhea that stubbornly persisted; knowing what usually happens with diarrheas, I could not stop worrying. In the end, God was served. Just by consuming good foods in moderation and at the beginning of my meals eating some toasted bread soaked in good barrel wine replete with powdered cloves, spices, cinnamon, and sugar, I was liberated.[7]

Some writers created the illusion of a clinical encounter by speaking directly to the reader. Gregorio Méndez, for example, instructs his readers in verse:

> Get up at the break of day, stretch your body and give thanks to God. . . . Don't forget to wash your hands and brush your teeth.

[Es que te levantarás / ya quando fuere de día/ el cuerpo menearás / a
tu dios gracias darás. . . . Las manos no oluidarás / que sean bien alim-
piadas / los dientes fregarás.] (*Regimiento de salud* fols. 6v–7r)

Strategies such as direct discourse, combined with frequent self-references
and extensive discussions in the first person, encouraged sickly readers to
imagine that there was a physician in and behind the text, who in effect was
always "on call," available at the opening of the book to address the reader's
needs.

Making Belief in the Physician

For late medieval and early modern readers, the imagined presence of a
medical authority did not translate readily into a desirable mediator for their
ailments. Over the past four hundred years, our modern systems of medical licensing and control have encouraged us to believe that the authorized
practitioner is knowledgeable and competent. This faith was not so readily
assumed in the medieval and early modern periods. What Michael McVaugh
has noted of the early fourteenth century holds true well beyond the sixteenth
century:

> every physician would at the onset have had to convince his patients
> that he knew something they did not—what was wrong with them,
> and how it could be cured—and that they should concede him au-
> thority and power over them in treatment. He could not have felt at
> ease until he was sure that his patients fully believed in him and ac-
> cepted his authority. (*Medicine Before the Plague* 166–67)

Although the authorizing mechanisms of modern medical practice—
university degrees, examinations, and licensing—emerged and were beginning to take hold during the early modern period, it would be well past the
sixteenth century before a physician could expect that the majority of his
patients would trust him solely on the basis of his academic or official credentials.[8] In fact, there was no occupation in late medieval and early modern
Spain that simultaneously inspired more blind trust and more intense suspi-
cion than the medical profession. Physicians were both desperately needed
and thoroughly detested—frequently by the same patient—and the line between a "good" physician and a reprehensible charlatan was often tenuous.

Thus, every physician had the ongoing obligation to convince the public that he was successful and skilled at his art, and most of all, that he could cure the patient.

The art of making the patient believe in the physician was often considered as valuable as the science of medicine itself. Estéfano de Sevilla, writing at the end of the thirteenth century, argued that a physician's ability to make patients imagine his virtuous traits and good works is the physician's most productive medical instrument:

> And this is because good and virtuous works invigorate the physician. His good reputation spreads and consequently the sick imagine their health in his goodness and confide more in him than in others because of his good life and works. More than the physician, this imagination and confidence, with divine assistance, are the cause behind the curing of many diseases ...because the patient's lively imagination is more useful to the good physician than all his other instruments.[9]

Controlling the patient's faith in the practitioner was thought to be so fundamental for successful healing that some works on bedside manners outlined what appear to be ruses and tricks to keep the patient's confidence and trust. In the brief treatise *De cautelis medicorum*, dubiously attributed to Arnau de Vilanova and included in sixteenth-century editions of Arnau's *Opera*, we find a series of strategies that a physician could use to preserve his professional integrity and avoid being deceived by devious patients. For example, the work recommended that if a physician could not satisfactorily interpret a urine sample, he was to announce the diagnosis, "oppilatio in epate" [obstruction in the liver] "and particularly use the word *oppilatio*, because they do not understand what it means, and it helps greatly that a term is not understood by the people."[10] In addition to detailing basic bedside manners, the *De cautelis medicorum* is particularly interested in teaching the practicing physician defensive ploys to either distract or silence mistrustful patients:

> When you come to a patient, you should always do something new, lest they say you cannot do anything without books. . . . Entering the sickroom do not appear very haughty or overzealous, and return with the simple gesture, the greetings of those who rise to greet you. After they have seated themselves you finally sit down facing the sick; ask

him how he feels and reach out for his arm, and all that we shall say is necessary so that through your entire behaviour you obtain the favour of the people who are around the sick. (136–37)[11]

There was a performative aspect to practicing medicine that required the physician constantly to stage healing events in ways that would not undermine the patient's trust, or worse, discredit him and his practice. For example, in the *Repetitio*, a work Arnau de Vilanova wrote for his students, he recommended that when the physician

doesn't know how long the illness will last or when it might return, he should never promise that any particular treatment is going to be the last, because when the treatment is complete the patient will lose hope if he hasn't recovered, and the physician will be accused of falsehoods. Thus the prudent physician will always tell the patient and his friends that he is using this drug or that in order to bring about a preliminary state, so that the patient can look forward to a further important treatment and will not give up hope; and meanwhile, if health returns, the physician will win praise for his preliminary treatment as having reinforced the power of nature.[12]

It is easy to see how such practices could be abused, and indeed in subsequent centuries physicians were harshly criticized for deceiving the patient. Especially denounced was the devious or incompetent physician who attempted to seduce his patient by using learned words and seemingly erudite concepts. In his late sixteenth-century treatise on medical ethics, Enrique Jorge Enríquez levels his criticism upon these so-called physicians:

Those whom I most ridicule are the miserable quacks on the corners, in the streets, and in the pharmacies who make much noise, shouting out those authorities whom they know by memory so that the commoners take them for learned men; when taking the pulse of a sick person, they pronounce a word in broken Latin, and examining the urine they say *oppilatio* and give two hundred considerations to matters that are against all the rules of medicine, so that with these lies they can trick the common people; for the most part these are charlatans, blabbermouths, entertainers, everything that a perfect physician must not be.[13]

Enríquez's criticism forms part of a broad denunciation of incompetent and deceitful practitioners in works of literature and in vernacular medical treatises. As I shall argue later in this chapter, when these outcries appear in a vernacular medical treatise, they may be best understood as a strategy to configure the author in benevolent and heroic opposition against other competing physicians. For the patient, however, the unambiguous message is that they must carefully choose their physician:

> For this reason we must come to the following conclusion; ignorant physicians should be completely thrown out, and the learned physicians should be doubted, and a great part of what they do should come under suspicion. This art is dubious, and people must necessarily choose with great deliberation such people for physicians for their great science, charity, and wisdom to administer this science in which so many dangerous uncertainties are near their words.[14]

The physician in the late medieval and early modern vernacular medical treatise, like the physician in the flesh, had to take steps to insure that his implied patients would trust his advice and believe that his remedies would actually work in making them healthy. Thus, the authors of vernacular medical treatises attempted to propagate belief by broadcasting their academic and institutional credentials while pointing to their extensive experience and medical ingenuity.

The most direct way was for the author or publisher to make references to the physician's academic degrees and institutional positions. These appear prominently in the title pages, approbations, and prologues of many treatises. For example, we read on the first page of his plague treatise, *Tratado util* (1507), that El Licenciado Forés was "licensed in medicine"; we learn that Fernando Alvarez, author of the *Regimiento contra la peste* (1501), was "cathedrático de prima en medicina en la universidad de Salamanca" [first chair of medicine in the Universidad de Salamanca] (1r). Many authors, editors, and publishers were eager to promote the author by pointing to his current or past affiliations with the court or the royal family: "Here begins the plague treatise by Master Valasco de Taranta, most excellent chief physician to the king of France" (*Tratado de la epidemia y pestilencia* [1507] fol. 42r); "[a treatise] recently composed by Doctor Bernardino Montaña de Monserrate, his Majesty's physician" (*Libro de la anathomía del hombre* [1551] fol. 1v); "Francisco Franco, physician to the very serene king of Portugal" (*Libro de las*

enfermedades contagiosas [1569] cover); "composed by the Licenciado Martínez de Castrillo de Onielo, residing in the court in service of his Majesty"
(*Tratado breve y compendioso sobre la maravillosa obra de la boca y dentadura*
[1570] fol. 1r).

The *aprobaciones, licencias, cartas, privilegios, elogios*, and poetic compositions that appear in the prefatory material of sixteenth-century works offer
additional testimony of the author, his academic and institutional credentials,
and the legitimacy of his work. In the *aprobación* that appears on the second
folio of Pedro de Torres's *Libro que trata de la enfermedad de las bubas*, the
physician Francisco Gonçalez de Sepulveda, physician to the king and the
holy inquisition, acknowledges that he has read Torres's work and has found
it "very useful with many good doctrines, practices, and experiences."[15] In the
Licencia at the beginning of Núñez de Coria's *Libro intitulado de parto humano*, Phillip II grants permission to publish the work based on the king's observation that the book written in Romance was very useful and valuable for
midwives and wet nurses.[16] Likewise Philip II granted Martínez de Castrillo
license to publish a second edition of his 1557 *Coloquio breve y compendios*,
retitled as *Tratado breve y compendioso sobre la maravillosa obra de la boca y
dentadura* (1570) because the king had found this revised and extended edition replete with "many remedies and things very necessary and tested that
will provide great benefit and utility."[17]

The prefatory material to the vernacular treatise, with royal approbations
and references to academic degrees and royal appointments, told the sickly
reader that the author had been trained in a university and had passed the
necessary examinations, and thus had earned the trust of men of high standing. These degrees and titles—often abstract and often only vaguely understood by many patients—began to gain weight in the minds of a public who
still considered professional medical practice as only one of several ways to
deal with illness. Moreover, many practitioners had been trained in what
García-Ballester calls an "open system" in which the physician, surgeons, and
other paraprofessionals learned their trade as an apprentice without formal
university training.[18] Thus, as an additional mechanism to cultivate the patient's confidence and generate a believing disposition, authors attempted to
demonstrate that they had a command of knowledge that remained inacces-
sible to the patient without their aid. This knowledge was of two types. On
one hand, authors endeavored to show that they were completely familiar
with canons of academic medicine, including a thorough knowledge of the
ancient and medieval authors as well as the most celebrated contemporary

authorities, and that they possessed a firm command of Latin, the language of erudite medicine. On the other hand, authors also wanted their public to know that they held an empirical knowledge that emerged from years of experience and interaction with hundreds of patients. As I shall argue, the vernacular medical treatise not only served as a vehicle for disseminating information but also as a performative space within which the author could demonstrate his academic and empirical knowledge.

Fictions of Erudition and Professional Collaboration

Non çesse en su çiencia de estudiar e con buenos maestros participar e con ellos consejo tomar. (Estéfano, *Libro de visitaçione e conssiliaçione medicorum* fol. 73v)

According to sixteenth-century treatises on medical ethics, one of the basic skills that a competent physician must acquire before attempting to practice medicine is a solid knowledge of Latin. "First of all, he must be a great Latinist" [Primeramente ha de ser gran latino], wrote Alfonso de Miranda in his *Dialogo da perfeyçam* (fol. 10r). Enrique Jorge Enríquez reiterated this idea in his *Retrato del perfecto médico* (1595), insisting that physicians also know Greek and Arabic (fol. 185r). The requirement that medical practitioners know Latin appears in most sixteenth-century discussions on medical deontology. Even subspecialists such as surgeons and pharmacists needed to be able to understand Latin. Antonio de Aguilera, in his treatise on the apothecary arts, argued that the first requirement for a good apothecary is to "understand the Latin language well, or at least moderately well, having studied it in the university or with competent teachers for four years."[19] For the sickly reader, a demonstrated knowledge of Latin verified the physician's preparation and ability to extract useful information from the works of the great medical authorities.

Latin abounds in vernacular medical treatises. From simple technical terms and expressions to references, quotations, and entire prologues, the use of Latin provided a spectacle of erudition for the sickly reader. Some authors limited themselves to set phrases, such as Ruy Díaz de Ysla, who punctuated his writing with Latin terms such as "Pro manibus," and "in honesta"; or Pedro Arias de Benavides who, for example, defended his observation that the extreme nature of Palo de las Indias causes many diseases because "omnia estrema sunt vitiosa."[20] Others, in a more user-friendly gesture, offered vernacular translations, paraphrases, or glosses for their Latin insertions. Damián Carbón in his *Libro del arte de las comadres*, explains, "as Cicero says 'Homo autem qui rationis est particeps &cetera,' which means that almighty God gave men the capacity and understanding to use reason by which man differentiates himself from other animals."[21] Francisco Núñez de Coria, discussing the physical implications of lust and sexual desire provides a citation from Ovid's ars amandi: "Mollibus in pratis admugit saemina tauro faemina cornipedi semper adhinnite quo mitior in nobis nec tam furiosa libido est legitimum finem flamman uirilis habet." He then provides his readers with a loose translation:

> [He says that in the soft field the cow with its moo calls the bull, and the mare always calls the stallion with its bay, but in us, lust is more powerful, although not as furious, and the flames of lust are extinguished and end in men, but not in women.][22]

In visual terms, Luis Lobera de Avila's *Vergel de sanidad que por otro nombre se llamava Banquete de cavalleros* (1542) offers the most striking use of Latin in a vernacular medical treatise. On each page, the Spanish text appears in a small box against the backdrop of an extensive Latin commentary in smaller typeface (see Figure 4). As the treatise progresses, the vernacular is frequently reduced to two or three lines (Figure 5). For the sickly reader, this layout offers a visual demonstration of many of the claims of utility detailed in the previous chapter. Unlike the small type and alienating demeanor of the Latin text, the vernacular version, smaller in physical space but with a larger typeface, powerfully conveys the idea that the difficult professional information has been summarized and recast in a useful and easy-to-use format, while confirming the idea of medical deontologists such as Miranda and Enríquez who argue that a good physician must above all be a great Latinist.[23] Moreover, I would suggest that the sickly reader may have perceived in the vast sea of Latinity that surrounds the vernacular text not only a demonstration of the physician's competence and learning, but an affective quasi-clinical encounter with an absent physician whose presence becomes palpable through the spectacle of Latin erudition on the page. There is an indexical quality to Lobera's visual presentation of the Latin text that directs the sickly reader toward the physician the way a footprint indexes and makes present in the imagination the absent human being who left his or her trace in the dirt.[24] For the sickly reader, Latin in the 1542 edition of Lobera's *Garden of Health*

¶Porque los Caualleros y señozes

assi de España y de francia y de Alemaña como de Italia/
y otras partes vsan agoza y tienen mucho en costum
bze de hazer se los vnos a los otros banquetes
y beuer autan que agoza dizen:dire las co
sas quel buen banquete ha de lleuar:
y los daños q̃ de vsar los mu
cho se siguen/y particular
mente de cada cosa q̃
en los tales ban
quetes en
tran:
y el daño y pzouecho que
hazen/y sus complexiones/y de to
dos los manjares que mas se pudieren
dezir/y sus complexiones/daños y pzouechos.

¶Banquete de nobles Caualleros.

IHIL *deterius quam diuer*
sa nutrientia in una mensa si
mul. Auic. III.pri. Doct. II.
Cap. VII. Nulli ergo gau
deat malo regimine utentes,
quod si in psen
tia no̅ noceat,
postea nocere so
let. Auic. Rasis.
& Co̅stantinus.
Non pura cor
pora quantum
cu̅q, magis nu
triens magis le
des filippo .II.
Apho. Voras
ces frequenter
ægrotat, & pa
rum uiuunt, & nu̅q ad naturalem perueniu̅t
senectutem. Auic. III.p Rasis. IIII.li. Varietates
salsameto̅ru̅ ad diuersa cibaria præparatorum

V̈ vn
buen ba̅
quete ha
de auer
muchas frutas de
principio y cosas o̅
leche y queso y mu
cha diuersidad de car
nes: assi como carne

ro/vaca/ternera/
venado/tocino/ceci
na/cabzito/lecho
nes y ansarones. &c.
Muchas maneras
de aues: ansi como
faisanes/frácolines/
codoznices/pdizes/
esternas/gallinas/

pzouocant sumentem ut plus de uiaticis assu̅
mat, q̃ stomachus digerere potest, ideo euita̅
da sunt, Galenus & Rasis asserunt hoc. Cibi
corrupti uel putrefacti, siue carnes, siue pisces, si
ue fruc̄9 q̃uis diuersimode p̅paretur semp̅ su̅
sceptibiles sunt
corruptionis et
putrefactionis:
q̃a in secla di
gestionis emen
dari no̅ possut:
Auice. & Gale.
ideo no̅ debent
uti, cum ad di
uersas maxime
putrefactio̅es p̅
paret morbos.
Dicit Auice. q̃d
cibus in masticatione p̅parationem suscipit, ut a
triens masticatio̅e aliquam habet digestionem.
Auicena. Indigestio & cruditas h̅uoris est cau

B

Figure 4. Luis Lobera de Avila, *Vergel de sanidad que por otro nombre se llamaba Banquete de caballeros* (Alcalá 1542). Biblioteca Universidad Complutense, Madrid (fol. 1r).

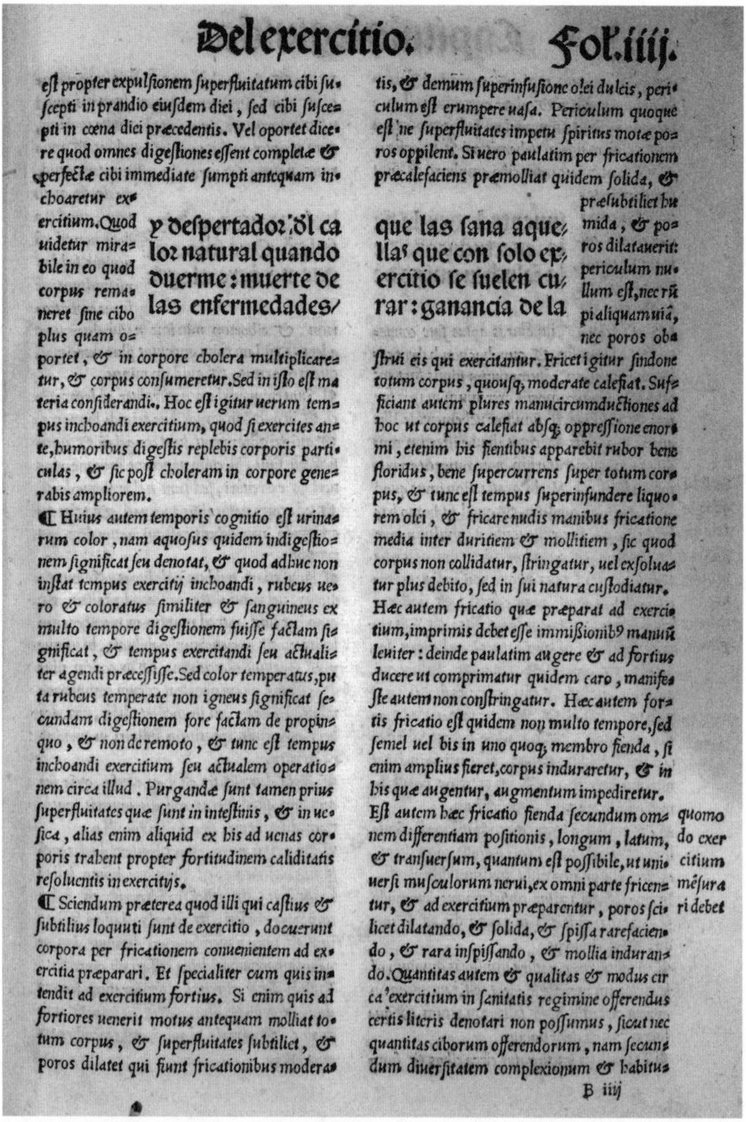

est propter expulsionem superfluitatum cibi suscepti in prandio eiusdem diei , sed cibi suscepti in cœna diei præcedentis. Vel oportet dicere quod omnes digestiones essent completæ & perfectæ cibi immediate sumpti antequam inchoaretur exercitium. Quod uidetur mirabile in eo quod corpus remaneret sine cibo plus quam oportet, & in corpore cholera multiplicaretur, & corpus consumeretur. Sed in isto est materia consideranda. Hoc est igitur uerum tempus inchoandi exercitium, quod si exercites ante, humoribus digestis replebis corporis particulas, & sic post choleram in corpore generabis ampliorem.

℃ Huius autem temporis cognitio est urinarum color , nam aquosus quidem indigestionem significat seu denotat, & quod adhuc non instat tempus exercitij inchoandi , rubeus uero & coloratus similiter & sanguineus ex multo tempore digestionem fuisse factam significat, & tempus exercitandi seu actualiter agendi præcessisse. Sed color temperatus, puta rubeus temperate non igneus significat secundam digestionem fore factam de propinquo , & non de remoto , & tunc est tempus inchoandi exercitium seu actualem operationem circa illud . Purgandæ sunt tamen prius superfluitates quæ sunt in intestinis , & uesica , alias enim aliquid ex his ad uenas corporis trahent propter fortitudinem caliditatis resoluentis in exercitijs.

℃ Sciendum præterea quod illi qui castius & subtilius loquuti sunt de exercitio , docuerunt corpora per fricationem conuenientem ad exercitia præparari. Et specialiter cum quis intendit ad exercitium fortius. Si enim quis ad fortiores uenerit motus antequam molliat totum corpus , & superfluitates subtiliet, & poros dilatet qui sunt fricationibus moderatis,

y despertador: öl calor natural quando duerme: muerte de las enfermedades,

que las sana aquellas que con solo exercitio se suelen curar: ganancia de la

& demum superinfusione olei dulcis, periculum est erumpere uasa. Periculum quoque est ne superfluitates impetu spiritus motæ poros oppilent. Si uero paulatim per fricationem præcalefaciens præmolliat quidem solida, & præsubtiliet humida, & poros dilatauerit: periculum nullum est, nec rumpi aliquam uiã, nec poros obstrui eis qui exercitantur. Fricet igitur sindone totum corpus , quousq; moderate calefiat. Sufficiant autem plures manucircumductiones ad hoc ut corpus calefiat absq; oppressione enormi , etenim his sentibus apparebit rubor ille floridus, bene supercurrens super totum corpus, & tunc est tempus superinfundere liquorem olei , & fricare nudis manibus fricatione media inter duritiem & mollitiem , sic quod corpus non collidatur, stringatur, uel exsoluatur plus debito, sed in sui natura custodiatur. Hæc autem fricatio quæ præparat ad exercitium, imprimis debet esse immißionibus manuũ leniter : deinde paulatim augere & ad fortius ducere ut comprimatur quidem caro , manifeste autem non constringatur. Hæc autem fortis fricatio est quidem non multo tempore, sed semel uel bis in uno quoq; membro fienda , si enim amplius fieret, corpus induraretur, & in his quæ augentur, augmentum impediretur. Est autem hæc fricatio fienda secundum omnem differentiam positionis, longum, latum, & transuersum, quantum est possibile, ut uniuersi musculorum nerui, ex omni parte fricentur, & ad exercitium præparentur, poros scilicet dilatando, & solida, & spissa rarefaciendo , & rara inspissando , & mollia indurando. Quantitas autem & qualitas & modus circa exercitium in sanitatis regimine offerendus certis literis denotari non possumus , sicut nec quantitas ciborum offerendorum , nam secundum diuersitatem complexionum & habitus

quomodo exercitium mesura ri debet

B iiij

Figure 5. Luis Lobera de Avila, *Vergel de sanidad que por otro nombre se llamava Banquete de caballeros* (Alcalá 1542). Biblioteca Universidad Complutense, Madrid (fol. 4r).

and less extensive Latin insertions in almost all vernacular medical treatises functioned as a single sign of the physician-author's professional competence and provided an almost uncanny sense of the absent physician's presence in treatises that were designed for nonprofessionals.[25]

In addition to their knowledge of Latin, vernacular medical authors demonstrated their academic knowledge by citing and referring to medical authorities. The physician's competency was thought to be grounded in his extensive studies. Alfonso Chirino tells us that a good physician must "spend his time in profound study of all the books of medicine."[26] Likewise, Estéfano insists that a physician should not cease studying and working alongside good learned physicians and should take counsel from them.[27] References to Galen, Hippocrates, and Avicenna appear repeatedly on almost every page of most vernacular medical treatises. Very few opinions, therapies, or diagnostic strategies stand on their own without the reinforcing acknowledgment of great physicians from antiquity and the middle ages. For example, in the following brief passage from the *Tractado del uso de las mugeres* (1586) on the salutary benefits of coitus, Francisco Núñez de Coria incorporates references and statements by Galen, Avicenna, Almansor, Aristotle, and Averroes to support the well-known (and often repeated) claim that some men would improve or preserve their health by regularly expelling their excess semen:

Avicenna says the same thing (Avicenna 1, third treatise, chapter 5.8), and in the *Canticos* he said, "Coitus comendatur iuuenibus quatenus per eum a nocumentis perniciosis liberantur." The same from Galen in *De locis affectis* book six, where he recommends extensive elimination of such excess because, he says, by doing this one escapes many strong illnesses; he said that he knew of many who because they had avoided this act became cold and suffered great sadness and strange thoughts (this should be understood as happening to those who are accustomed to much coitus), and he uses the example of Diogenes who refused all women for his pleasure, using them only for preserving his health. Hence, Almansor affirms (book 4, chapter 6) that moderate coitus alleviates and empties a full body, makes the spirit rejoice, calms anger, eliminates thoughts, lightens the head and the senses. . . . Likewise, we find this in Aristotle (*Proberbia* 3, 1) and Averroes (*Colliget* 5), and Galen (*De sanitate tuenda* 6), who more than the rest said that if one has great quantities of warm semen, he should not refrain from coitus."[28]

Perhaps the delicate subject matter—Núñez recognized that his advice might present problems for members of the clergy—encouraged him to attribute the origin of this information to the great authorities of medicine. But references of this type are common throughout his treatise. In the following chapter on the danger of excessive coitus, Núñez uses a similar number of ancient and medieval authorities, referring to Avicenna, Rasis, Almansor, and Aristotle to support the idea that excessive coitus can damage the patient's vision, nerves, and stomach while leading him to premature death (fols. 5v–6r).

In vernacular medical treatises, the copious citations of diverse medical authorities may have established more than an erudite image of a learned practitioner for the sickly reader. There is evidence to suggest that, when possible, patients in the medieval and early modern period preferred to be treated by a team of collaborating physicians. Michael McVaugh has documented such cooperation among the practitioners of the Kingdom of Aragon at the beginning of the fourteenth century. He argues that physicians regularly consulted with one another and collaborated in the treatment of patients, especially those of the upper class who could afford to pay for more than one practitioner (*Medicine Before the Plague* 108–13). Arnau de Vilanova promoted cooperation and collaboration as a deontological ideal. In his commentary on Hippocrates's first aphorism in his *Repetitio*, Arnau depicted physicians working on cases in consultation with other physicians, seeking advice and opinion from fellow practitioners. According to McVaugh, "the message communicated tacitly by Arnau's *Repetitio* to his students was that cooperation and collaboration among physicians are certainly normal and probably indispensable" (*Medicine Before the Plague* 112). Medieval and early modern medical practice was firmly grounded in a perpetual act of consultation, and even physicians who did not turn to other living physicians regularly consulted medical treatises and their corresponding authorities for advice and information related to a particular ailment. Likewise, if patients could afford it, and if more than one physician was available, they appreciated and even demanded this type of collaboration.

I suggest that many vernacular medical treatises provided the illusion of a collaborative medical practice, allowing the patient almost permanent access to medical opinions and experiences from diverse authors and authorities. For example, a patient with Soriano's *Libro de experimentos médicos* (1599) in hand would learn after reading the first folios that the author had consulted with a legion of medical authorities who appeared "in text" to comment, clarify, and opine on the various maladies that afflict the human body.[29]

In addition to acknowledging and confirming the validity of Soriano's remedies and cures, these authorities confirm the opinions of other physicians as well: "Averroes thought likewise, and one can confirm it with the authority of Mesue" (fols. 11r–12v); "Antonio Mizaldo verifies it . . . Guaynerio advises the same, saying one should eat it at the beginning of lunch and dinner" (fol. 13v); "This advice is from Benedicto Victor de Faeza and Amato Lusitano holds it to be certain, and very good after universal evacuation" (fol. 18v); "This appears to be from Dioscoridies and Antonio Mizaldo confirms it" (fol. 20r–v); "Habi, Valesco de Taranto, Leonello de Faenza, and Pascual in their Practica advise . . ."(fol. 25v); "Along with this you can use the counsel of Cardano and Alonso Lupeyo" (fol. 38r); "Two apothecaries have made it, Hieronymo Valeujo and Juan Dolio, men extremely capable in their art" (fol. 42r).

The idea that the health-related interests of the patient are best served through collaboration is fully present in the introductory lines of the popular *Tesoro de los pobres* (the vernacular translation of the *Thesaurus pauperum* attributed to Petrus Hispanus [Peter of Spain]):

Here begins a very useful book of medicine called the Treasure of the Poor, which Pope John ordered to be made by his physician Master Julian, a very wise man with great medical experience, who in order to serve his Holiness, and to serve God, and for the good of his fellow man, sought as many doctors and masters of medicine as there were in that time. For this work he united fifty-six doctors so that men would know how to cure themselves without a physician when there was not one and when there was great need.[30]

A table identifying these fifty-six physicians with whom Master Julian had allegedly consulted in preparing the work appears prominently inserted at the beginning or attached to the end of sixteenth-century editions (Figure 6).

What did names mean to the sickly reader? Clearly, lay readers would not recognize many of the sixty authorities such as Maestre Ricardo, Maestre Pedro Barbaroxa, and Pedro Logrero. Even more familiar names such as Avicenna, Aristotle, Dioscorides, Galieno (Galen) and Ypocrates (Hippocrates) may have eluded many less-educated patients. Although the authorities grounded the medical advice in a historical specificity, its greatest effect was to promote a myth of copious collaboration and consultation.

In addition to the idea that vernacular treatises were the result of extensive collaboration, the treatises themselves may have prepared the way for a

Thesoro.

os que son mucho cansados de camino o de otro trabajo grande corporal: conuiene le lauar las piernas y los braços con agua caliente en que ayan cozido mançanilla y maluauiscos y eneldo o qualquier destos. E luego duerma: y si mas fuere menester vnte los lugares del dolor y mayormente las coyunturas con azeyte de eneldo o de mançanilla. Y estas cosas cozidas en azeyte vnten conello: y esto si fuere tiempo frio: y si fuere tiempo caliente sea azeyte de oliuetas o rosado y duerma lo mas q pudiere. Y despues de dormir trayanle las espaldas blandamente con paño de lino y el lauar delas piernas y raer delas suelas o los pies conuiene en todo tiempo vna vez enel mes con agua caliente. E cumple para el regimiento de sanidad.

¶ Deo gracias.

Los dotores y maestros desta obra son los siguiétes.

¶ Maestre Macedo. Maestre Caton.	Maestre plateario. Maestre matasi.
Maestre Ricardo. Maestre Yrato.	Platon. Maestre nicolao.
Maestre Diatico. Maestre Romero.	Pedro logrero. Ypocras.
Maestre Auicena. Maestre Allano.	Tulio. Maestre ysaac.
El esperimentador. Maestre Intino.	Teodorique. Maestre Casto.
Maestre Diascorides. Maestre Crisostomo.	Maestre yran. Aristotiles.
El cometador aueruys. Maestre macencio.	Maestre megiraldo. Maestre isidoro.
Maestre Laberto. Maestre Cabecarasa.	Maestre Rogero. Maestre Caso.
Ase pedro barbaroca Maestre Dirdiro.	Maestre Alberto. Esculapio.
Maestre Plinio. Maestre Ramon.	Maestre Rogel. Galieno.
Maestre Biliberte. Maestre Balterio.	Constantino. Enrrique.
Maestre Justiniano. Maestre Sisto.	Maestre bartolome Maestre jacobo.
Maestre juliano. Maestre Octauiana:	Maestre Lucano. El lapidario.
El libro delas naturas. Maestre Raymundo.	Maestre Giraldo. Guido de cauliaco.

❧ Aqui se acaba el Libro llamado Tesoro de

Pobres, con el regimiento de Arnaldo de villanoua. Obra vtilissima en medicina: tal q en los lugares donde assi facilméte no se pudiere auer medico: cada qual lo podra ser de si mismo: porq guiado por este regimiéto biuira sano: y si alguna efermedad sobreuiniere: por el se podra curar: y con tal intencion el papa Juan caritatiuo pontifice lo mado fazer a maestre Juliano doctissimo medico.

¶ Fue Impreso en la muy Noble y Muy leal ciudad de Seuilla en las casas de Juan Cromberger: que Sancta gloria aya. En doze dias del mes de Setiembre. Año del nacimiento de nuestro redemptor Jesu Christo de Mill y Quinientos y Quarenta y tres Años.

✠

Figure 6. List of 56 medical writers consulted. *Libro de medicina llamado thesoro de pobres con un Regimiento de Sanidad* (Sevilla 1543). Biblioteca Universidad Complutense, Madrid (fol. xxxviii v).

second type of collaboration. This is, no doubt, what Francisco López de Vil-lalobos had in mind when he suggested that his vernacular summary of Avicenna's *Canon* would be "useful and valuable for the nobility and the learned in other fields who want to learn something about medicine so as to be able to speak with their physicians, ask questions, and experiment."[31]

Fictions of Experience

Lo que vemos, atestiguamos, y lo que atestiguamos es verdad. Como ninguno de razón pueda escribir en los libros sino lo que ha visto y aprendido de los pasados. (Valesco de Taranta, *Tratado de la peste* fol. 42r)

Vernacular medical treatises contain abundant claims of the author's extended experience, including often exaggerated descriptions of prolific and extraordinary healings. Juan de Aviñón, for example, reminds his readers that he has labored in the city of Seville for thirty years, during which time he became familiar with the complexions of the majority of its inhabitants, and thus he claims he is able to undertake the difficult task of prescribing the correct amount of food that each citizen must consume in order to maintain his health (*Sevillana medicina* fol. 22r). In the absence of or in addition to the ability to cite ancient or modern medical authorities, authors wanted their public to know that they "had tested" (*probado*) firsthand the therapies and remedies in their treatises. Arias de Benavides introduces his compendium of recipes by making the claim that his remedies would be effective and valuable for his patients because he has tested them himself (*Secretos de chirurgia* fol. 4v). Ruy Díaz de Ysla tells us that he has seen all the cures and experiments related to syphilis, that he has included in his treatise treatments that he himself has used and tested with an "infinite number of people who were cured."[32] Emphatically, writers announce that they have seen a particular therapy work "muchas veces" [many times] with "muchas personas." As Agustín Farfán explains, his remedies and recommendations are valuable because (referring to his observation on the benefits of the matlaliztlic root), "I have seen it used for many years. We give it with complete certitude to children, the elderly, and pregnant women."[33] Typical is the way Alfonso Chirino ends his descriptions of various remedies in his *Menor daño de medicina*; for a headache remedy, "I have seen more than five men try this remedy and it worked well for them"; for the pains of gout, he recommends an ointment and claims, "I have seen this used and it has been very beneficial for many"; for chronic abscesses, he advises using a remedy made from green fig leaves: "I saw someone who had used it many times, and he said that he had not found a medicine that worked better to reduce the inflammation, to clean and dry the abscess, and to promote the growth of new skin."[34]

Such referencing of the author's medical experience points to practical implications of the longstanding controversy over whether medicine should be regarded as a science or as an art, and over the relative value of knowledge gained through experience versus that derived from medical theory.[35] At the heart of this controversy was the belief derived from the Galenic corpus that successful medicine addressed individual circumstances and "could not be reduced to a perfectly universal theory" (McVaugh, ed., *Tractatus de intentione medicorum* 136). This meant that in practice the physician could not rely on general rules found in medical books when treating his patients. As Juan de Aviñón explains, particulars cannot be written or written with certainty; these lie in the understanding and "clear experience" of the good physician.[36] Although most medical writers would never reject the value of theoretical knowledge, those of the Galenic persuasion would increasingly argue in favor of the value of personal experience, as did Ruy Díaz de Ysla when he cited Avenzoar (Ibn Zuhr): "I am certain that nobody can perfectly use medicine without having much practice and a great deal of experience in this art, and by no means by relying on logical and invented arguments."[37] Thus vernacular medical writers frequently argued in favor of the benefits gained from personal experience, because, as Juan Cornejo points out in his *Discurso particular preservativo de la gota* (1594), "in the art of medicine, and in its great remedies, personal experience is more powerful than reason."[38] The Italian apothecary, Saladino de Ascoli, would emphasize this point in the fifteenth-century Spanish translation of his *Compendium aromatariorum*; citing an argument Arnau de Vilanova made several centuries earlier, he explains that "it is necessary that the physician be efficacious in practice and not in speaking, because diseases are not cured with words."[39] In practical terms, and in the eyes of the ailing patient, this debate translated into an effort to identify remedies and therapies that were successful in curing the patient over those based on medical theories or the teachings of venerable medical authorities.

For medical writers, having seen or "experienced" firsthand the effects of a particular remedy or cure made a powerful argument for its efficacy. Vernacular medical treatises are replete with personal accounts and testimonies. Typical is Jerónimo Soriano's description of a plague remedy that an

Italian physician, Antonio Fumanello, developed: "it cures amazingly. This is a great truth for I have seen and tested it."[40] Likewise, Nicholás Monardes, in his *Primera y segunda y tercera partes de la historia medicinal* (1580), offers his own testimony and personal experience to support his description of the medicinal properties contained within New World plants: "I saw a man who suffered from sores in his nose" cured with tobacco juice (fol. 43r); "I cured a young man of the tercian fever" using pills made from rhubarb ("pildoras de rahabarbaro") (fol. 50v); "I cured a gentleman" with sassafras water who "could not write because every time he started to write the pen would drop from his hand after writing five or six letters" (fols. 54v–55r). As we shall see in the following chapter, this emphasis on tested or proven drugs, therapies, and hygienic advice was bolstered by a number of factors, including the discovery of new botanical resources from the New World and novel pharmaceutical combinations that benefited from the empirical approbation of those physicians who had successfully employed them in their practice. Pedro Arias de Benavides defended his treatise in which he describes newly discovered remedies from the New World, stating that although "in new lands there are new cures," he has limited himself to describing those "new and secret things," which he had tested in the city of Toro: "I have cured more than two hundred in the Indias and in the city of Toro, and all are well and healthy, and none of those whom I have cured have fallen ill again."[41]

As the sixteenth century advances, eyewitness accounts of proven remedies and successful cures tend to proliferate and become more detailed, incorporating specific dates and the names of patients and cities. Jerónimo Soriano in his *Libro de experimentos médicos* (1598) tells us that in the year 1564, in the city of Teruel, he successfully cured a shoemaker named Juan de la Bastida of leprosy.[42] Cristóbal Méndez describes how he witnessed in Mexico the removal of a bladder stone the size of an egg from the son of an "honorable man" named Villaseñor.[43] As a cautionary tale against the remedies of illicit practitioners, Bernardino Gómez Miedes recounts, in his treatise on gout, the fate of Don Martin de Ayala, archbishop of Valencia, who in the year 1566 suffocated in his own urine after a Moorish healer blocked the archbishop's urinary tract as part of a procedure to relieve his pain.[44] Bernardino Montaña de Monserrate reports in his *Libro de anathomia del hombre* the unfortunate case of a knight's misery:

> In the same year of 1513, in route to Spain, I saw in Tolosa a gentleman with a hard apostema in his groin. After recognizing that the

numerous mollifying plasters the surgeons had applied proved to be
of little benefit, he followed my suggestion to open the lump with a
hot iron from which a ball of lead emerged. It was then discovered
that two years previously the knight had been shot in the sinew, but
they had not been able to discover the ball, thus causing him great
headaches for over a year.[45]

Case studies such as these were not unique to vernacular or popular
medical writing. Frequently Galen himself had exemplified his theoretical
discussions with firsthand accounts of his clinical experiences. Throughout
the middle ages and Renaissance, clinical narratives appeared in Latin medical works and in the highly respected *Consilia* in which physicians detailed
their interaction with specific patients.[46] These narratives often served as a
pedagogical device or, as we shall see, as a means to promote the author. For
the sickly reader, however, the clinical anecdotes related in first person with
references to local place names and specific dates had the effect of turning
an abstract theoretical principle into a concrete object of therapeutic belief
and a clear demonstration of the physician's competency and of the efficacy
of his advice and cures. Moreover, the "I" of the physician in these narratives
becomes the surrogate "eyes" of the patient, allowing the sick to diagnose
("to see through" as the etymon suggests) their bodies, availing themselves
of the physician's ability to perceive what they cannot see for themselves. "A
religious man suffered greatly from hemorrhoids," Jerónimo Soriano tells his
readers, "and I advised him to use the following ointment, which he did, and
which cured him and all who have used it very well."[47] The vernacular case
study invited the sickly reader to observe in the remedies of others an effective remedy for themselves.

The Physician's Tale and the Heroics of Disease

Yo he curado más de veinte mil personas y que se han sanado mas
de otras veynte mil. (Ruy Díaz de la Ysla, *Tractado llamado fructo de
todos los auctos* fol. 63v)

The image of the physician that emerges from the case histories and other
narratives in the popular medical treatise is that of a learned and experienced
practitioner whose previous triumphs allow him to recommend the most
beneficial medicines and cures for his readers. This image of the heroic healer

is bolstered by that of a heroic personality. Authors would have their readers believe that they are girded by a host of virtues including diligence, benevolence, resourcefulness, and ingenuity. Ruy Díaz de Ysla, for example, describes his benevolent practice of searching out syphilis victims to be treated in his hospital in Lisbon:

> And in the time that I resided [in Lisbon], there was a purveyor, a great captain of the very serene king don Manuel, whose name was Gonçalo de Miranda. There were so many afflicted that left [our hospital] cured from this illness, that many times the aforementioned purveyor and I sought out the sick in the doors of the churches and monasteries to bring them to this famous hospital and cure them. I do not believe that they do this in any hospital in Europe. . . . In Europe there are sumptuous and rich hospitals, but I do not believe that any of them go out to look for the sick.[48]

Other writers eagerly express their diligence in hunting down a cure for their patients' disorders. Common is the claim that Alvarez Chanca makes at the beginning of his plague treatise, *Tratado nuevo* (1506): "[In preparing this book] I have given a great deal of attention with the greatest diligence, searching through all the writings of the ancients and the moderns."[49] Pedro Arias de Benavides explains that other physicians have not made the kinds of discoveries in the New World that he has, because they prefer the "riches and the good life" that they have at home in Spain.[50] In one of his more spectacular professional interventions, Arias de Benavides relates how he cured a leather tanner in Mexico who suffered from three fistulas or holes at the base of his penis; when the time came to relieve himself, rather than urinate through the end of the penis, his waters would splatter from the three holes, wetting his legs and genitalia, and causing him a great deal of irritation:

> The first time I examined him, a cure appeared to be impossible. Nevertheless, I told the patient that I would go searching through the works of authors such as Juan de Vigo and Guido, but I could not find a cure or anything like it. Hence I resorted to my ingenuity and decided that I could cure him in the following way and none other.[51]

The ingenious physician goes on explaining in detail how he filled the fistulas with wax and created a lead belt, which he snugly attached to the base of the penis covering the wax-filled fistulas. The result was amazing, he tells us; "all the physicians and surgeons from Mexico came to examine [him] and marveled at the cure" (*Secretos de chirurgía* fols. 111r–14v).

Writers often describe themselves as resourceful and innovating, even praising themselves for being the first to investigate and develop a cure for a particular disease or condition. Speaking of his innovating use of caustics, Francisco Díaz claimed openly, "I was the first to do it . . . something that other physicians have not even dreamed."[52] Ivan Sorapán de Rieros, author of a curious treatise that collected popular refrains and glossed them to show their hygienic applicability, applauded his ingenuity in being the first to present medical information in a new, more productive form:

> I have been the first to walk this new shortcut by which the memory and principles of things pertaining to the preservation of the individual can be more easily obtained; although short and frank, the reader will discover all the substantial information that the Arabs and the Greeks, rational masters of medicine, have said, leaving the superfluous for those who desire to walk the long and wide road that they invented.[53]

At the heart of this self-promotion is the author's desire to have the public accept him as a powerful advocate who has fought tirelessly to improve his patients' health.

With this in mind, medical writers began to employ heroic metaphors to portray their professional interventions. They described themselves agonistically, as warriors who not only battled human illness but also combated the incompetence of their fellow practitioners. Whereas late medieval writers regularly pointed to Christ and Christian charity as their professional model and prime virtue, sixteenth-century physicians tended to cast themselves as medical reincarnations of secular figures, such as Alexander the Great, and claim the status of a great military leader who was prepared to protect the republic against pestilence, bodily affliction, unrelenting pain, and spurious practitioners. The exaggerated number of healings claimed by many authors rivals the battle-inflated casualties in epic poetry. "I have treated more than twenty thousand people and more than twenty thousand have been cured," Ruy Díaz de Ysla boasts.[54] Juan de Cornejo contends that he has put all his thought, attention, and work into resolving the obscure enigma of a cure for gout, which previously had frustrated physicians as if it were a battle against a

Hydra who upon cutting off one head sprouted seven more, frustrating even the military skills of a Hercules.[55] Licenciado Forés speaks in terms of the plague inflicting battle blows ("golpes de la batalla") and wounds ("feridos") on its victims, reminding them that they should not lose hope for believing that there is no cure (*Tratado útil* fol. 11r).

Authors are keen to have their readers see physicians as playing an essential role in the development and preservation of the republic. Frequent are the reminders that many brave and powerful military men owe their great deeds to the vigor and health provided by physicians: "We can take this as a certainty, Phillip, Alexander the Great's physician, did nothing less in defeating Dario than Alexander did in battle; just before the victory, he had restored Alexander's health and recovered his lost strengths from a very serious illness; without his health, Alexander would not have reigned victorious."[56]

As early as the late thirteenth century, a lay concept of health as a public good (*publica utilitas*) surfaced in the Crown of Aragon, where steps were taken to establish sanitary policies that included the control of foods such as meat and fish, and the removal of garbage and other common health-related matters (García-Ballester, "Changes" 120). Although authors never abandon or reject the idea of Christian charity as the motive behind the writing of a vernacular medical treatise, from the beginning of the fifteenth century they increasingly point to the idea that their treatises would benefit the *res publica*. A defiant Alfonso Chirino defends his use of the vernacular in his *Espejo de medicina*: "I do not regret [writing this work in Romance] because it is for the benefit of the republic." Chirino compares his medical writing with Alfonso X's vernacular legal corpus, *Las siete partidas*, commenting that the use of the vernacular must have troubled many learned jurists but was necessary for the public good.[57]

The popular image of the physician as a quasi-military defender of the public health gained momentum from a shifting emphasis toward ontological notions of disease. The frequent waves of plague during the period covered in this study were increasingly thought to be caused by external entities that attacked the body from the outside, rather than by a physiological imbalance.[58] The burgeoning mechanics of contagion, often visualized in plague treatises as a host of arrows riddling the body of Saint Sebastian, patron saint of the plague (Figure 7), promoted an agonistic concept of medical practice in which the physician was called on to defend the individual and the republic from often unseen yet dangerous enemies. For the sickly reader, these enemies could be identified as bad air, spoiled food, or more vaguely as simply

Oratio deuotissima ad san-
ctum sebastianum·ad impe
trandum salutē contra pestem·

O Sancte sebastiane semper vel-
pere τ mane horis cūctis τ mo
mentis duz adhuc sum sane mē
tis : me protege τ conserua : τ a me
marthyr enerba : infirmitatem noxiā
vocatam epidimiā. Tu de peste huius
modi me defende τ custodi : τ omnes
amicos meos : qui se confitetur reos
deo τ sancte marie : τ tibi o marthyr
pie · Tu mediolanus ciuis : hanc pes-
tilenciam si vis : potes facere cessare
τ a deo impetrare · Quia a multis est
scitum : qd ab hoc habes meritum·

joe mutā tu sanasti: τ sanatam resta
rasti : nichostrato eius viro : hoc fa
ciens modo miro : in agone consola-
bas : marthyres τ promitebas : eis se
piternam vitam : τ marthyribus de
bitam · O sancte sebastiane : tu no
biscum semper mane : atqz per tua
merita: nos quesumus in hac vita :
defende sana τ rege: τ a peste nos pro
tege: presentās nos trinitati :τ virgi
ni christi matri:vt sic vitam finiamus
quod mercedē habeamus : τ marthy-
rum consortiuz : τ deū videre primū·
Oratio·
C O sancte sebastiane magna est fides
tua : intercede pro nobis ad dominuz
nostrum ihesum christum : vt a peste
epidimie siue morbo liberemur ·v.
Ora pro nobis beate marthyr sebastia
ne · Et digni efficiamur promisioni-
bus christi·
Oratio·
C Omnnipotens sempiterne deus : q
meritis τ precibus beati sebastiāi glo
riosissimi marthyris tui : quandā ge
neralem pestem hominibus mortife
rā reuocasti : pra supplicibus tuis: vt
qui pro consimili peste reuocāda: sub
tua confidentia ad ipsum configiunt:
ipsius meritis τ precibus : ab ipsa pes
te epidimie : τ ab omni tribulatione
liberentur · Per dominum nostrū ihe
sum christum filium tuum·τ c.

Deo gratias·

Figure 7. Image and prayer to Saint Sebastian. Opening folio of Vasco de Taranta's *Tratado de la peste* (Burgos 1495). Biblioteca Universidad Complutense, Madrid.

the ailing pains of disease itself. But whereas medical writers would insinuate that their fight was against the pains of gout or the devastation caused by a particular fever, the explicit enemies of individual and public health were almost always other healers, both medical subalterns and university-trained physicians.[59]

Vernacular medical treatises often bristle with direct and indirect denunciations of incompetent, immoral, deceiving, and evil practitioners, who at best do little to help the patient and at worst lead the afflicted to an early death. At the heart of Alfonso Chirino's entire vernacular project is his insistence that patients learn to regain their health with the least amount of medicine possible, including little or no intervention from physicians, and especially from surgeons, whom he deems particularly incompetent. His work on medical ethics, *Espejo de medicina*, outlines the tricks and deceits used by ignorant and unscrupulous physicians. He warns readers that these men invent diseases and persuade healthy patients—most often rich ones—that they are sick, and thus prescribe cures that make the healthy sick and the sick more ill. Chirino claims that other practitioners try to convince patients who have been cured or improved by works of another physician that they are not truly healed; using the power of the imagination, these avaricious physicians are able to make these patients feel sick and hence in need of further treatment. According to Chirino, many malevolent physicians will insist that patients will be cured only after a protracted treatment lasting a year or more; others, when they have brought their patients to the brink of death with their purges, bleedings, or other dangerous treatments, check the patient's pulse or examine his urine only to conclude he will die from the very ailment that the physician himself had caused; and others present expensive and elaborate treatments and medicines from faraway lands and diverse regions, some taken from the bottom of the sea and others from the surface, others from human flesh and fluids, the organs of the fox, the broth made from turtles, the fat from lions and bears, and bones of elephants (fols. 49v–54r).

In vernacular medical treatises, the term *medico* seldom appears alone and is often qualified as "el buen médico" [the good physician] or "el médico sabio" [the wise physician]. These benevolent practitioners stand in opposition to "médicos locos" [mad physicians] and "médicos necios" [foolish physicians]. Jerónimo Soriano recommends that in the case of a high fever, his readers "call a physician, and not just any, but a very learned one to whom you can entrust your health and life." He warns, "Do not let yourselves be treated by physicians who are friends of potions, who are of lesser standing or charlatans; I see these every day."[60] The Spanish translation of Teodorico Borgognoni's treatise on surgery is more direct:

> It is necessary that the surgeons be learned and not idiots, because the idiots with their experiments fall into error. A surgeon can hardly learn the art of surgery if he doesn't know how to read. Almansor says that the majority are crazy, thickheaded idiots, whose madness engenders illnesses in men because they do not practice using a certain amount of science or logic, and as such they kill men.[61]

Standing against difficult, almost incurable diseases and incompetent, dull-witted practitioners, medical authors offer their readers personal narratives in which they emerge as the triumphant victor on the patient's behalf. We can clearly see the common rhetorical structure of these heroic narratives in the following anecdote found in Teodorico's treatise on surgery:

> I healed a man from Salerno who had an injury in his spine that had originated from outside. Eight months had passed since he had been wounded. And the lesion had become a fistula that went inside and from which a very thick pus emerged. And also when he coughed, he would expel this pus. All the physicians in Salerno had diagnosed him as *phthisic* and *enpico* and *eptico*, but were never able to cure him. (*Enpico* is he who spits out blood that emerges from the lung passage and the diafram; *eptico* is he who is consumed by the radical humor). Finally, that man from Salerno came to me, and using my advice he was healed very well in a short time, causing all the physicians of Salerno to marvel greatly.[62]

Teodorico's clinical account offers basic components of many healing narratives from the late middle ages and early modern period: (1) a description of a difficult medical problem (wound to the spine exuding pus); (2) a report of the failed therapies and misdiagnoses of other practitioners (all the physicians of Salerno offered diverse explanations for the ailment); (3) an account of the author-physician's successful intervention, which results in curing the patient ("using my advice he was healed in a very short time"); and finally, (4) onlookers and fellow physicians provide a public acknowledgment with direct praise or gestures of wonderment ("all the physicians of Salerno greatly marveled").[63]

Nancy Siraisi has observed that although initially "[s]uch anecdotes are indeed much more often found in books by surgical rather than by medical writers," they become increasingly common in all kinds of medical treatises during the fifteenth and sixteenth century ("Girolamo Cardano and the Art of Medical Narrative" 589). In the vernacular medical treatises, the interpolated accounts of heroic interventions and marvelous healings—accounts often embellished with vivid descriptions and lively dialogues between physicians and patients—not only offered the patient the image of a powerful medical advocate behind the text in hand, but also served the physician as a mechanism for promoting his professional skills.

Making the Physician's Place: Juan Méndez Nieto and the *Discursos medicinales*

The use of first-person narratives in a vernacular medical treatise reaches its most extensive manifestation in Juan Méndez Nieto's curious manuscript, *Discursos medicinales*. Penned in 1607 when the author was seventy years old, the treatise offers readers an autobiographical account of Méndez's medical education and fifty years of itinerant practice from Salamanca to Seville and finally to the New World. In his *Discursos*, he describes the way he confronts tenacious diseases and seemingly irremediable ailments while exacting marvelous cures with ingenious—sometimes outrageous—therapies that restore health to hundreds of patients whose conditions had frustrated other physicians.

At first glance, the *Discurso medicinales* is an unusual work. The author combines lively episodic adventures—often enlivened with extensive dialogues—with generous and highly detailed descriptions of pharmaceuticals, dietary guidelines, and concoctions and remedies that he insists will be of great value for his readers. For Marcel Bataillon, one of the few modern critics to have carefully examined the *Discursos medicinales*, the mixture of autobiography and direct medical information constitutes a work *sui generis* (46). Méndez's work, however, is firmly grounded in the vernacular medical tradition. The autobiographical narratives are broken frequently by lengthy recipes and detailed instructions on how to administer particular remedies. Although never published in the early modern period, Méndez clearly wrote his treatise with the idea that it would circulate among interested readers for whom the work would be of great use. In fact, Méndez attributes his motive for writing the work to not being able to administer his cures in person everywhere, suggesting that with his book in hand as a surrogate, readers could benefit from his medical knowledge.[64] He laments not having published his "useful and beneficial" remedies sooner for the public good.[65]

It is difficult to ignore the picaresque elements that resonate through Méndez's work. Beginning with his training in Salamanca, he relates in vivid detail his itinerant medical adventures in which his patients' recovery and his own survival as a medical practitioner often depend less on his formal university training than on his wit and ingenuity. Casting himself as a snubbed underdog, he repeatedly confronts hostile yet (according to Méndez) always professionally inferior medical authorities, whose jealousy and incompetence are as difficult to treat as his patients' bodily afflictions. Truly, Méndez spends as much time defending himself against medical authorities as he does fighting the diseases that afflict his patients.

If there is a picaresque element to Méndez's work, that is because during the early modern period the *pícaro* and the physician shared an ambiguous status within analogous systems of power that forced them to employ similar strategies to ensure their own survival and ultimately to create and maintain an enduring place for themselves in that system. For the *pícaro* and the physician, telling one's own story is yet another strategy of emplacement designed to preserve a delicate parasitical relation between system and subordinate. Michel de Certeau's opposition between strategies and tactics offer a useful point of departure from which we can compare the way physicians and *pícaros* learn to operate in the corresponding systems that engulf them.

> [A strategy is] the calculation (or manipulation) of power relationships that becomes possible as soon as a subject with will and power (a business, an army, a city, a scientific institution) can be isolated. It postulates a place that can be delimited as its own and serves as the base from which relations with an exteriority composed of targets or threats (customers or competitors, enemies, the country surrounding the city, objectives and objects of research, etc.) can be managed. (*Practice of Everyday Life* 36–37)

By contrast, a tactic "is a calculated action determined by the absence of a proper locus." What is useful in Certeau's paradigm for understanding the plight of the *pícaro* and the practicing physician is the struggle to create a proper place from which one can "capitalize acquired advantages" and manage exterior forces and resources (36).

In the late Middle Ages and early modern period, the working physician was forced to establish and defend a proper place for himself within the villages, towns, and regions in which he practiced. For these men, all bodily intervention had to bear fruit almost immediately. Unlike the theologian or natural philosopher, who could demonstrate his knowledge with metaphysical proofs or defer the confirmation of specific precepts to the hereafter, the medical practitioner constantly had to prove his worth and the value of his treatments in the ameliorated human body. Hence, the physician recognized that every piece of hygienic advice, every diagnosis, and every therapeutic procedure was not only a strategy designed to assist the patient, but also a mechanism to preserve the physician's place in the community. The fame acquired by a series of successful treatments could evaporate instantly in the wake of a failed remedy or unconvincing diagnosis.[66] Moreover, factors such as the professional envy and competition that frequently arose among practitioners, the success of popular subaltern healers—folk healers, non-licensed practitioners—and even the inevitability of death itself all conspired to undermine his reputation. Many practicing physicians found themselves migrating from town to town and from country to country.[67]

For physicians such as Méndez, the vernacular medical treatise promised a unique mechanism to stabilize their professional identity. Within the pages of a medical work, the physician's reputation, including his erudition and university training, remained secure while his most effective and ingenious cures became a matter of enduring public record. In effect, the vernacular treatise offered the author-physician a "proper place" from which, as Certeau describes, one can "capitalize acquired advantages" and begin to manage exterior forces and resources.

Faith in the Text

Assi dize Seneca, que ninguna cosa aprovecha más al enfermo, que tener confiança en el médico. (Enrique Jorge Enríquez, *Retrato del médico perfecto* fol. 200r)

Regardless of the benefits that the physician/author may have derived from the self-promoting elements in a vernacular treatise, the professional image of the physician that emerges from these texts served to garner the sickly reader's confidence (*fiducia*) in the text as an extension of a successful practitioner. As Winfried Schleiner points out, Avicenna's dictum, "Illum medicum curare, cui plurimum confidunt" [The physician in whom patients most trust is able to cure], established what was thought to be the basis of a productive patient/physician relation in the late medieval and early modern period (25). A patient's faith in the practitioner actively contributed to a sickly reader's recovery. Conversely, the frequent referencing of the author's credentials, his knowledge and experience, and the accounts of his most efficacious cures served to convince the sickly reader that the physician in the text warranted the same confidence as the physician in the flesh.

In the *Retrato del perfecto médico*, Enrique Jorge Enríquez took the idea of the patient's *fiducia* a step further and argued along with the Consiliator, Peter of Abano, that confidence in the physician could be understood within the hygienic paradigm of the non-naturals. In the fictitious dialogue between the physician (the bachelor Enríquez) and his interlocutor (the theologian, Doctor Palomares, archdeacon of Coria), the archdeacon asks how it is that Avicenna, who wrote extensively on the way proper diet and control of the non-naturals could cure disease, failed to mention the patient's need to confide in the physician. Enríquez replies:

> When Avicenna said that a good diet could cure diseases, he was referring to the non-natural things, which are happiness, fear, sadness, and others. The confidence that the physician has earned from the patient should be put among these. Thus, Avicenna affirmed, good confidence in the physician is worth more to the patient than all the medicines that he can apply. As the Arab authors Avicenna and Algacer wrote, the reason for this is because when one has great and efficacious confidence one's actions become efficacious and powerful. And just as the non-natural things—as the physicians call them—and food and drink alter the body, so does confidence alter it.[68]

In this sense, the vernacular medical treatise, to the degree that it is able to inspire confidence in the physician-author, takes on a hygienic, even pharmacological quality. As I will argue in the following chapter, the vernacular medical treatise, in its tangible form as well as in its content, functioned as a type of *pharmakon* that circulated alongside ointments, pills, and other drugs that patients believed would provide relief for their ailments.

CHAPTER THREE

Fictions and Pharmaceuticals

Todas sus partes (que son muchas) [de la medicina] son
muy dignas de saber, mas la que trata de las yerbas, paresce
ser la más excelente, útil, y sobre todo deleitosa. . . . [las
yerbas] provienen, y manan, una abundantísima copia de
remedios, una recreación tan grande que no hay otra que
se le iguale. ¿Quién ser el que no se holgara de saber las
virtudes dellas, y los secretos tan excesivos que en ellas
están ençerrados?

—Juan de Jarava, "Prefatión a los lectores,"
Historia de las yerbas y plantas (1557)

In the early summer of 1374 the Aragonese queen Elionor de Sicília received a
letter from her daughter-in-law, Mata d'Armagnac. Mata had just given birth
and was suffering from "mal de mamella," an unspecified mammary ailment
that medieval physicians may have attributed to excessive milk or milk that had
thickened in the breast, a common disorder that Damián Carbón described in
the sixteenth century as one that occurs on "infinite occasions."[1] In her letter
to Elionor, Mata wrote, "I have heard that you have a good recipe with which,
if you have it, I will be immediately healed."[2] The exchange between Mata and
her mother-in-law provides rare medieval documentation for the act of sickly
reading. Once again, we have a patient who, while suffering from a particular
malady, has imagined that her future well-being lies in the possession of a
medical text. In this case, however, the medical text is not an extensive treatise
replete with medical advice, surgical procedures, and dietary regimens, but
rather a brief text that succinctly describes a pharmaceutical remedy.

Over the ages, pharmaceuticals have enjoyed a longstanding if not privileged tradition in Western medicine. Professional healers, subaltern practitioners, and self-medicating patients regularly turned to pills, powders, ointments, herbs, plants, animal parts, stones, syrups, balms, and plasters for their healing and hygienic needs.[3] During times of illness and the accompanying conditions of pain, discomfort, and bodily dysfunction, pharmaceutical cures gain a commanding ability to encourage patients to imagine that a particular substance or concoction holds the power to remedy their disorder or eliminate the threat of disease. Pharmaceuticals provide a conceptual repository where patients can lodge their diverse therapeutic hopes, believing that once they have acquired and consumed a particular medicine the restoration of their health will be forthcoming. The medieval and early modern recipe promoted belief in a particular substance or concoction by describing it, revealing its mode of elaboration and consumption, and extolling its health-restoring benefits.

Recipes in the Vernacular

In the late medieval and early modern period, thousands of recipes in the vernacular circulated throughout the Iberian Peninsula.[4] Many appeared at the ends or in the margins of larger medical texts while others found their way into dedicated collections or *recetarios*. Even though some recipe collections were designed initially for the unique complexion of a single individual, such as the fifteenth-century *Recetario de Enrique IV*, this did not stop the entire collection or extracted recipes from circulating independently with claims for more universal applicability.[5] Rarely occupying more than five or six lines in a book or a manuscript, recipes constitute the most prolific form of discrete vernacular medical writing in the late medieval and early modern periods.[6] They appear in all vernacular medical genres from plague tracts and hygienic guides to treatises on surgery, anatomy, and pathology. Even the most reticent authors, such as Alfonso Chirino, who encouraged his patients to cure themselves without the use of medicaments, provided readers of his *Menor daño de la medicina* with over one hundred and fifty recipes, including remedies for gout, warts, toothaches, and female maladies such as "mal de la madre."

I use the term *recipe* in a very broad sense to refer to a written instruction for the creation or medicinal use of individual or compound substances that have been identified as being able to alter the human body. Unlike discussions of general dietary norms, surgical procedures, and other therapeutic practices that appear in vernacular treatises, recipes are focused on the health benefits derived from the application or consumption of a tangible object.[7] Within the vernacular treatises, a recipe is variably identified or introduced as *recetas* "prescriptions," *medicinas* "medicines," *remedios* "remedies," *experimentos* "experiments," or *secretos* "secrets."[8] Many are simply introduced with the name of the ailment they are designed to cure: "For toothaches, take . . ."; "To eliminate kidney stones, mix. . . ."

In its most minimal form, a recipe describes the medicinal use of at least one substance (usually its ability to cure or prevent a disease or ailment):

> Wash your hair with canine urine and you will not become bald. [lava la cabeza con la orina del can y non serás calvo]. (Gilberto, *Libro de recetas*, fol. 3r)

> [For a toothache] the mashed brains of a partridge placed in the tooth cavity take the pain away. [el meollo de la cabeza de la perdiz puesto en el diente cavado quebranta y tira el dolor]. (fol. 12r)

More commonly, recipes include a list of ingredients including quantities, a method of elaboration, and form and frequency of application:

> Recipe for melancholy: one ounce each of senna [*Cassia senna*] and epithymon; two ounces of lavender sugar; take one spoonful each day.[9]

Frequently, recipes are tagged with the name of the originator, inventor, or source author, and verification that it has been tested:

> [For nose bleeding] Macer says that when the herb called yarrow (*Achillea millefolium*) is put up to the nose it stops bleeding; and if the juice from this herb is placed in the nose, it makes it bleed more. Tested [Cosa probada].[10]

From a discursive standpoint, we can divide the recipes in the vernacular medical treatise into two types: one organized around the medicinal benefits of a particular substance (herb, plant, mineral) and a second focused on a specific disease or ailment (e.g., headache, toothache, stomach pain). The first emerges from the entries in herbals and treatises on *materia medica*, and follows the structure found in works modeled after Dioscorides's *Materia medica* including Andrés de Laguna's monumental translation into Spanish. These recipes usually identify a single plant, animal, or mineral, offer a description of its natural properties, and list its medicinal applications. For example, in the Spanish translation of Macer's herbal, following the structure of the Latin original (*Macer Floridus*), we find a separate chapter for each herb, ordered alphabetically so that those "in need can easily find" the appropriate substance.[11] The initial chapter on absinth begins with a standard description of the herb's properties—naturally hot, strong, and bitter—followed by a list of its therapeutic values; used properly, either solely or compounded, it settles the stomach, relieves itching, cures head wounds, removes earwax, clears up nebulous vision, induces menstruation, alleviates constipation, reduces inflamed tongues, provokes sound sleep, and helps men urinate well; it even can be used to create an ink capable of preserving paper and thwarting bookworms.[12]

Less extensive recipes of this type appear in general health guides. Alfonso Chirino, for example, provides a number of brief recipes under the rubrics of individual plants:

> Salvia benefits weak nerves, using it any way; put in bath water, soaking it in wine, etc. . . . Chicken eggs, cooked and the hard yolk pounded with saffron and rose oil, are for applying on top of an eye that hurts. . . . Ground madder, kneaded with vinegar, eliminates white spots on the body.[13]

This same discursive structure dominates the recipes in treatises that describe newly discovered medical material from the Orient and the New World, such as Cristóbal Acosta's *Tractado de las drogas, y medicinas de las Indias Orientales* (1578) or Juan Fragoso's *Discurso de las cosas aromaticas, arboles y frutales, y de otras muchas medicinas simples que se traen de la India oriental, y sirven al uso de la medicina* (1572). At the heart of each entry is a therapeutic description of uses and benefits:

> [Sandal:] the yellow, greenish-yellow, and white sandal benefit (primarily) head pain from hot origin; and those delirious who are on the verge of frenzy; applying it on the forehead and temples, ground and mixed with rose water and vinegar, eases burning in the stomach. Putting it in the mouth refreshes and gives strength in burning fevers.

Applying it with rose water to the heart, liver, and pulses, enlivens and revives the vital spirits when mixed with tonics.[14]

In some cases, entire treatises were dedicated to one particular herb, plant, or substance, such as Gómez de Salamanca's vernacular presentation of the *Propiedades del romero* and Nicolás Monardes's individual writings on the medical uses of iron and snow.[15]

The second type of recipe, usually associated with *antidotaria* and books of medical experiments, begins by identifying a particular ailment that the medicine will cure, followed by a list of ingredients (with proper amounts) and instructions for elaborating and applying the medicinal substance:

To cure a cough. Take sheep lard. Take a bit of pennyroyal and dry it, grind it, sift it, and knead it with the lard until it is mixed as one. Take a mouthful of this on an empty stomach and another at night. Do not eat or drink with it. It will cure the cough.[16]

Many recipes provide extensive instructions for elaborating and applying a particular medicament:

For those who cannot sleep. Take the green tops and stems of the elderberry plant [*Sambucus nigra*], mash them well, and extract the juice. Put them in the tube of the reed grass; close one end with a knot at the end of the reed; tie the other opening with a thread that will not break. Then wrap it well with two so that water cannot enter. Make as many of the tubes as are wanted or needed. Put them in a pot or kettle and boil them with good water until they are reduced by a third or more. And then dry the tubes and break them. You will find the unguent inside. Rub this ointment on the temples, forehead, and wrist. At this point, take the milk from the seeds of gourds. Rub it on the back of the head and cover it well. Have [the patient] lie down and sleep in a place where there is no noise, and he will sleep well. Do not wake him.[17]

In addition to plants, animals, and occasionally stones and minerals, human and animal byproducts are also extremely common in these recipes. Excrementa of all kinds, human and animal, were required to create plasters and ointments, and sometimes for making tonics and other orally administered medicines. For example, a recipe for intestinal cramps required that a plaster be made from pulverized excrement from humans, chickens, oxen, pigeons, hunting birds, and goats.[18] Women's milk (*leche de muger*) was called for in hundreds of recipes, most often for the treatment of eye and ear disorders.[19] Human and animal blood, urine, and saliva appear in many recipes designed to cure everything from hair loss to hemorrhoids. Díez Daza, for instance, cited Galen's observation that the people of Syria were liberated from the plague by drinking the urine of a child or a virile man (*Avisos y documentos para la preservación y cura de la Peste* fol. 22r). Arcane substances used in esoteric ways also appeared in many recipes: a medicament for intestinal cramps called for the foot of a wolf to be tied around the neck of the patient, and a remedy for constipation required the leg bone of a dead man to be filled with feces and boiled (Gilberto, *Libro de recetas* fols. 22v, 19v); a tonic for insomnia employed the wax from a dog's ear (Enríquez, *Secretos de la medicina* fol. 4r). Frequently, recipes called for the use of prayers and other logotherapeutic practices in combination with herbs and other material substances. For example, one recipe for a toothache required patients to place a burned date pit on the tooth while reciting a paternoster (Enríquez, *Secretos de la medicina* fol. 8r). Still other recipes required the patient to write words, prayers, and sometimes gibberish on paper and either hang them on their body or consume them in liquefied form. Fernando de Córdoba writes, "I have heard that if you write these words in a notebook [cartilla] and place it on the neck, it will take it away [the toothache]; this is the prayer, 'leçio lijbri job cancaris cancaris cancaris tantani tantani, tantani.'"[20]

The Popular Appeal of the Medical Recipe

The medical recipes, like the pharmaceuticals they described, captured the imagination of sickly readers by appealing to patients in seven ways: (1) recipes tended to acknowledge the patient's sense of illness rather than the physician's concept of a particular disease; (2) these works enthusiastically promoted the efficacy of the described medicines; (3) many recipes purported to reveal for patients esoteric and concealed medicinal powers in common substances heretofore held in great secret; (4) when abundantly collected in dedicated chapters or complete recipe books, recipes often provided the comfort of having access to copious remedies; (5) recipes made known newly discovered plant and animal remedies and novel combinations of more familiar substances; (6) recipes allured readers by identifying drugs with universal properties capable of treating multiple ailments and diverse bodily complexions; and (7) the written recipe responded to the patient's need to possess tangible forms of medicine.

Pain and the Symptoms of Illness

The late medieval and early modern medical recipe tended to address the patient's symptoms of illness rather than the abstract concepts of disease held by the learned physician. Medical anthropologists have long acknowledged that patients experience bodily disorder in different ways from physicians. A patient tends to focus on the presence of pain and discomfort or the experience of immobility and social stigmatization associated with an illness. Physicians, on the other hand, are trained to treat specific pathologies and physiological disorders and are often criticized for acting with indifference to the patient's experience of ill-being. Reading early recipes, we can sense that a patient wants the body to stop aching, whereas a physician might be concerned with identifying and rectifying a patient's humoral imbalance. In the discourse of late medieval and early modern medical recipes, the concerns of the patient frequently prevail over abstract concepts of disease. This is most notable in the regular references to pain in vernacular recipes.

Although illness brings on a variety of negative conditions such as immobility, alienation, loss of sensory powers, and a general retreat from the customary habits of daily life, nothing is more compelling, and in many ways more destructive, than pain. The vernacular medical recipe constantly promises readers that the described remedies will eliminate that pain. A list of the rubrics for the recipes contained in Alfonso Chirino's *Menor daño de la medicina* makes this clear, offering remedies for back pain, head pain, general bodily pain, side pain, stomach pain, pain from animal bites, pain from abscesses and sores, pains of indigestion, eye pain, toothaches, hemorrhoidal pain, painful urination, liver pain, gout pain, joint pain, mouth pain, foot and leg pain, sciatic pain, pain caused by cold, hot pain, light pain, and persistent and profound pain. Medicinal plants and herbs are frequently described according to their ability to alleviate pain, as Chirino comments about rue: "Rue is good for all pains caused by coldness."[21] Many recipes conclude by assuring the reader that a remedy will "take away" (*tirar* or *quitar*) or "mitigate" (*mitigar* or *amansar*) the pain, as in a recipe for "reuma" or head congestion: "take three parts of leek juice, one part of honey, and put in the nose by drops"; the recipe ends by reassuring the reader that the remedy "takes away strong pain in the head."[22] While readers would clearly understand that they were suffering from the disease of "reuma," their immediate concern was to eliminate the effects of the disease—in this case, the intense head or sinus pain. In general, the vernacular recipe appealed to the patient by addressing the pain and other symptoms of illness rather than focusing on the nature of the disease.

Efficacy

Recipes frequently make explicit claims for a medicine's efficacy. Many are marked with tags and testimonies promising or illustrating how the medicine has worked for others. In addition to tags such as the common assertion that a remedy is "proven" (*probado*), many recipes present enthusiastic testimonials. Bernard of Gordon tells us that a cosmetic facewash "cleanses marvelously" [marauillosmente la alimpia] (*Lilio de medicina*, Biblioteca Nacional MS I-315, fol. 186r); Jerónimo Soriano asserts that his recipe for easing hemorrhoidal pain produces a "marvelous effect" [effecto maravilloso] (*Libro de experimentos médicos* [1599] fol. 60r); Gilberto claims that a remedy from Constantine for forehead and eye pain has not only been tested and proven [probado] but is a "marvelous recipe" [rreçebta maravillosa] (*Libro de recetas* fol. 6v); and Fernando Alvarez's prophylactic concoction for avoiding the plague is "marvelous and great for the prevention and cure of this disease" (*Regimiento contra la peste* [1501] fol. 5r). Nicolás Monardes can hardly contain his enthusiasm for the virtue of tobacco juice in healing chronic sores and abscesses:

> For chronic sores [llagas viejas], the workings and great effects of this herb are marvelous, because it cures and marvelously heals them, cleaning them and eliminating any putrid superfluities, promoting the growth of skin, and returning them to perfect health. This is so common in this city [Seville] that everybody knows about it. And I have administered it to many people, numerous men as well as women, and with only this remedy I have healed—to the amazement of all—the putrid and chronic sores on the legs and other parts of the body that had persisted for ten, even twenty years.[23]

Some recipes come with anecdotal commentaries related to the medicament's usefulness in treating a particular disorder:

Celandine [*Chelidonium majus*] is an herb that according to Prinius clears up vision in the eyes. And believe that this is true. Test it in this way: during the season when the swallows raise their young, a boy took the small swallows, poked their eyes, and afterwards returned them to the nest. The mother came with this herb celandine and put it in their eyes and they lost their blindness and recovered their sight. Prinius proved this to be true.[24]

Testimonies of efficacy are notably present in descriptions and recipes for New World drugs, which, because of their very newness, required special corroboration. Monardes claims that the oil from the *Higuera del Infierno* (*Datura stramonium*, thorn apple) has "great virtues as has been seen by the use of it, in the Indies as well as in our country; and all that I will say is from great experience and much use of it with diverse people."[25] Likewise, in support of his claim that tobacco juice counters the poisonous resin used by hunters to kill wild beasts, he details an experiment that the king ordered to prove the effectiveness of the drug:

Desiring to ascertain [the efficacy of tobacco juice], His Majesty ordered an experiment. They wounded a little dog in the throat and applied *yerba de Ballestero* [*helleborus*] in the wound; a while later, they put in the same wound in which they had rubbed *yerba de Ballestero* a good quantity of tobacco juice with the compressed mass [of the tobacco leaves], and tied it; the dog escaped [injury] not without the great admiration of all those who saw it.[26]

In continuation and to emphasize the empirical certainty of the experiment, Monardes transcribes a marginal annotation in which the king's chamber physician relates in first-person the details of the experiment:

I did this experiment by order by His Majesty. I wounded a dog with a knife [covered with] *yerba Ballestero*, and then applied more fresh *yerba Ballestero* to the wound; the dog was overtaken by the herb, but after placing tobacco juice in the wound, the dog escaped and remained very healthy.[27]

Secrets of the Quotidian

Much of the popular charm of sixteenth-century pharmaceutical medicine emerged from a reenchantment with and medicinal indexing of the familiar world. Although some recipes included exotic plants, animals, and minerals from the Far East and the New World, a great majority called for the use of common materials that were often overlooked or misunderstood.[28] Vernacular recipes promoted the idea that even seemingly useless substances could produce extraordinary results when used in arcane yet potent ways. The discarded urine of a small child, for example, when properly combined with other ingredients and specifically applied or consumed, was thought to alleviate earaches and improve eyesight.[29] Household substances could hold secret properties: "An onion, baked and mashed with oil or lard, is beneficial when placed on hemorrhoids" (Chirino, *Menor daño de la medicina* fol. 195v). Even an ordinary chicken could be exploited in extraordinary ways. Zamudio de Alfaro, for example, offers what he calls "a miraculous and speedy remedy" for treating carbuncles and glandular tumors by using the sucking quality of a chicken's deplumed anus:

> Take large, living chickens. Remove the feathers from the place where they purge their stomach and place it on the tumor until they die. When one dies, apply another one.[30]

At the heart of the vernacular recipe is what we might call the concept of contingent utility. The key for the sickly reader was to know which substance to use for a particular ailment, when to use it, and how it should be used. The line between the useless and useful substance depended on the specific part of the plant or animal used, the method of elaboration, the manner of application, and the frequency by which the final medicine was consumed. Human excrement can heal eye ailments, but it must be burned, pulverized, and put into the eyes.[31] Chick peas, according to a recipe found in Soriano's *Libro de los experimentos médicos*, can cure melancholy and "sad thoughts," but they must be put into the open air during a crescent moon, rubbed with oil, and soaked in water for three hours, then cooked and finally given to the patient to eat.[32] The hairs of a hare can stop nose bleeds, but they need to be soaked in water with vinegar and then placed in the nose.[33] The medical recipe captured the imagination of the sickly reader by detailing how common and seemingly inert matter could acquire astonishing medical potency.

The Appeal of the Copious

In many cases, recipes circulated in copious format, often in collections of hundreds. Traditionally, the pharmaceutical profession was closely linked with the responsibility of storing abundant varieties for *materia medica*. The term *apothecary* (Spanish *boticario*) derives from the Greek word for warehouse. Vernacular medical compendiums provide the textual equivalent of a pharmacy where readers could find remedies for hundreds of ailments. For example, the Catalan and Spanish translations of the *Tesoro de los pobres* (published in Spanish at least sixteen times from 1500 to 1650) contains hundreds of recipes for treating, among other ailments and pathological conditions, fleas, lethargy, headaches, insomnia, toothaches, nosebleeds, sore throats, accelerated heartbeats, hemorrhoids, snake bites, broken limbs, and upset stomachs. Divided into chapters corresponding with a particular ailment, the majority of entries contain no fewer than ten recipes for a given ailment. In the case of eye diseases (chapter IX), we find sixty-eight recipes; nineteen for general eye ailments, nineteen types of eyewashes, and the remaining treating bloodshot eyes, running eyes, cataracts, eye pain, swollen eyes, dry eyes, and blindness. Even greater abundance characterizes recipe collections. Gilberto's *Libro de recetas* contains more than 1,250 recipes for more than fifty disorders; in many cases, the number of remedies for a particular disease exceeds fifty or sixty, as is the case for loose bowels (57 recipes), syncope (54 recipes), and general eye disorders (67 recipes).

Copious recipes centered on a particular type of bodily affliction appealed to the sickly reader, if nothing more than for the comfort one finds in abundance and the practical option of having additional remedies to turn to if the first one fails. This is what Agustín Farfán had in mind when he offered his readers recipes for two different eyewashes designed to clear clouded vision: "Test both of them and use the one that works best to complete the cure."[34]

The Allure of New Cures

The driving force behind many sixteenth-century vernacular treatises is the desire to broadcast the discovery, recovery, and invention of new drugs and innovating methods to cure disease. The sixteenth-century pharmaceutical imaginary abounds with the prospect that the remedy for stubborn ailments and chronic illnesses might soon be found at the hands of devoted physicians and apothecaries who searched for new drugs in distant lands,

in the overlooked pages of ancient medical treatises, and through the frequent experimentation with new combinations of well-known materials.
Valeria Finucci has recently discussed the extraordinary account of Duke
Vincenzo Gonzaga I whose desire to cure his impotency "led him to send
an apothecary, Evangelista Marcobruno, on a secret two-year journey by
coach, boat, galleon, mule, llamas, and foot from Mantua to Genoa, and
then to Barcelona, Madrid, Segovia, Seville, and Cádiz in Spain, and later
to numberless stops in the New World—including Cartagena, Portobelo,
Panama, and Manta in Ecuador; Callao, Lima, Cuzco, and Potosì in Peru;
and Chuquiabo (La Paz) in Bolivia—to say nothing about the return trip—
to find a Viagra-like remedy in that expanse of lands where all marvels were
contained" (523).[35]

Humanism, with its philological return to classical works of ancient
medicine, set in motion the idea that overlooked or misunderstood pharmaceuticals and other remedies could be found by carefully undertaking direct
readings of the great medical works from antiquity (Pastor Frechoso 14). In a
more extended sense, this often called for a reconsideration of the traditional
understanding of these methods. Agustín Farfán, for example, introduces
what he calls "another way of curing ulcers, sores, and wounds." He offers the
following caveat:

> This is not my invention, rather a return to the use and practice of
> that which the ancient wrote, having substantiated over many years
> with much study and work. I have tested this new way of curing ulcers
> [llagas] many times and I do not tire in giving thanks to our good
> God upon seeing the ease and swiftness that wounds and ulcers be-
> come healed. And having experienced this that I say, I determined to
> take the trouble of putting it here so that all may take advantage and
> acquire such great benefits.[36]

Philological rigor and pharmaceutical innovation went hand in hand. Such is
the result of Lorenzo Pérez's treatise on the multiple pharmaceutical benefits
of the ancient compound *Theriaca andromachi*—an antidote for poison and
venomous animal bites made with sixty or more ingredients. Pérez explains
that he has spent his study time writing his little treatise in the vulgar language in a common style so that from him those who cannot read Greek or
Latin can benefit from the "delicate ingenuities" of the past and have this "new
fruit" [nuevo fructo] free from the "celebrated errors" that have undermined

the use of this medicine.[37] By collating various ancient writings and references to the medicinal use of *Theriaca andromachi*, Peréz promotes the drug as a panacea for all kinds of ailments from kidney stones and asthma to leprosy and gout. He concludes by saying that "this antidote is very excellent for all ailments that cannot be cured with other remedies; regardless of its gravity, almost without hope of a cure, such a disease has been incredibly cured with the help of *theriaca*."[38]

Paradoxically, much medical innovation in the sixteenth century originated in new readings of old texts. In his treatises on gout, Gómez Miedes describes a medicine that has been "newly discovered," and although "the medicine is ancient, the method and true use is modern." He ends his treatise reflecting that in discovering how the human body has been liberated from many ailments and diseases with this medicine, "we should make reference to the many benefits and health that come along with it; there are so many that it would be necessary to write a new treatise on them alone."[39]

Deeply embedded in the ancient, medieval, and early modern medical imaginary was the idea that pharmaceutical innovation was linked to the discovery of therapeutically potent substances in distant lands and remote places. When Arias de Benavides succinctly stated, "In new lands there are new cures," he not only crafted an axiomatic formulation but also encapsulated a professional imperative.[40] Even before the extraordinary reports of newly found plants from the New World, legends and anecdotal material promoted the idea that the great physicians found new remedies by traveling from region to region. According to Amato Lusitano, Hippocrates's and Galen's fame as perfect physicians was grounded in their knowledge that they gained from extensive travel:

> He [Hippocrates] went through various lands and regions (as he writes in his works), which is of no little importance for one to become a perfect physician. Galen did the same, as he tells us in diverse places in his books. He went to Rome two times, sailed to Lycia, was in Thrace, Cyprus, Macedonia, Syria, Alexandria, Sicily, Phoenicia, Palestine, Crete, Italy, Bithynia, and Egypt and many others that he sought out. And he traveled to find simple herbs, and various types of medicines, and diverse kinds of diseases that are usually found in each place. And he also wrote that Hippocrates taught in the book of the air, waters, and regions, the regional diseases that each different land generates. Likewise others wrote that for this reason Hippocrates is

depicted with his head covered, a sign that he was a friend of traveling and seeing lands.[41]

In *The Virtues of Rosemary*, a brief treatise appended to Maestre Gil's translation of the *Macer Floridus*, we find an apocryphal account of Arnau de Vilanova's discovery of a recipe for rosemary oil. While traveling throughout the world in search of secrets of natural philosophy, Arnau encountered in Babylon a "learned Moor" who was a great physician, astrologer, and philosopher. With the idea of learning some secret, he made friends with the Moor and pleaded with him to reveal the secret of making oil from the leaves of the rosemary plant. After much diligence, Arnau was able to convince him to divulge the formula that had never before been revealed.[42]

Ancient and medieval myths and legends surrounding the discovery of new medicines in distant lands provided an enthusiastic foundation for the reception of medicinal materials from the New World. Such is the basis upon which Nicolás Monardes introduces his *Historia medicinal*.[43] After describing the riches from the New World—gold, silver, pearls, turquoise, emeralds—he draws the reader's attention to the medicinal riches from this new land:

> Beyond these great riches, our West Indies sends us many trees, plants, herbs, roots, juices, gums, fruits, seeds, liqueurs, and stones that have great medicinal value, in which has been found and will be found great effects that greatly exceed their value and price. . . . And it is not marvelous that it is thus so, as the philosopher Aristotle says, not all lands produce the same plants and fruits, because one region or land has such trees, plants, fruits, another does not have them. We see that *diptamo* only grows in Crete and *encienso* in the regions of Saba, *almaciga* in the Isle of Chio, cinnamon, cloves, and pepper and other spices only in the island of Maluco. And there are many things in diverse parts of the world that have not been known until our time. . . . And since our Spaniards have discovered new regions and new provinces, they have brought us new medicines and new treatments that can cure and heal many diseases that, lacking these, would be incurable and without remedy.[44]

The various parts of Monardes's *Historia medicinal* published between 1565 and 1574 enjoyed a phenomenal popularity in Spain and Europe. Before his death in 1588, nineteen editions of the work had been published in five languages. The phrase "Joyfull Newes," which the English merchant John Frampton used for his 1577 translation of Monardes's *Historia medicinal* (*Joyfull Newes out of the New Found Worlde*), refers not only to the fortunate notices of medicinal substances from the New World, but also to Monardes's detailed discussion on the preparation and application of this material.[45] Most of the botanical specimens discussed in the *Historia medicinal* had already been described in earlier works by authors such as Fernando Gómez de Oviedo. The novelty in Monardes's work lies in establishing a medicinal use for these substances for vernacular readers.

In this sense, Monardes anticipated Francisco Hernández's extraordinary expedition in 1570. Phillip II had charged Hernández to travel to the New World, consult with all those involved in the healing professions—physicians, surgeons, herbalists, Indians, and "other curious people in this practice"— and then to provide a written account of the medicines derived from trees and plants, including their proper method of cultivation. Unfortunately, Hernández's opus containing descriptions and medicinal uses for over three thousand plants and animals never made its way into the vernacular until the early seventeenth-century, when Francisco Ximénez, a Dominican working in the hospital of Huaxtepec, published a Spanish version of the Latin summary that the Napolitano Antonio Recchi had made at Phillip II's request. Although far from Hernández's orginal twenty-two volumes, Ximénez's translation contains the workings of popular medical treatises designed with a nonprofessional reader in mind.

At the heart of the projects undertaken by Monardes and Hernández is a desire to find medical applications for new substances through empirical methods. Locating new plants and animals was only the first step. Once found, these substances needed to undergo experimentation to determine their value in treating disease. "Many are the concealed virtues" [E muchas y son de las yerbas sus virtudes encubiertas] of plants and herbs, the Spanish translator of the *Macer herbolario* tells his readers (1r). Juan Jarava introduces his Spanish translation of Leonhard Fuchs's highly respected *Historia stirpium* (*Historia de las yerbas, y plantas sacada de Dioscoride Anazarbeo y otros insignes autores*) informing readers that there are astonishingly "abundant remedies" [abundantissima copia de remedios] in herbs whose hidden secrets are copious.[46] Experimentation involved stripping away this metaphorical covering and revealing those secret virtues and hidden remedies. Of course, in the sixteenth century this amounted simply to trying out medicines, usually on patients and occasionally on animals. Monardes grounded his knowledge of

New World drugs in the forty years in which he had "experimented on many and on diverse people, with all diligence and observation possible, and with a very successful outcome."[47]

For sickly readers, an additional benefit from the reports of medicinal substances from the New World was the possibility of obtaining inexpensive and efficacious substitutes for costly and rare drugs that were often prescribed but difficult to obtain. For example, balsam from Matariyya in Egypt was frequently recommended by ancient and medieval medical writers such as Dioscorides, Constantine the African, as well as major Arabic writers including Avicenna for its amazing curative properties.[48] Used to anoint kings, embalm the deceased, and as a panacea for a host of diseases, the aromatic resin and oil was extremely costly and difficult to find in Western Europe. We find it most frequently in recipes for healing wounds and in surgical procedures. Saladino de Ascoli explains that there is nothing more sublime than balsam for reducing and removing scar tissue. But he also laments that the price of this substance is so great that only the powerful and great lords can obtain it on account there is only one plantation in the world and it is under the control of a great Muslim sultan.[49] According to legend, the infant Christ during the Holy Family's sojourn in Egypt stopped in Matariyya where he broke Joseph's staff into several pieces from which the balsam trees sprang forth (Milwright 205). Limited supply and high cost made this highly valued and symbolically charged substance almost impossible for use in general medical practice.

Although balsam appears as an ingredient in vernacular medical writing and recipe collections, authors were not indifferent to the practical impossibility of treating patients using what would become known as "true balsam." It is common to find recipes for oils, waters, and other concoctions that were praised as being "as useful as" or "as valuable as" balsam.[50] These substitutes for true balsam proliferated with the notice of new botanical substances from the New World.[51] García Pérez Morales's *Tractado del balsamo* (published in Sevilla in 1530) offered an entire treatise on the curative powers of this "precious liqueur" (2r). Nicolás Monardes dedicated a chapter of his *Historia medicinal* to what he called an "excelentísimo" botanical liqueur whose profuse medicinal properties led Spaniards to name it balsam (bálsamo) after the "true balsam" that was once cultivated in Egypt. The discovery of a substitute drug in the New World was timely since, according to Monardes, the plantations that produced true balsam in Egypt had dried up and it was no longer available. Monardes's enthusiasm for balsam from the New World sprang not only from the substance's ability to cure everything from asthma to bladder afflictions, but also from its accessibility. He explains how when the substance first arrived in Spain the price was between ten to twenty *ducados* per ounce. By the time it had arrived in Rome the price had jumped to a hundred *ducados* an ounce. But as the supply increased to the point of abundance, the price dropped to almost nothing.[52] Monardes implicitly warns readers that the price of a drug does not change its healing powers and its current abundance makes this marvelous substance highly available for use in surgery, for curing wounds, for comforting upset stomachs, for purging the uterus, for nervous disorders, for joint pains, for encouraging the flow of urine, and for preserving the youthfulness in old men. Monardes tells us: "I met a very healthy person who used it, and although he was very old, he looked like a young man and he lived with out pains after using it."[53] The idea of a plentiful, inexpensive, and highly effective substitute from the New World certainly would have appealed to sickly readers. Esteban de Villa, writing in the first part of the seventeenth century, confirms Monardes's belief that the new balsam was more advantageous than that from Egypt or Siria, and that it could be use every time a recipe required true balsam.[54]

Empiricism and experimentation with new and old drugs provided yet another avenue of pharmaceutical innovation that captured the imagination of sickly readers in search of new cures for vexing ailments. Medieval and early modern pharmacology was based on the specific qualities of individual medicines. In addition to the benefits acquired from the use of individual medicines, the sixteenth-century pharmacological imaginary shared by patients and professionals thrived on the assumption that the qualities and powers of individual substances could produce astonishing effects in combination with other medicines. To a degree, this assumption was backed by a longstanding pharmacological theory. According to Avicenna, the specific qualities of individual medicines gained unexpected and largely unpredictable results when combined with other single or complex medicines. A compounded medicine was thought to produce a unique complexion (*forma specifica*) by virtue of its combinatory nature. As Michael McVaugh notes, pharmacists could "systematically predict many properties of a compound, those derived from its simples, but the property that results from its *forma specifica*, a quality peculiar to the individual medicine, can be determined only through experience in its use" ("Development" 17–19). It is the unpredictable aspect of compounded medicines that opened the door for extensive pharmacological imaginings. The power to heal a troubling ailment may lie in the combination of an additional ingredient. In this sense, the frequent "probatus est" tags at the end of many compound drugs and concoctions was meant to tell readers that the alleged effects of new drugs, often promoted as marvelous and astonishing, were not the results of mere theoretical speculation, but rather had been verified by use and experience.

The Attraction of Universal Medicines

Juan de Aviñón, writing in the later part of the fourteenth century, argued that the doctors of medicine "did not prescribe one medicine for all the ailments that require purging," and thus concluded, "it is not possible to purge many ailments with one medicine."[55] As a devoted Galenist, Aviñón endorsed the concept of radical individualism that required physicians to monitor the particular complexion and exogenous conditions related to each patient. Fernando Alvarez also supported this idea and reminded readers of his short plague treatise that the dozen or so recipes attached to the end of the work should be used with the assistance of a physician who could moderate the medicine "according to the age, complexion, and personal habits" of the patient.[56] Nevertheless, in the sixteenth century we see a tendency to promote drugs and medicinal substances that were allegedly capable of treating multiple disorders in all types of patients with indifference to age or a particular bodily complexion.

The idea that one medicinal substance could cure multiple ailments in all kinds of people is notably associated with certain plants and herbs. Rosemary (*romero*), for example, was frequently promoted as this type of wonder herb. In the final part of Maestre Gil's translation of the *Macer Floridus*, we find an appended version of the *Virtues of Rosemary* falsely attributed to Arnau de Vilanova. The work begins with the following rubric:

> A very marvelous recipe for the virtues of rosemary, especially the flower from which is made an oil with which you will use and cure infinite afflictions of diseases [passiones de enfermedades].

The author then proceeds to list the benefits of the oil:

> First it comforts the heart and gives strength to all weakened bodily members; it cures those whose head and hands tremble; it removes spots on the face, and the person who rubs it on his face will stay

young; a drop in the eye eliminates cataracts in those who have them, or spots or tears that disrupt vision (it will clear it; use it three times). Likewise, it benefits greatly those whose members suffer from a great ailment; rub on this oil and they will be healthy. Furthermore, it treats all pains caused by coldness or by descending humors in the joints. It also benefits those patients who suffer from colic and treats the diseases of women suffering from the wandering womb. Furthermore, it helps any patient with abscesses.[57]

Additionally, the author explains how rosemary, used in various ways, soothes stomach pains and colic, preserves youthfulness, serves as a mood enhancer, protects against abscesses, rejuvenates the face, eliminates bad breath, protects the teeth and gums, reduces all types of fevers, counters the effects of poisons, quiets bodily tremors, remedies phthisis, prevents hair loss, helps women conceive, relieves the pains of gout, and alleviates constipation. In conclusion, the author emphatically informs the reader, "know that whatever ailment you have in your body, you will be healthy and preserved" [Sepas que quanto mal tovieres en el cuerpo, de todo serás sano y conservado] (30v).

Universal medicines are markedly present in sixteenth- and seventh-century works on the plague and contagious diseases. It is common to find recipes for cure-all pills, powders, and ointments. The growing acceptance of ontological epidemiology and the development of contagion theory no doubt turned attention toward universal medicines over the benefits of mere physiological adjustment. In Martinez de Leyva's late sixteenth-century *Remedios preservativos y curativos para en tiempo de peste* (1597), we find among the pharmaceutical remedies in the final chapters of the treatise a recipe for *diaromatico*. According to Martinez, this is a drug with very great virtues for "all illnesses, internal and external." A mixture of sugar, ground pearls, saffron, cinnamon, and musk, the great benefit of this drug is not only its universal effects but also its incorruptibility and its ability to be stored for long periods of time. It has "infinite" benefits, and by testing this "unique" [singularissimo] remedy, readers will be able to see how it "cures all types of illnesses and all kinds of people."[58]

For the sickly reader, the benefits of possessing such a drug, or even a quantity of a potent medicinal herb such as rosemary, is obvious; a single substance promises to take care of hundreds of possible ailments. It can be stored, redistributed, and easily applied without the complicated process of searching for more specific remedies.

The Charm of Tangible Medicine

Throughout the 1980s and 1990s medical anthropologists explored the over-whelming popularity of medicines in relation and in opposition to other heal-ing practices. It appears that when given a choice, patients in Western cultures almost always prefer to take a pill, rub on an ointment, or drink a medicinal tonic rather than undergo surgical procedures or submit themselves to di-etary and behavioral modifications. According to van der Geest and Whyte, when "medicines are lacking, people stop visiting health care services, for medicines are seen as the essence of health care. A clinic without medicines is, one could say, like a bar without beer" ("The Charm" 246). Moreover, in many cultures, physicians and healers who do not prescribe medicines risk leaving patients with the sense that the practitioner has failed to intervene on their behalf.

The orienting question for these anthropologists is what makes medicines popular as solutions in moments of bodily distress. For van der Geest et al.,

the secret of their attributed power lies primarily in their concrete-ness. Their "thinginess" provides patients and healers with a means to deal with the problem at hand. Medicines are tangible, usable in a concrete way; they can be swallowed, smeared on the skin, or inserted into orifices—activities that hold the promise of a physical effect. By applying a "thing," we transform the state of dysphoria into something concrete, into some thing to which the patient and others can address their efforts. ("Anthropology of Pharmaceuticals" 154)

The possession of objects deemed as having pharmaceutical power can pro-duce a liberating effect. Medicines can be warehoused, exchanged, and saved for future ailments. Patients who can secure a supply of drugs gain a sense of independence from the costs and inconvenience involved in consulting phy-sicians and other healthcare practitioners ("The Charm" 346–50).

I suggest that the concreteness that anthropologists have identified as the charm of modern medicines also drove the late medieval and early modern popularity of medicaments. In the late medieval and early modern medical imaginary, the perceived concreteness of a particular herb, pill, ointment, or concoction was supported by the very physicality of the materials upon which the recipes for such pharmaceuticals was written. Written on a sin-gle piece of paper or bound among hundreds of others in a medical treatise, recipes offered the sickly reader a tangible link to the body-altering effects of medicines. And recipes, like pills and other drugs, can be stored, transported, sold, and exchanged. Having a written recipe at hand was, on the level of the imaginary, tantamount to possessing an actual medical substance.

Near the end of Martinez de Leyva's treatise on the plague (*Remedios preservativos y curativos para en tiempo de peste*), in the chapter following the descriptions of various medicines designed to remedy plague-related conditions and ailments, the author makes the following observation:

> Having written this present regiment on the plague, in which is written the method to make some notable and very important remedies for use against said plague, I do not want to forget to talk about the way to use these remedies for many other kinds of diseases in the hope that this book will be good and beneficial at all times and in all occasions, and that I can serve everyone according to his will when necessary.[59]

As Martínez would have it, the plague-related remedies merely form part of a larger pharmaceutical project that extends itself universally to all people at all times. In effect, this medical compendium takes on the role of a pharmaceutical compound, a potent universal drug designed to meet hundreds of medical needs and to provide fodder for an equal amount of therapeutic fictions. It may be that the most powerful characteristic of the popular medical treatises lies in the way these writings offered sickly readers a tangible, palpable, "touchable" form of medicine. The various discursive characteristics that I have detailed throughout this study—tropes of utility, claims of efficacy, presence of the physician, first-person accounts of healings, copious remedies, and the vernacular exposition of medical information—converged to create one potent medicament, a type of pill or drug capable of stoking the imagination of sickly readers and encouraging them to create salutary fictions of their future well-being.

Fictions of Ill-Being

Among the most astonishing things in the study of
medicine is seeing the multitude and variety of diseases.
Every day we come across new ones in addition to those
about which the splendid Greeks, elegant Romans, and
curious Arabs wrote.

—Francisco Díaz, "Prólogo al lector"

Belief kills; belief heals. The beliefs held by persons in a
society play a significant part in both disease causation
and its remedy. In different societies, such categorizations,
beliefs, and expectations are culturally organized, to various
degrees, in enthnomedical systems. The significance of
these beliefs in disease causation and cure is the same
as that of microorganisms and medicinals; given certain
conditions of host and environment, pathology or healing
consistently follows belief.

—Robert A. Hahn and Arthur Kleinman,
"Belief as Pathogen" 3

"The Body," a popular website that disseminates information on HIV prevention and treatment, regularly fields questions from men who, following
a lower-risk sexual encounter—such as protected sex with a prostitute—
suddenly experience the many symptoms related to acute retroviral syndrome
(ARS) and conditions associated with AIDS—thrush, folliculitis, lipodystro-
phy. Often these symptoms (and the corresponding anxiety) persist even

after the patient has received numerous negative results from HIV testing. "Worried well hell," as one poster calls it, is not limited to those who fear HIV ("Worried Well"). The perceived threat of SARS, mad cow disease, cancers, multiple sclerosis, lupus, Lou Gehrig's disease, tapeworms, diabetes—almost any disease or affliction—can cause individuals to suffer from hypochondriasis or a related somatization disorder.

Curiously, the considerable information available on the Web seems to exacerbate and perhaps even to produce the suffering of the Worried Well. Patients report spending hours online, either trying to confirm that certain bodily symptoms—rashes, swollen limp nodes, tingling arms and feet—are the result of a specific disorder or generating fears that a particular disease they have read about is festering in their bodies.[1] "Cyberchondria," as it has been coined, is the result of having too much medical information at hand, too many accounts of debilitating diseases, and too many lists of symptoms. As one journalist writes, "if hypochondria is the excessive fear of illness, then cyberchondria is that fuelled by the huge amount of medical information that is now available on the internet" (Valley).

From a pathological standpoint, the psychosomatic nature of the modern worried well syndrome would have given medieval and early modern medical writers little pause. They would have quickly acknowledged that the very thought of a pending illness could make a patient sick and account for the paradoxical onset of the very disease that had initially arisen only in the patient's imagination. As Estéfano de Sevilla reminded his readers: "And we see that a healthy man who fears becoming sick, becomes ill."[2] We might ask ourselves, if vernacular medical treatises could help readers envision their well-being, as I have argued throughout this study, might these works generate in some cases the opposite effect, producing anxiety and promoting sensations of ill-being?

In the vernacular medical treatises that circulated in the late medieval and early modern period, we find account after account of troublesome diseases, frightening symptoms, and professional malfeasance. As I have discussed, many authors took time to remind readers that diseases and afflictions lurk around every corner, threatening to destroy the good health of all. Indeed, the fear of developing the very disease described in a medical treatise could have turned a general work on pathology into a hypochondriac's handbook, converting hundreds of possible ailments, *a capite ad pedes*, into anxious contemplation. Case studies, embedded in many medical works, point to strange conditions: Nicolas Monardes tells of a man whose infested nasal passage was eaten away by twenty or more worms; Pedro Arias de Benavides describes a man who developed multiple fistulae at the base of his penis from which his urine leaked, leaving his groin painfully chafed and ulcerated.[3] Whereas most treatises offer the afflicted hope in the way of proven and innovative remedies for the disorders they describe—Monardes cured his patient with tobacco juice and Arias de Benavides remedied the fistulae-ridden man by concocting a truss that plugged the holes—it is not uncommon to find descriptions of diseases for which even the most illustrious physicians argued that there was no cure. In the Spanish translation of Bernard of Gordon's *Lilio de medicina*, the author addresses physicians about the impossibility of curing epilepsy.

> I want to talk to you about epilepsy. I have had in my care young, old, poor, and rich men, and women suffering from every type of epilepsy, but I have never seen anybody cured either by me or anyone else. . . . And I tell you this so that if patients come to you, you do not dishonor yourselves with vain and false promises to cure them.[4]

Given that many vernacular works are translations of treatises written for professionals or paraprofessionals, and promoted as "useful" for lay readers, it not surprising that sickly readers could come across information better reserved for professionals that was discouraging, disheartening, and perhaps disadvantageous for the nonprofessional's well-being.

In addition to descriptions of ailments that may have frightened readers, the accounts in vernacular treatises of medical malpractice and professional incompetence, which led to horrific and complicated afflictions, were certain to cause some unease. Bernardino Gómez Miedes, under the rubric "How a man wanting to be cured from gout, died from a urinary disorder," explains that often when incompetent practitioners try to cure an ailment, they only succeed in making it worse:

> About this, we have an account of a sad case from our days that occurred in 1566 to don Martin de Ayala, the very learned and vigilant pastor and archbishop of Valencia in 1566. . . . As this archbishop was suffering greatly from gout, a Moorish empiric, they say from Granada, advised him to allow him to cut or burn certain small, tenuous veins, almost imperceptible that run parallel to the emulgent arteries where the receptaculum is formed, and which is the main conduit for the urine to pass from there to the kidneys and consequently to the

bladder. By closing these small veins, gout's cold humor would be diverted and he would be cured of it. The Archbishop liked the idea and with his health in mind, he went to some baths, not far from Granada, where the procedure took place. Having done this, he felt completely alleviated from gout, and he returned to Valencia very happily, pleased with his cure. Halfway back, he stopped urinating and felt a notable blockage, for which he had physicians come to him. When they could not find the cause of the blockage in the bladder or further along, they started with baths and many other remedies for treating the disorder as they understood it, but it did no good. The amount of urine continued to increase, and given that the passage to the kidneys had been closed, little by little it regurgitated upward beyond his chest into his throat until he expelled urine from his mouth and thus, drowned.[5]

The rise of vernacular medical writing, with its extensive talk about diseases, disorders, symptoms, and cures, was likely to have promoted the development of a new culture of pathology in which humans increasingly envisioned their disorders in more specific terms. Speaking of the late medieval period, Luis Granjel argues that the most frequent bodily afflictions were presented under the rubric of imprecise pathologies and localized pains ("La medicina europea" 13–16). It is true that a work such as Chirino's *Menor daño de medicina* tended to speak of diseases in terms of undesirable symptoms, most notably in relation to the presence of pain. We find recipes and remedies for "pain in any member," "pain in the stomach," "pain in the ribs," "back pain," "headaches," "toothaches," "eye pain," "kidney pain," "pain in the joints," "profound bodily pains," "hemorrhoid pain," "pain in the throat," and "mouth pains," to name a few.[6] Yet by the middle of the sixteenth century, the learned terms for diseases and afflictions began to displace vague, symptomatic-based terminology in works directed towards the lay public. In the table of contents of Lobera de Avila's *Remedio de cuerpos humanos y silva de experiencias* (1542), a work simply organized and explicitly designed for use by nonprofessionals, we find chapters on disorders such as spinancia, *peripleumonia, emopthoica, syncopis, hidropesía, ictericia, apolexia, perlesía, scotomia, çollipo, lienteria, fluxo epatico*, along with chapters on *dolor de cabeza* [headaches], *dolor de los oídos* [earaches], and dolor del estómago [stomach pain].

New diseases (or new names for familiar disorders) and their accompanying etiologies provided fresh ways to think about the body and new ways to conceptualize illness and disease. In fact, it is quite possible that within this new culture of pathology, a more learned notion of disease could prove liberating and useful in resolving difficult social problems. In Arias de Benavides's *Secretos de chirurgia, especial de las enfermedades de morbo galico....* [The secrets of surgery, especially those maladies related to the French Disease . . .], the author acknowledges that syphilis is usually transmitted when the patient comes into contact with "women who are not clean" and from drinking from the same glass as someone infected with the disease or by sleeping with an infected person. But he also notes that syphilis can develop independently of contagious contact. In fact, he claims that a particular combination of corrupt humors can produce this disease in anyone. If contagion was the only cause of this disorder, he argues, then how could the first human to suffer from the disease become infected? He backs his argument pointing to many nuns who have entered the convent without the disease only to have it appear later in abundance. "I have seen this happen to religious men, as well" he concludes.[7]

In the sixteenth century we find similar attempts on part of nonmedical professionals to explain or cast problematic human behavior in medical terms so as to reduce or eliminate negative theological and moral implications. Melchor Bajaen Español has recently documented the case of the Jesuit, Miguel Pérez, who attempted to "medicalize" certain "poluciones" (a euphemism for the practice of masturbation) experienced by monks and nuns. According to Pérez, these people suffer from an intense discomfort and itching in the genital region that compel them to touch themselves. Pérez employed various medical explanations to argue that inept sperm ("esperma no apto") caused by a mixture of strange humors created an uncontrollable urge to expel by manual methods the corrupt substance. For Pérez, the medical explanation served to absolve those who attempted to alleviate themselves of this "disorder."

The continued circulation and subsequent readings of vernacular medical information during the late medieval and early modern period helped to create communities of medicalized subjects who increasingly began to understand their bodily sensations—painful as well as pleasurable—in medical terms. On one hand these readers could take comfort knowing that the information stored in a vernacular, well-organized, and understandable medical text could provide not only relief from their ailments and sufferings but also new and useful ways to understand their bodies and their behaviors. On the other hand, extensive talk about disease and bodily maladies could create anxieties, and as Michel Foucault has forcefully argued, lead to new disciplinary projects in which "the pathological must be constantly centralized," requiring that the "relation of each individual to his disease and to his death passes through the representatives of power" (*Discipline and Punish* 195–97). Future studies on vernacular medical works will need to address the way this writing aided authorities in exercising control over individuals through the creation of what Foucault identifies as binary divisions and branding that sought to clearly determine who was mad, who was sane, who was dangerous, who was harmless, who was normal, and who fell into the ranks of the abnormal (197).

NOTES

Preface

1. According to Latour, "By definition, a technological project is a fiction, since at the outset it does not exist, and there is no way it can exist yet because it is in the project phase" (*Aramis, or The Love of Technology* 23).

2. I am greatly indebted to the transcribers who have worked on the Hispanic Seminary's medical texts series under the direction of John Nitti, María Teresa Herrera, Nieves Sánchez, and María Estela González de Fauve. These include Enrica J. Ardemagni (Alfonso Chirino, *Menor daño de la medicina*), Andrea L. Arismendi (Pedro Arias de Benavides, *Secretos de chirurgía*), Mirta Alejandra Balestra with Patricia Gubitosi (Bernardino Montaña de Monserrate, *Libro de la anathomía del hombre*), Andrea María Bau (Juan Cornejo, *Discurso y despertador*, and Francisco Núñez de Coria, *Libro intitulado del parto humano*), Fabián Alejandro Campagne (Marsilio Ficino, *Libro compuesto por Marsilio Ficino*, and Francisco Núñez de Coria, *Libro intitulado del parto humano*), Gabriela Canavese (Francisco Núñez de Coria, *Tractado del uso de las mugeres*), Thomas Capuano (Maestre Gil, *Libro de medicina llamado Macer*), Patricia de Forteza (Martínez de Castrillo, *Tratado . . . de la boca y dentadura*, and Jeronimo Soriano, *Libro de experimentos médicos*), Victoria García Serrano (*Cirugía Rimada*), Patricia Gubitosi (Ruy Díaz de la Isla, *Tractado . . . contra el mal serpentino*), Cecilia Estela Incarnato (Bernardino Gómez Miedes, *Enchiridion*), Eric Naylor (Juan de Aviñon, *Sevillana medicina*), Alejandra Piñeyrua (Damian Carbón, *Libro del arte de las comadres*), Ruth Richards (Isaac Israli, *Tratado de las fiebres*), María Purificación Zabía (Diego Alvarez Chanca, *Tratado Nuevo*; Fernando Alvarez, *Regimiento contra la peste*; Licenciado Forés, *Tratado útil* y *Tesoro de la medicina*; Valesco de Taranta, *Tratado de la epidemia*).

Introduction

1. For an overview of Berenguer Sariera's professional involvement with the royal household, see McVaugh, "Royal Surgeons"; see also Batllori, ed., "Regiment de sanitat" 75–77.

2. "E prec los legidors d'aquest que, si per ventura in lo romanç ho en la senténcia del libre trobaven nuyla cosa qui·ls semblàs no raonable, que ans que ho reprenguesen, que ho corregisen ab aquel del latí, per ço cor moltz vocables e [en]tenimentz ha en los

libres de medicina, que a penes se poden metre en romançˮ (Arnau, "Regiment de sanitat,ˮ trans. Berenguer, ed. Batllori 99).

3. "E per ço con la art de medicina és fort longua, e·ls savis metges entichs ho agen
longuament escrit (així que·ls grans senyors qui an los grans neguocis, ne encare lo poble
comú, bonament no o poden entendre), lo dit maestre Arnau, a nonor del molt alt senyor En Jacme seguon, rey d'Araguó, ha ordonat aquest libre per donar doctrina de viure
san e de venir a natural velea a aquels qui ho volran entendra e metre en obraˮ (Arnau,
"Regiment de sanitat,ˮ trans. Berenguer, ed. Batllori 99–101).

4. Although the relation between the reading subject and vernacular medical writing in the Iberian Peninsula has never been studied extensively, recent works by medical
historians offer us a remarkable point of departure for undertaking such an endeavor.
Expanding considerably on the earlier works of José López Piñero, scholars such as Luis
García-Ballester, Michael McVaugh, María Estela González de Fauve, Jon Arrizabalaga,
and Marcelino Amasuno have produced a significant corpus of studies on all aspects of
late medieval and early modern medical theory and practice. Students of these scholars,
such as Montserrat Cabré and Lluís Cifuentes, have contributed impressive work on the
social aspects of medical writing, especially in the Kingdom of Aragon. In addition to
the historical and social contributions of these scholars, a group of philologists under
the direction of María Teresa Herrera and Nieves Sánchez, and in collaboration with
John Nitti and the Hispanic Seminary of Medieval Studies, have painstakingly genera-
ted critical editions, modernized versions of machine-readable paleographic transcriptions of vernacular medical treatises, as well as an impressive two-volume dictionary
of medieval medical vocabulary. These works provide an extraordinary set of tools for
researching all aspects of medical knowledge and practice during the late middle ages
and early modern period.

5. See, for example, Beaujouan, "Manuscrits médicaux du moyen âge conservés en
Espagneˮ; and López Piñero, *Bibliografía médica hispánica (1475–1950)*.

6. "Yo quir parlar per aço en aquesta raho e complir e be declarar, per so que entenen
tot hom quil vulle guardarˮ (*Speculum al foderi* fol. 35r; my emphasis throughout); "que
todo lo que aquí fallardes escripto non será por vocablos de medeçina nin por palabras
escuras salvo fablando vulgarmente que qualquier omne puede entenderˮ (Chirino, *Menor daño de la medicina* fol. 3r); "cada vno en su casa se pueda aprovechar del en tiempo
de tanta necesidadˮ (Franco, *Libro de las enfermedades contagiosas* fol. 3r).

7. See respectively, with my emphasis: "la conservación de la salud de todosˮ (Monardes, "Prólogo,ˮ *Sevillana medicina* fol. 3v); "ha ordonat aquest libre per donar doctrina de
viure san e de venir a natural velea *a aquels qui ho volran* entendra e metre en obraˮ (Arnau, "Regiment de sanitat,ˮ trans. Berenguer, ed. Batllori 100); "sacar a luz este pequeño
tratado, del *qual quien lo* leyere, sacará por lo menos algún consuelo, con remedios im-
portantes para la conservación suyaˮ (Manuel de Escobar, *Tratado de la essencia, causas,
y curación de los bubones y carbuncos pestilentes*, "Al lectorˮ); "me ha parecido hazer este
breve tratado para que *cada uno que quiera* pueda conocer la dicha peste preservarse y

curar con poca ayuda de médicos" (Antonio Pérez, *Breve tratado de peste* fol. 5v). See Eamon (99–105) for a discussion of the notion of "common man," or *gemeine Mann*, as the implied reader in sixteenth-century German translations of medical works.

8. ". . . muy útil y necesario a los médicos y cirujanos que quieren ser perfectos en su arte, y apacible a los otros hombres discretos que huelgan de saber los secretos de naturaleza" (Montaña de Monserrate, *Libro de la anathomía del hombre* fol. 1r). Elsewhere Bernardino explains, "Nos ha sido hecha relación que vos habéis hecho un libro de la compostura del cuerpo humano que a vuestro parecer será provechoso a los médicos y cirujanos y *agradable a otras personas* que desean saber secretos de naturaleza" (fol. 1v).

9. "Otrosí, es muy útil y provechoso para los señores y para letrados de otras facultades que quieren saber algo en la medicina" (López de Villalobos, *Sumario de la medicina* fol. 2v).

10. "Por ende confiando en el señor de las sciencias entiendo tractar cosas comunes fáciles y provechosas a provecho de los pobres y de los humildes" (Bernard of Gordon, *Lilio de medicina* fol. 2r). On Christian charity as a motive behind the vernacular translation of medical treatises, see Faye Marie Getz's study, "Charity, Translation, and the Language of Medical Learning in Medieval England."

11. ". . . ruegue a su hijo precioso me quiera infundir espiritu de saber para que pueda rectamente escribir en mi propósito a servicio honor y alabança suya alguna cosa provechosa a la salud de la miserable y flaca humanidad que es: habiendo consideración quan afligida y quan lastimada ha sido y aun esta la gente en esta provincia y aun en las circunstantes de peligrosas y aun mortales enfermedades de las quales gente sin número es pasada desta vida en el año pasado de quinientos y .v. y en el presente de quinientos y .vj. así de fiebres pestilenciales como de dolores de costado" (Diego Alvarez Chanca, *Tratado nuevo* fol. 2r).

12. For recent studies on the philosophy and social attempts to provide for the sick and poor in the Iberian Peninsula (1540–1700), see Brodman, *Charity and Welfare*; Grell et al., *Health Care and Poor Relief*, notably Arrizabalaga, "Poor Relief in Counter-Reformation Castile: An Overview"; and López Terrada, "Health Care and Poor Relief in the Crown of Aragon."

13. "Y por eso movido de caridad, en esta obrezica les demostraré su arte y las reglas y forma que tienen de tener para ser suficientes; y en buena conciencia puedan tal arte usar y aconsejar para la salud de las preñadas, paridas, y criaturas" (Carbón, *Libro del arte de las comadres* fol. 2r).

14. "La caridad y obligación que como hombre cristiano debo al próximo" (Luis de Toro, *Discursos o consyderaciones sobre la materia de enfriar la bevida*, "Al lector" fol. 3r).

15. "Experiencia tanto quanto es más comunicable tanto es más noble: y por tanto todo hombre en alguna sciencia o arte enseñado es obligado según sentencia del philosopho Platón de aprovechar con sus letras a su patria y a sus amigos como no para si solo haya nacido" (Ruy Díaz de Ysla, *Tractado contra el mal serpentino* fol. 2v).

16. "... movido con celo de hazer algún provecho en la republica ayudado con la persuasión de algunos amigos ..." (Francisco Martínez de Castrillo, *Tratado breve y compendioso sobre la maravillosa obra de la boca y dentadura* fol. 7r).

17. For specific examples, see Schleiner, "*Mentiamur sane*: Lying for Health in Renaissance Medical Ethics," in *Medical Ethics in the Renaissance* 5–48.

18. On the difficulties of establishing a universal and transhistorical definition of disease, see my discussion and related bibliography in "Disease, Discourse, and Illness: The Structure of Healing in Late Medieval Spain," in *Literature of Misogyny* 17–19.

19. For a concise overview of the dominant theories of reception, see Machor and Goldstein, "Theoretical Accounts of Reception," in *Reception Study* 1–6. Understandably, these critics are concerned with the reception of literary works rather than what would superficially appear to be simple information-bearing texts in the vernacular.

20. I have taken care to use the word illness in the context of sickly reading rather than the term disease. Most medical anthropologists distinguish between the symptoms and conditions experienced by the individual and the classification the physician assigns to the patient's biological disorder. In this study, the terms *illness* and *sickness* refer to the highly subjective and individual experience of bodily disorder. Again, see the discussion and related bibliography in Solomon, *Literature of Misogyny* 17.

21. García-Ballester describes this case taken from a Valencian inquisitorial record of the process against Jerónimo Pachet: "Los procedimientos terapéuticos por analogía y transferencia, basadas en la reproducción mimética del proceso curativo, utilizando la propiedad del espejo de ver reflejada en él la imagen, aparece también entre los moriscos. Por ejemplo, una metgessa de Turís (Valencia) que 'hablava con un espejo para curar mirándose en él' curaba proyectando sobre el espejo las páginas de un libro, cuyo contenido debía presumir que fuera medicinal y cuya virtud recogía y transmitía el espejo, puesto 'que la dicha muger no sabía letra sino que tenía el espejo detrás del libro'" (*Los moriscos y la medicina* 123).

Chapter 1. Fictions of Utility

1. "... los llibres qui parlen en molt foder són molts atrobats, may jo viu d'ells negun compliment en aital fet, ans los trobe desviats e escampats en manera que era major lo dany que havien que lo profit. E jo quir parlar per açò en aquesta raó e complir e bé declarar, per ço que entena tot hom qui el vulle guardar, e que es pusque[n] aprofitar d'ell també los fisics e los cirurgians e moltes d'altres gents" (47). All orginal citations of the *Speculum al foderi* are taken from Anna Alberni's recent edition (*Speculum al foder*, 2007).

2. Discussions on the health benefits (and dangers) of coitus are couched within larger compendiums such as Galen's *On the Affected Parts* and Avicenna's *Canon*, and in complete treatises such as Constantine the African's *Liber de coitu*, the anonymous *Liber minor de coitu*, and Maimonides' *Treatise on Cohabitation* (see Gorlin, *Maimonides "On Sexual Intercourse"*; and Rosner, *Sex Ethics in the Writings of Moses Maimonides*).

For an overview of medieval treatises on coitus, see Jacquart and Thomasset, *Sexuality and Medicine* 116–38. In general, the treatment of coitus formed part of a larger discussion on the six non-naturals. The hygienic notion of the non-naturals dates back at least to Hippocrates and was adapted by Galen and later developed in Islamic medicine. Non-natural hygiene requires individuals to control six exogenous phenomena: air and environment, food and drink, motion and rest, sleep and vigilance, the excretion of superfluous matter, and control of the emotions. Coitus fell under the non-natural idea of excretion and required that men and women, according to their temperament and other factors, regularly rid themselves of excess semen as a preventative measure for avoiding illness. For more detailed explanation of the non-naturals and the development of the concept during the Middle Ages and early modern period see García-Ballester "On the Origin," Niebyl, Jarcho, and Emch-Dériaz.

3. Although the first chapters of the *Speculum* are a loose translation of the anonymous *Liber minor de coitu*, critics have noted that the final three chapters related to aphrodisiacs, female sexual response, and coital position do not correspond to the Western models, suggesting the incorporation of Arabic sources (Montero Cartelle, "Sobre el origen árabe"; Alberni 6-7).

4. The *Liber minor de coitu* begins abruptly on the dangers of sexual intercourse: "Scias inmoderatis veneris usibus naturalem calorem extingui et extraneum augmento plurimo excitari, ideoque omnis nature invisibles operaciones infirmari" (56).

5. To my knowledge the term *foder* (*joder* in Castilian) does not appear in any of the vernacular treatments of coitus. Most authors simply left the vernacular equivalent of the Latin term (*coyto* or *coito*) or employed more euphemistic expressions such as "uso de las mugeres" [use of women] as we see in the title of Nuñez de Coria's treatise *Tratado del uso de las mugeres* [*Treatise on the Use of Women*] and throughout works such as Alfonso Chirino's *Menor daño de medicina* [*Least Harm from Medicine*]: "E este es el tienpo onde es más dañoso el uso de las mugeres" (21v); "Quando con el grant perdimjento del apetito de comer es mucha la flaqueza o es mucho flaco el omne por mucho usar con mugeres" (138r).

6. "Ansi que como del tal acto se sigua no pequeña utilidad, usándose bien como debe para la salud del cuerpo y conservación de la generación, parecióme no dexar de dezir y tractar algo dello" (Núñez de Coria, *Tractado del uso de las mugeres* fol. 1v).

7. "Y aunque yo no sea digno de sacar a luz este tractado, que ansí mismo tracta de algunas cosas de medicina, y secretos particulares de cirugía, que yo he experimentado, en las quales he hallado mucho provecho y benefficio para mis enfermos" (Arias Benavides, *Secretos de chirurgía* [1567] fol. 4v).

8. ". . . halle un libro en medicina llamado Macer que traslado en Romançe castellano un físico del rey de Francia que se llamaba maestre Gil de nación castellana, el qual me paresçió útil y provechoso" (*Libro de medicina llamado Macer* [1518] fol. 1v); "E puesto en mejor romançe que solía. Porque la primera vez estaba en romançe viejo. E mal puesto. E agora está como debe" (fol. 32r).

9. "... nos ha sido referido que abeys compuesto un libro intitulado *Tratado sobre la maravillosa obra dela boca y dentadura*, en el qual ay muchos remedios y cosas muy necessarias y experimentadas, de que redundará muy gran provecho y utilidad a los que dellas se quisieren valer y aprovechar" (Martínez de Castrillo, *Tratado breve y compendioso* fol. 3v).

10. "Por quanto vos, maestre Rodrigo de Ysla, me hezistes relación que vos hezistes y ordenastes un libro para la cura y remedio de la enfermedad de las bubas, el qual es provechoso y muy necessario y conviene imprimirle" (Díaz de Ysla, *Tractado llamado fructo de todos los auctos* fol. 1v).

11. "Porque el ingenio pobre y pequeño las cosas difíciles y estrañas no sostiene. Por ende confiando en el señor de las sciencias entiendo tractar cosas comunes, fáciles y provechosas a provecho de los pobres y de los humildes copilar libro: conviene a saber libro de práctica. E porque para los humildes escribo: por ende los soberbios son desechados y el convite dellos apartado" (Bernard of Gordon, *Lilio de medicina* 2r).

12. "Leyendo en el séptimo libro de las Políticas de Aristótiles hallé que dezía: "si queréys [se quiere] curar el alma, curad al cuerpo. Y, considerando el precepto divino (que diximos), fui movido con mucha razón a buscar (quanto lo que toca a medicina) la más fácil cosa que se puede hazer para alcançar esta salud corporal, de donde la del alma algunas vezes se sigue. Y, con gran cuydado y diligencia inquirido, hallé que con sólo hazer exercicio (como diximos), se podría emprender y conseguir tan gran bien y utilidad" (Méndez, *Libro del ejercicio corporal*, ed. Alvarez del Palacio 243).

13. "Otros remedios pusiera aquí, pero como el intento que llevo, es solo traer remedios, faciles de hazer, los que han de costar trabajo, y tienen dificultad en hazerse, no quiero cansarme en ponerlos aquí" (Soriano, *Libro de experimentos médicos* fol. 54v).

14. "... con estilo y modo tan claro y llano, que qualquier ingenio las pueda bien entender, y con obra tan fácil y segura, que el hombre varón prudente, prevenido y sin temor, se pueda servir y aprovechar" (Cornejo, *Discurso y despertador preservativo de enfermedades* [1594] fol. 9v).

15. "Aquí hallara el lector algunos vocablos que al parecer no se entienden: los quales si los bien mira con la contestura de la letra serán fácilmente entendidos" (Monardes, *Sevillana medicina*, "Prólogo" fol. 4v).

16. "... e vull guardar que no haja llongues raons, mas que es pusquen aprofitar de la cura e de l'obra mellor" (47).

17. "Por lo cual siendo yo médico, y bien necesitado de salud, viéndome tan cercado de males y enemigos, y tan cargado de aforismos y preceptos, de medicamentos y medicinas de tanto número de receptas, con tanto aparato de boticas, de tantos remedios empíricos y racionales, de tantos humos y çumos del tabaco, y del eleboro venenosos y vomitivos de olios y polvos de minerales de oros potables y quintas esencias de alquimistas, y en una perpetua contienda desta temerosa confusión, considerando la facilidad y brevedad de las dos partes de definición y demostración: y que la verdad no requiere muchas palabras, porque consiste en un punto indivisible, me resolví de

entenderlas bien, y comprenderlas y perfeccionarlas, acomodándolas para mi con estilo y modo tan claro y llano, que cualquier ingenio las pueda bien entender, y con obra tan fácil y segura, que el hombre varón prudente, prevenido y sin temor, se pueda servir y aprovechar" (Cornejo, *Discurso y despertador preservativo de enfermedades* 9r–v).

18. Andrés de Laguna, *Discurso breve, sobre la cura y preservación de la pestilencia* (1566); Agustín Farfán, *Tractado breve de medicina* (1592); Francisco Ximénez de Carmona, *Tratado breve de la grande excelencia del agua* (1616); Pedro Barba, *Breve, y clara resumpta, y tratado de la essencia, causas, prognostico, preservación, y curación de la peste* (1648).

19. Examples are numerous: "en esta obrezica les demostraré su arte y las reglas y forma que tienen de tener para ser suficientes" (Damián Carbón, *Libro del arte de las comadres* [1541], fol. 2r); "Querria que el benigno lector recibiese mi voluntad y deseo de servir a la República con este pequeñuelo trabajo" (Pedro de Torres, *Libro que trata de la enfermedad de las bubas* [1600] fol. 8v); "he determinado sacar a luz este librito de los experimentos médicos" (Jerónimo Soriano, *Libro de experimentos médicos* fol. 7v); "poniendo en effecto mi propósito acorde de hazer este breve tractado" (Díaz de Ysla, *Tractado llamado fructo de todos los auctos* fol. 2v).

20. "... nuestro propósito es, solamente dezir las verdades en toda cosa que trataremos sin disputa, lo mas brevemente que pudiéremos con tanto que por la brevedad procuraremos que no se haga obscura la doctrina" (Montaña de Monserrate, *Libro de la anathomía del hombre* fol. 12v).

21. "... y porque el beneficio sea común y todos lo entiendan, y puedan aprovecharse dello, dexaré disputas agudas y prolixas, y escribiré en lengua común y vulgar, bastara saber que aquellas cosas que yo dixere, dado que no serán muchas teniendo respecto a la brevedad, serán aprobadas con muchas buenas razones, y con el autoridad de todos los doctores antiguos y modernos y experimentadas de muchos" (*Libro compuesto por Marsilio Ficino* [1598] fol. 9r–v).

22. "... ordené para vosotros aqueste breve compendio de medeçina" (Chirino, *Menor daño de la medicina*, Escorial MS b.IV.34 fol. 1v).

23. Lope de Saavedra's *Regimiento preservativo en romançe* (1522) and Fernando Alvarez's *Regimiento contra la peste* (1501) provide instruction on avoiding the plague in treatises consisting of a mere four folios; Alvarez Chanca's *Tratado nuevo* (1506) and Alonso Espina's *Tratado contra toda pestilencia* (1518) each contain ten folios; Lluis Alcanyís's *Regiment preservatiu e curatiu de la pestilència* (1490) and Andrés de Laguna's *Discurso de como se ha de preservar y curar de pestilencia* (1600) consist of fourteen folios each; and the two 1507 editions of Forés's *Tratado muy util* each contain eighteen folios.

24. Most editions of Chirino's popular *Menor daño de la medicina* vary from 24 to 36 folia; Gregorio Méndez's versified *Regimiento de salud* (1562) has 17 folios; and the numerous sixteenth-century editions of the *Tesoro de los pobres*, a work that almost always includes Arnau de Vilanova's *Regiment*, usually contain between 28 and 30 folios.

25. For a detailed description of the Latin editions of the *Canon* used in sixteenth-century medical training, see Siraisi, *Avicenna in Renaissance Italy*.

26. "Ypocras que dijo, la vida es breve: el arte es luenga, el juicio grave, el tiempo angosto, y la prueba dudosa. E la razón porque esta arte es muy luenga, según dijo Boecio, es por razón que ella es departida en siete partes y en cada parte ha menester luengo tiempo para alcanzarla" (*Sevillana medicina* fol. 5r). Juan de Aviñón goes on to explain that a physician must not only know medicine but also be instructed in each of the seven liberal arts: "Ca estas requieren que el físico sea en las siete artes liberales entremetido: conviene a saber: gramática: lógica: retórica: geometría: aritmética: música: astrología. E por esta razón dijo Ypocras: que la vida del ome es breve a respecto de esta arte de la medicina, señaladamente por razón que el subjeto de esta arte es el más acabado del mundo terrenal" (fol. 5v).

27. "Los quales sin discrepar alguno dizen, y afirman, que esta doctrina de la templança y compostura del cuerpo que se dize anathomía, es como alphabeto por donde han de començar a estudiar los que quieren ser médicos. Estoy muy maravillado como en personas de buen juicio, se puede asentar tan grande yerro: y creo cierto que la causa de todo ello consiste, en que los varones excelentes antiguos y modernos, en esta arte de anathomía, que hasta agora han escripto della, han hecho libros tan grandes que aunque toda la vida se estudiasse, habría harto que hazer de saber lo que en ellos se contiene: y por esto espantados de obra tan largo dexan los médicos de estudiarla" (Montaña de Monserrate, *Libro de la anathomía* fol. 9v).

28. As an example, Siraisi points to the way the author of the *Flores Avicennae* (1508) compressed Gerard of Cremona's Latin version of Avicenna's chapter on the elements from 550 words to a mere 53 ("Changing Fortunes" 21).

29. "E de regiment de preservació pot tot hom usar ab aquest present tractat sens de metge, sens tot periyll. Mas lo regiment de curació és apropriat al metge en lo qual cascú sens de la art de medicina porie leugerament errar." (Jacme d'Agramont, *Regiment de preservació a epidèmia o pestilència e mortaldats*, "Próleg," eds. Ardeiu and Roca).

30. ". . . yo he visto y han passado por mis manos todas las curas y experiencias que en esta enfermedad se pueden hazer; por donde he conoscido su origen, causas, definición y efectos" (Díaz de Ysla, *Tractado llamado fructo de todos* fol. 2v).

31. "E he escogido entre todos los libros de la sobredicha arte de la curugía por escusamjento del trabajo que los curujanos toman en levar las grandes volumenes de los libros de una tierra en otra quando algunas partes habían de ir" (Fernando de Córdoba, *Suma de la flor de cirugía*, fol. 148r).

32. "Mas, que·s pusquen aprofitar della cura e della obra mallor, he siu per capítols, per so que sia leuger de trobar so que sercaran en aquesta rahó" (*Speculum al foderi* fol. 35r).

33. "Emperó jo vuyl enadir en aquest libre alscunes notes per los marges en manera de rúbliques, per ço que aquels qui legiran en aquest libre pusquen pus leugerament trobar la proprietat del ajudament ho del noÿment de les coses que açí són nomenades per regiment de santitat; per ço cor aquels qui s'an ajudar ab los libres qui són en romanç, no poden aver estudiatz tantz libres que leugerament pusquen trobar la proprietat del

regiment dejús escrit, lo qual lo dit maestre Arnau ha aordonat en .XVIII. Capítols" (Berenguer trans., "Regiment de sanitat," ed. Batllori 101).

34. The translator of Guido's *Anatomía* makes the same claim: "Porque las materias de que se trata en este libro se puedan fallar más ligeramente, será provechoso anteponer en el principio las rúbricas de los tratados y capítulos de todo el libro" (Guy de Chauliac, *Guido en Romance* [1498] fol. 2r).

35. "Ut scolares qui saepius in libris Galeni quarerendo materias noctes ducent insompnes a laboribus et sollicitudine releventur et citius inveniant id quod eorum anima sitibunda et fatigata videre desiderat" (McVaugh's translation in *Tractatus de intentiones medicorum* 131).

36. ". . . me ha parecido hazer este breve tratado para que cada uno que quiera pueda conocer la dicha peste, preservarse y curar con poca ayuda de médicos" (Pérez, *Breve tratado de peste* [1598] fol. 5v).

37. ". . . para que los hombres se sepan curar sin médico, donde no lo obiere y obiere mucha neçessidad" (*Libro de medicina llamado tessoro de los pobres* [1540] fol. 3r).

38. "Pueden se de cada día ayudar deste libro mientras que no han físico a la mano por cuyo seso se pueda cumplidamente guiar. E quando les acaesçiere alguna cosa a que no abaste, lo que en este libro es escripto, demanden consejo de algunos de los físicos que cumplidamente saben esta arte" (Gil, *Libro de medicina llamado Macer* fol. 2r).

39. "Otrosí es muy útil y provechoso para los señores y para letrados de otras facultades que quieren saber algo en la medicina para hablar con los médicos preguntar y experimentar y también si estos deprenden a entender el dicho sumario alcançarán harto y aun se podrán por algunos días aprovechar en tanto que viene el físico do hubiere falta dél" (López de Villalobos, *Sumario* fol. 1v).

40. "Examine el libro intitulado Tractado breve de mediçina compuesto por el padre doctor fray Agustín Farfán, y halló ser útil y provechoso para todo genero de gente en esta nueva España specialmente para los que tienen su habitación y moradas en las ciudades villas e lugares donde ay falta de médicos y mediçinas de botica" ("Ortiz de Hinojosa's examination report," in the prefatory material from Agustín Farfán, *Tractado breve*, fol. 2r–v).

41. "Por los que están fuera de esta cuidad en minas y estancias, pueblos y partes remotas, que carecen de los remedios convenientes, hice este libro para que cualquiera que supiere leer hallare el remedio para la pasión y enfermedad que tuviere que en este libro se hace mención; y sabrá la causa de que procede y es hecha la tal enfermedad y cómo se ha de curar" ("El benigno lector" 77 [Academia nacional de medicina, México edition] 1977).

42. "Que andando en la conquista del Reyno de Valencia, teniendo cercada a Burriana villa fuerte, en un assalto los de dentro hirieron malamente de una saetada a un tío suyo muy querido, llamado Don Guillen de Entença, al qual mandó el Rey traer luego a su tienda Real, donde con sus proprias manos le sacó el yerro de la saeta que se le abía enclavado en la pierna, y le lavó la herida, y se la envendó en presencia de todos

los médicos, y cirujanos del campo, con tan buen arte, y felice sucesso, que fue por ello muy alabado de todos" (Gómez Miedes, *Enchiridion* [1589] fols. 10v–11r).

43. ". . . digo que desta enfermedad se mueren los físicos y sanan los rústicos pastores. Digo que yo he visto muchos físicos famosos morir desta enfermedad y en esta ciudad, dende el año de mil y quinientos y quarenta y dos en treynta meses murieron desta enfermedad ocho físicos y cirujanos; en que de los cirujanos otros tales no quedaron: donde se cumple la palabra del santo evangelio que dize muchas cosas son escondidas a los sabios y prudentes las quales son reveladas a los pequeños donde dixo Dios, revélame mis secretos a los ignorantes y encobrillos a los sabios y se ha visto en esto muy claramente y a lo que digo que sanan los rústicos pastores es desta manera que yo vi un pastor muy perdido desta enfermedad serpentina y de no poder exercitar su cuerpo andando todavía en su oficio hinchóse de ladillas y ellos traen consigo un cañuto de sebo y azogue porque donde les pica el piojo sacan su cañuto y toman tanto de aquel sebo como una cabeça de alfilel y póneselo donde le picó el piojo, y desque el piojo torna por aquel lugar pica allí y muere; . . . a cabo de quinze días remanesció muy perfectamente sano con toda la buena disposición del mundo" (Díaz de Ysla, *Tractado llamado fructo de todos los auctos* fol. 78v).

44. "Onde nuestro señor nos manda amar así a nuestros próximos commo a nos mesmos y así por nesçesidat somos constreñidos a amar nuestra salud temporal y en tanto que si por nuestra culpa o desidia, aquella perdemos somos homiçidas de nos mesmos, el qual homiçidio es digno de mayor pena que fecho en el próximo segunt sant Agustín en el terçero de la *Cibdat de Dios*" (Chirino, *Menor daño de la medicina*, Escorial MS b.IV.34, fol. 1r–v).

45. "Todo se acaba con la salud. Todo tiene fin. Todo lo desseado se vee cumplido. ¡Oh valerosa, oh generosa, oh grandiosa salud, digna de ser amada! Y en tanto se ha de tener como la vida, pues que sin ella, aunque biuamos [vivamos], muertos nos pueden decir" (Méndez, *Libro del ejercicio corporal*, ed. Alvarez del Palacio 250).

46. "La joya más preciosa que en este mundo el hombre puede poseer, el la salud: y assí tuvieron por conclusión llana los mas de los sabios antiguos, que ni el rico, ni el fuerte, ni el docto, ni el bien afortunado, ni el que esta en la cumbre de la honra, ni el que tiene fieles amigos, ni aun el que tiene hijos, y muger a gusto, se puede llamar dichoso, o feliz, si no goza de la dulçura de la salud" (Sorapán de Rieros, *Medicina española* [1616] 1).

47. "Ca el fuego nos quema y el agua nos ahoga, y el ayre nos mata de frío o de calentura, o con otra alguna mala calidad o pestilencia. E la tierra nos mata con su pesadumbre, si nos cae de suso. Otrosí muchas de las piedras de las yerbas y muchas de las cosas que nascen en los mineros de la tierra han poder de nos matar con enconamiento e mala propriedad que en ellas ha para esto. E en esse mismo peligro somos con las bestias, y con las otras animalias de la tierra. Ca muchas dellas nos matan con ponçoña y con enconamiento que en ellas ha. Assí como son las serpientes, y las culebras, y las otras cosas enconadas. Y muchas dellas nos matan despedaçando nos muy cruelmente

con su braveza. Así como son los leones y los osos y los toros, y las otras tales bestias fieras. Y aun por la nuestra desaventura somos en peligro muy grande con las viandas mesmas que comemos y bebemos para nuestro mantenimiento. Ca si las no bebemos y comemos, morimos de hambre o de sed. E si las comemos, nascen nos dellas muchas enfermedades y mucha congoxa y muchas dolencias de que habemos de morir" (Gil, *Libro de medicinas llamado Macer* fol. 3r).

48. ". . . pues que no ay cosa en ella grande o chica, perfecta o imperfecta, que no estuvo o está, o en alguna manera pueda estar enferma; por lo qual, con muy justa razón se ha de estimar y apreciar y tener en mucho la salud" (Méndez, *Libro del ejercicio corporal*, ed. Alvarez del Palacio 250).

49. "E a las tribulaciones del cuerpo nos acorrió nuestro señor alumbrando nos los entendimientos de los philosophos y de los sabios antiguos porque pudiesen hallar sabidoria y sciencia de la phísica, con la qual sopiessen los hombres mantener y guardar la salud de sus cuerpos mientras que la han. E otrosí, se supiesse guarescer y guardar y curar sus dolencias y enfermedades quando las tienen. Por que cobren su salud natural que perdieron tal qual, la pueden y deben cobrar por natura, en manera que con ayuda desta sciencia, la nuestra salud sea bien guardada y sostenida en su estado natural (Gil, *Libro de medicinas llamado Macer* fol. 3v).

50. "Todo lo que aquj fallardes escripto non será por vocablos de medeçina nin por palabras escuras salvo fablando vulgarmente que qualquier omne puede entender" (Chirino, *Menor daño de la medicina*, Escorial MS b.IV.34, fol. 3r).

51. Francisco Franco: "paresciome cosa mas conveniente escribir este libro en lengua castellana, para que cada uno en su casa se pueda aprovechar del en tiempo de tanta necessidad" (*Libro de enfermedades contagiosas* [1569], "Epístola dedicatoria" fol. iv; cited by Martín Ferreira). Francisco Díaz: "quise y determiné escribir esta obra en castellana para que hombres curiosos, y tocados deste mal puedan preservarse del, y aun cursarse apartándose de muchas cosas que podrían ofender, y causar acrecentamiento del daño" (*Tratado nuevamente impresso de todas las enfermedades de los riñones, vexiga, y carnosidades de la verga* [1588] fol. 3v).

52. "Antes que te de cuenta de mis trabajos y peregrinaciones (discreto lector), te quiero dezir la ocasión que me movió a escrebir en nuestra lengua española antes que en latina, que cierto a mi me fuera muy más fácil sin comparación, y de menos trabajo hazerlo en esta más que en aquella, y la razón es evidentissima porque si escribiera en latín no fuera necessario buscar la propria interpretación del vocablo que usan los cirujanos, ni traduzir los textos de los antiguos y modernos que me a sido grandissimo trabajo, sino pusiera los en latín que ellos los pusieron. Pero dexado esto a parte, como yo viesse y considerasse quan decayda va la cirugía en nuestros Reynos de España (cosa de grañidísima lastima) quan poquitos buenos cirujanos ay, y quanta ocasiones da para que del todo se acabe. Y habiendo yo examinado en la corte más de dose años (por mandado y en presencia del doctor del Aguila, y del doctor Juan Gutiérrez de Santander, médicos de cama de su Majestad, y sus prothomédicos generales) a los cirujanos romanistas, que

se iban a examinar, vi muchos que tenían muy buenas habilidades, y que por falta de no tener libros en su lengua estaban muy atrás de lo que pudieran saber. . . . Assí que por estas este libro en romance bueno y polido, no le tengays en menos que si estuviera en latín pues he querido enriquecer mi lengua, porque para mi en tanto tengo quando me dan una buena razón en romance, como si la dixiessen en latín" (Daza Chacón, *Practica y teórica de cirugía*, [1609] "Prólogo al lector").

53. "E holgado de escribir este libro en romance, porque muchos cirujanos y otros hombres discretos que no saben latín, se querrán aprovechar de leerlo y también porque hallo, que en este tiempo los médicos están tan aficionados al latín, que todo su pensamiento emplean en la lengua: y lo que haze al caso, que es la doctrina, no tienen más pensamiento dello que sino la leyessen. Y esta es una de las causas potissima, por la qual el día de hoy se hallan pocos médicos que sepan medicina, y muchos que la escriban" (Montaña de Monserrate, *Libro de anathomía del hombre* fol. 10r).

54. See Gil Fernández, *Panorama social del humanismo español* 74.

55. "Y por proveer al bien común de nuestra nación española, al qual todos tenemos obligación, saque a la luz este libro en el vulgar castellano. . . . Y si porque a nuestra lengua la llamamos vulgar, imaginan algunos que no podemos escribir en ella sino vulgar y baxamente, es grandissimo error: que Platón escribió no cosas vulgares en su lengua vulgar: y no menores ni menos levantadamente las escribió Cicerón, en la lengua que era vulgar en su tiempo. Pues que diremos de S. Basilio, y Chrysostomo, y Gregorio Nazianceno, Cyrilo, con toda la antiguedad de los griegos, que en su lengua materna griega (que cuando ellos vivían la mamaban en la leche los niños, y la hablaban en la plaça las vendedoras) escribieron los mysterios divinos de nuestra Fe. Y por dezir lo que es más vezino a mi hecho, Cornelio Celso, caballero y médico romano, escribió en su lengua vulgar la medicina y cirugía, tan exquisita y elegantemente que le llamaron el Hipocrates latino: y Avicenna escribió en su arábigo un gran volumen de la arte medicinal. . . . Assí que por estas razones, y otras que no digo, he porfiado a publicar este libro como siempre, desseando que de tal suerte los no sabios tomen del lo que les pareciere" (Juan Fragoso, *Cirugía universal* [1627], "Al lector").

56. Nieto laments the poor level of Latin use and instruction at the Universidad de Salamanca during the mid-sixteenth century: "tierra tan estéril en aquel tiempo de buen latín y buenas Artes, que todo era barbarie y sofistería" (quoted in Ser Quijano and Rodríguez-San Pedro 7).

57. In the decades surrounding Monardes's publication of the *Sevillana medicina*, Spain produced a flurry of vernacular medical treatises. For example, in Seville alone, Chirino's *Menor daño de la medicina* was published five times (in 1536 by Dominico de Robertis and in 1538, 1547, 1550, and 1551 by Cromberger), while the popular *Tesoro de los pobres* enjoyed four editions (in 1535, 1543, and 1547 by Cromberger and 1548 by Dominico de Robertis). In 1542 three of Luis Lobera de Avila's works were published in Alcalá in the house of Juan de Brocar: *Vergel de sanidad, Remedio de cuerpos humanos y silva de experiencias*, and *Libro de pestilencia curativo y preseruatio*. Ruy Díaz de la Ysla's

Tractado llamado fructo de todos los auctos was published twice during these years (1539 and 1542).

58. "Vemos que el hombre es frágil, nascido para trabajos, y que en todo lo que vive le es contrario; pues, el ayre le corrompe, y el agua le ahoga, y el fuego le consume, y la tierra le es madrastra, dándole cosas que le aflijan y acaben: y si algún bien dellos recibe, dales cien males en recompensa que le ofendan" (fols. 1v–2r).

59. Mucho debe todo hombre conservar su salud; pues della se siguen tantos bienes y de no tenerla tantos males. De Septimo Severo Emperador leemos que por ser desordenado en comer y beber, padeció dolores de gota intolerables en tanto grado que quiriendo acabar con ellos y con su vida comió tanta carne y manjares crudos que súbitamente murió . . . Flavio Vespasiano nunca tuvo enfermedad con fregarse cada día el cuerpo y dexar de comer un día cada mes. . . Lo mismo leemos de Pythagoras, Lhrysyppo, Platón, Galeón, Antonio Catón y de otros muchos que vivieron con reglas y horden muchos y sanos años usando de aquella parte de medicina que nos enseña como nos avemos de conservar en salud: la qual ya que no nos haga immortales; es mucha parte para que el hombre dentro de los límites de su vida pueda vivir con más salud y menos enfermedades. Porque cierto es que este nuestro cuerpo no es hecho de diamantes ni de acero. . . . Verdad es que todo aquello que Dios repartió a los otros animales por propriedad quiso que lo uviesse en el hombre por razón y entendimiento rational mediante el qual se gobernase y con sciencia y reglas adquiriese lo necessario a su conservación . . . y para esto los sabios y antiguos médicos usaron de reglas en el uso de todas las cosas a la vida necessarias y quisieron hazer horden como el hombre se gobernase por razón porque difiriese de los animales brutos que sin ella siguen sus apetitos y inclinaciones naturales. Y por esto sirven los libros a este propósito hechos; que enseñan como cada uno se debe de gobernar en el comer y beber y en las demás obras pertenecientes a la conservación de la vida humana. . . . Por tanto he procurado que saliesse a luz obra de que tanto contentamiento y provecho esta ciudad recibiría, la qual no solamente aplazerá y aprovechará ala conservación de la salud de todos, pero holgarán de ver y leer en ella cosas antiguas que ha avido y passado" (2v–3v).

Chapter 2. Fictions of the Physician

1. Letter written April 6, 1305 (Finke 872). For the relation between Jaume's desire to have Arnau present at his bedside and the preparation of the *Regimen sanitatis*, see Paniagua and García-Ballester, "El Regimen Sanitatis" 868–69; and McVaugh, *Medicine Before the Plague* 14–16.

2. ". . . dijo Galieno que era un noble omne de Roma que habie esta dolençia que echaba por deyuso mucha sangre y mucha podredumbre e tenie llagas en los estentinos. Y melecinábanlo nobles físicos que moraban en Roma. Y cuanto más lo melecinaban tanto más la podredumbre de las llagas se acrecentaba. Y a tanto, empero, que los físicos decían a sus amigos en poridat que por çierto non poder escapar desta dolencia. Y el enfermo oyó que yo era en Roma y envió por mí, y yo fui a vesitallo. Y cuando entré, a

él fallé que desesperaba de su vida. Y primeramente, començé lo de confortar con palabras en que tómase placer y pregunté le en que manera le acontesçiera esta dolencia. Y díjome la razón y la melecina quel fizieran los otros físicos. Y paré mientes y vi que la virtud desta enfermedat podrie haber remedio" (Israeli, *Tratado de las fiebres* fols. 80v–81r).

3. Physicians inspired by Galen and Hippocrates recognized the need to treat the patient at the bedside: "Galen and Hippocrates were careful and subtle clinical observers, something that was implicit or explicit in almost everything they wrote…. [A]bove all, the physician had to observe the patient directly and closely, and in addition take his history" (McVaugh, "Bedside Manners" 204–5).

4. This very assertion appears in the title of Gregorio Méndez's rhymed treatise, *Regimiento de salud: Arte para conservar el dinero en la bolsa . . . que se gasta con el orinal* (1562) [Health regimen: The art of keeping money in the purse . . . that is usually wasted in the urine flask].

5. ". . . he volgut trabayllar de fer lo tractat seguent. Lo qual humilment e ab reverencia deguda, jo Maestre Jacme dagramont present a vosaltres honrats seynnors pahers e conseyll de la Ciutat de leyda axi com a aquells qui representats tota la damont dita Ciutat" (Jacme, *Regiment*, ed. Ardeiu and Roca 1); "Por ende, yo, maestre Alfonso Chirino, entre los profesores de medeçina . . . ordené para vosotros aqueste breve compendio de medeçina" (Chirino, *Menor daño de la medicina*, Escorial MS b.IV.34, fol. 1v); "Yo, Saladino, dotor en artes y medicina, físico de su señoría, propuse de componer este tratado el qual quiero que se llame *Compendio de los boticarios*" (Saladino de Ascoli fol. 2v).

6. "Yo suelo dezir que . . . ; Y assí yo daría por consejo . . . ; Y por esso digo yo muchas vezes . . . ; Y yo le dixe . . . ; Yo juro que . . . ; Yo estaba presente . . . ; Yo pensaba que . . . ; assí lo hago yo . . . ; Para lo qual yo respondo . . . ; Yo no aconsejaría . . . ; Yo bien lo creo . . . ; Yo tengo determinado . . . ; yo lo tenía por burlería . . . ; yo he sido informado . . . ; yo no lo sé dezir . . . ; yo no hallo para ella mejor medicina . . . ; Quando yo miro alguna cosa . . . ; Preguntaba yo . . . ; no hablo yo destas . . . ; yo no siento que . . . ; yo no hallo escrito . . . ; quiero yo poner por obra . . . ; yo vi . . . ; Yo conocía un señor . . . ; Yo vide en México . . . ; yo mandé . . ." (Méndez, *Libro de ejercicio corporal*, ed. Alvarez del Palacio).

7. "Solo quiero contar, lo que el año 1587 me sucedió. Acometióme una caeliaca. Tuve trabajo con ella, y sabiendo lo que de las caeliacas suele suceder, no dejé de tener temor. Fue Dios servido, que sólo con el comer de bueno, y con orden, y tomando al principio de la comida unas tostadas de pan, remojadas en buen vino de tonel, y cargadas de polvos, de clavos, de especias y de canela y açucar, me libre" (Soriano, *Libro de experimentos médicos* fol. 54v).

8. On the rise of medical licensing in the Iberian Peninsula see García-Ballester, McVaugh, and Rubio, *Medical Licensing and Learning in Fourteenth-Century Valencia*.

9. "Et esto porque por las buenas obras virtuosas ávidas en el médico. La fama buena es divulgada y per conssequens la imaginaçión buena del en los enfermos es contenida

y ssanidat en él más que en otris son confiantes por causa del bien vivir y obrar. La qual imaginaçión e confiamiento con la ayuda divinal es causa de muchas enfermedades curar, más que al médico . . . porque más vale la imaginaçión del enfermo ávida en el buen físico que el otro con todos sus estrumentos" (Estéfano, *Libro de visitaçione e conssiliaçione medicorum*, Biblioteca Nacional, Madrid, MS 18052, fol. 42v).

10. *De cautelis medicorum*, trans. Sigerist, "Bedside Manners in the Middle Ages: The Treatise *De cautelis medicorum* Attributed to Arnald of Villanova" 135. Also see McVaugh, *Medicine Before the Plague* 139.

11. For a more extensive study of the concept of *dolus ad bonum* and the tricks and ruses physicians used on their patient's behalf, see Schleiner, "*Mentiamur sane*: Lying for Health in Renaissance Medical Ethics," in his *Medical Ethics in the Renaissance* 5–48.

12. See McVaugh, *Medicine Before the Plague* 169.

13. "De lo que yo mucho me burlo, es que los miserables a los cantones y calles, y en las boticas dan vozes, claman trayendo luego aquellas authoridades, que saben de memoria, para que el vulgo los tenga por sabios, y tomando el pulso a enfermo, luego dizen van palabra medio latina, y presentándole una orina, luego dicen *oppilatio*, danle doscientas vueltas; lo cual es contra toda regla de la física, para que con estos embustes y embaimientos engañen la gente vulgar; y por la mayor parte son estos unos charlatanes, habladores, juglares, de lo qual todo ha de carecer el perfecto médico" (Enríquez, *Retrato del perfecto médico* 60–61).

14. "Por lo qual debemos venir a este fin; que los médicos ignorantes deben ser desechados de todo en todo y los físicos letrados deben ser dudosos y sospechados gran parte de lo que fazen. E pues esta arte es dubdosa, y la gente la han por nesçesaria debían ser escogidos con grande deliberaçión tales personas para físicos de mucha sçiençia y caridad y muy mucho sabios para administrar sçiençia en que tantas dubdas peligrosas están çerca de la su platica" (Chirino, *Espejo de medecina* fol. 7r).

15. "Digo yo el Doctor Francisco Gonçalez de Sepúlveda, médico del Rey nuestro Señor, de la Santa y general Inquisición, que por Vuestra Alteza se me mandó viesse este libro que compuso el Doctor Pedro de Torres, médico y cirujano de la Magestad de la Emperatriz, intitulado, De la origen, causas, y señales y cura del mal de bubas, el qual es bien trabajado, y de mucha y buena dotrina y plática y esperiencias, y muy útil, y se le debe mandar dar licencia para imprimirle" (Torres, *Libro que trata de la enfermedad de las bubas* fol. 2r).

16. ". . . un libro en romance, intitulado el parto humano, que era muy útil y provechoso para las parteras, y cura de las paridas y niños, y para las amas que los crían" (Núñez de Coria, *Libro intitulado de parto humano* fol. 2r).

17. "Y agora de nuevo le habiades corregido y enmendado y añadido muchos remedios y cosas muy necessarias, provechosas y experimentadas" (2v).

18. For an overview of the extra-academic training that many early physicians received, see García-Ballester, "El charácter extraacadémico de la circulación y producción intellectual médica," in his *La búsqueda de la salud* 268–410.

19. ". . . la primera es que el que justa y rectamente viere de usar la arte de boticarios conviene que sea latino y que a lo menos entienda la lengua latina bien, o moderadamente habiéndose ejercitado en ella, procurándola y estudiándola en universidad, o con maestros fuera della competentes, espacio de cuatro o a lo menos tres años, y pues es el tiempo necesario y que se requiere para ayer de entender la gramática y fundamentos de la lengua latina: sin la qual ciertamente no podrán ser buenos ni perfectos boticarios" (Aguilera, *Exposición sobre las preparaciones de Mesue* [1569] fol. 17r).

20. "Yo digo, que cría y engendra otras enfermedades de mal de orina y de ijada, y de riñones, a causa que como dicho tengo, el palo delas Indias se cría en tierra muy caliente y es seco en mas del tercero grado, que creo llega a mas de dos partes mas del tercero grado, y 'omnia estrema sunt vitiosa'" (Arias de Benavides, *Secretos de chirurgía* fol. 19v).

21. ". . . como dize Tulio en el primero de sus oficios capítulo quarto diziendo: 'Homo autem qui rationis est particeps &cetera.' Que quiere dezir: que Dios poderoso dio capacidad al hombre y entendimiento para usar de razón: por la qual es muy differente de los otros animales" (Carbón, *Libro del arte de las comadres* fol. 6r).

22. "Y por esso dixo Ovidio en el libro de arte amandi, 'Mollibus in pratis admugit saemina tauro faemina cornipedi semper adhinnite quo mitior in nobis nec tam furiosa libido est legitimum finem flamman uirilis habet.' Dize, que en los blandos prados la vaca con su bramido llama al toro, y que la yegua siempre llama al caballo con su relincho, empero que en nosotros es más mite la luxuria, aunque no tan furiosa, y que el encendimiento de luxuria tiene fin y término en el varón, empero no en la muger" (Núñez de Coria, *Tratado del uso de las mugeres* [1572] fol. 291r).

23. I do not deny that some of the code switching or code mixing that occurs in these treatises may have been inadvert, or as Linda Voigts describes, a result of the author's "propensity to draw on the lexical resources of another code when one is at a loss for words in the base language, or for lexical amplification." Voigts also points out that language mixing in medical texts was often used to differentiate categories of texts ("What's the Word" 819–22). I do not, however, believe that the incorporation of Latin into vernacular medical treatises necessarily suggests that the author was writing for a bilingual reader, but rather that the Latin serves as a spectacle of erudition designed to demonstrate the writer's competence.

24. By "index" I am referring to one of the categories in Charles Sanders Peirce's semiotic trichotomy composed of symbols, icons, and indices. The index posits an indirect representation of its referent, often a physical mark left by the object. An example of an index is a footprint in the sand, animal tracks in the snow, stains on clothing, and the lingering scent of perfume. The index is inextricably linked with its object by virtue of a cause-and-effect relationship, and cannot function as a sign without forcing the interpreter to imagine the absent object. For an overview of Peirce's theory of signs, see Atkin.

25. For a more extensive discussion on the uncanny indexical quality of Lobera de

Avila's 1542 edition of the *Garden of Health*, see my electronic presentation, "Spectacles of Erudition," (Lawrence J. Schoenberg Symposium on Manuscript Studies in the Digital Age).

26. "Que aya trabajado su pensamiento e gastado su tiempo en estudiar profundamente todos los libros de medeçina e los libros de los naturales" (Chirino, *Espejo de medicina* fol. 17r).

27. "... non çesse en su ciencia de estudiar e con buenos médicos participar e con ellos consejo tomar" (Estéfano, *Libro de visitaçione e conssiliaçione medicorum* fol. 73v). Also see González de Fauve and Forteza, "Ética médica y mala praxis en Castilla" 17–19.

28. "... lo mismo dixo Avicena en la primera del .3. tractatu .5. capítulo .8. y en los cánticos, dixo: 'cuius commendatur inuentis quatenus pereum a nocumentis perniciosis liberantur.' Lo mismo Galeno en el sexto *De locis affectis*, adonde encomendo mucho la expulsión de la tal superfluydad, porque dize, que por el se escaparan de muy fuertes enfermedades, adonde dixo que conoció a muchos, los quales por apartarse del tal acto se enfriaron e incurrieron en gran tristeza, y en estraños pensamientos, entiendese de los que primero lo acostumbraron, y truxo por exemplo a Diogenes, el qual no quiso muger alguna por deleyte ni contento sino por conservacion de su salud. Por ende como lo affirma Almansor en su lib. 4. capitul 6. El coyto moderado descarga y aliviana el cuerpo repleto, alegra el animo, aplaca la yra, quita pensamientos, alivia la cabeça y los sentidos, lo mismo dixo Aristóteles en el .30 de los problemas, proble. 1. y Averroes enel 6. de su colliget y Galeno, el qual es sobre todos en el .6. de sanit. tuen. adonde dixo, que en las disposiciones de mucha y calida simiente, no conviene del todo apartarse del coyto" (Núñez de Coria, *Tratado del uso de las mujeres*, ed. Dangler fol. 293r).

29. Authorities cited in Soriano's *Libro de experimentos médicos* include Mathiolo Senes, "doctissimo varón en medicina" (fol. 9r); Jian Jacobo Vuerero (fol. 9v); Juan Villaroya, "doctor theólogo, racionero de la parrochial de Sanctiago de Teruel, y Rector de la villa de Scriche" (fol. 10v); Victor Trincauello (fol. 11v); Guillermo Rondoleto, "autor gravissimo" (fol. 13r); Alexandro Benedicto, "médico veronés doctissimo" (fol. 15v); El Doctor Uson, "natural de Alcañiz" (fol. 15v); Laurentio Iouberto, "Medico Regio, y cathedrático primario de medicina en la Universidad de Montpellier" (fol. 17r); Victor de Faenza (fol. 18v); Amato Lusitano (fol. 18v); Levinio Lemnio, "doctor gravissimo" (fol. 19v); Iuan Dolio (fol. 19v); Alcanzio, "médico árabe" (fol. 19v); Antonio Mizaldo (fol. 20r); Valesco de Taranto (fol. 25v); Leonello de Faenza (fol. 25v); Atonio Fumanello, "doctissimo médico Verones" (fol. 28r); Pedro Bayrio (fol. 30v); Maestro Francisco de Norsia (fol. 32r); Leonardo Fuctisio (fol. 33r); "El licenciado," Dionisio Daça Chacon (fol. 34v); Fallopio del Capricio (fol. 35v); Antonio Vallesio (fol. 37v); Alonso Lupeyo (fol. 38r); Hieronymo Valejo (fol. 41v); Paulo Aegineta (fol. 55v); and references throughout to Galen, Rasis, Arnau de Vilanova, Avicenna, and Pliny.

30. "Aquí comiença un libro muy provechoso en medicina llamado tesoro de los pobres. El qual mandó hazer el papa Juan a un médico suyo llamado maestre Juliano,

hombre muy sabio y experimentado en medicina, el qual por servir a su santidad, y por servicio de Dios y por bien de los próximos, buscó quantos doctores y maestros había en medicina en aquel tiempo, en que hubo cincuenta y seis doctores que allegó para esta obra: muy sabios para que los hombres se sepan curar sin médico donde no lo hubiere y hubiere mucha necesidad" (*Tesoro de los pobres* [1540] fol. 3r).

31. "Otrosí es muy útil y provechoso para los señores y para letrados de otras facultades que quieren saber algo en la medicina para hablar con los médicos preguntar y experimentar" (López de Villalobos, *Sumario de la medicina* fol. 1v).

32. ". . . yo he visto y han passado por mis manos todas las curas y experiencias que en esta enfermedad se pueden hazer. . . . yo porne en este capítulo lo mejor y más especificadamente que yo pudiere aquellas cosas que yo usé y experimenté con infinito número de gentes con que se remediaron" (Díaz de Ysla, *Tractado llamado fructo de todos los auctos* [1542] fols. 2v, 6v).

33. "La rayz del Matlaliztlic es de las nobles y seguras purgas que ay en esta tierra, como yo muchas vezes he esperimentado. Dámosla con toda seguridad a niños, viejos y a preñadas" (Farfán, *Tractado breve de medicina* [1592] fols. 9v–10r).

34. Chirino, *Menor daño de medicina*: "Para el dolor de xaqueca de mucho tiempo, tome çumo de yerba mora y amasen con ello y con unas tres yemas de huevos farina de trigo, çernida unas quatro vezes y frito fecho como buñuelos y comido con miel en ayunas. Esto probaron más de çinco omnes de lo que yo vi y le fallaron bien con ello" (fol. 103v); "Para el dolor de podraga. . . . yo lo vi probar y provecho mucho" (fol. 175r); "Para llagas muy viejas y para mataduras de bestias que non dexen de afanar pongan ençima dos o tres fojas de figera verdes una ençima de otra y tengo que es mejor majarlas y enchir las llagas dello y poner ençima. Yo vi quien lo probó asaz vezes y dixo que non falló melezina que así; tirase la hinchazón y alinpiase y ensugase la llaga, y cresca la carne fízolo en sy mesmo tres semanas poniéndolo dos vezes al día" (fol. 177v).

35. The scholarship on the relation between empirical and theoretic medicine is extensive. See McVaugh's introduction to *Tractatus de intentione medicorum* 139–54; Siraisi, "Girolamo Cardano and the Art of Medical Narrative" 586; Ziegler, "Ut Dicunt Medici: Medical Knowledge and Theological Debates in the Second Half of the Thirteenth Century."

36. Here Aviñón is arguing on the method for determining the correct amount of bread that a patient should eat: "ca las cosas particulares non pueden ser escriptas por escripto cierto; y esto finque en el entendimiento del buen físico: y alcançmiento cerca de la verdad y clara esperiencia sola finque" (*Sevillana medicina* fol. 21v).

37. "El Abenzoar dice en su primer libro, 'yo soy cierto que la medecina no se puede obrar por ninguno perfectamente sino después de larga costumbre y mucha esperiencia en su misma arte y no en ninguna manera por argumentos fingidos y logicales'" (Díaz de Ysla, *Tractado llamado fructo de todos los auctos* fol. 72v).

38. ". . . porque en el arte de la medicina, y en los grandes remedios della, tiene mas

fuerça la esperiencia propia, que la razón" (Cornejo, *Discurso particular preservativo de la gota* fols. 18r, 19r).

39. "El fin de todas las sciencias práticas es la obra, y ansí lo es de la medicina como sea una dellas. Y por esta causa dize Arnaldo de Vilanova en sus parábolas, conviene al médico ser eficaz en la obra y no hablador porque las enfermedades no con palabras, mas con las essencias o virtudes de las cosas se expelen y alançan de los cuerpos" (Saladino de Ascoli, *Compendio de los boticarios*, "Prólogo" fol. 2r).

40. "Antonio Fumanello, doctissimo médico veronés, dize, que darle al enfermo de pestilencia, luego al principio, seis onças de agua de nuezes verdes, destilada por alquitara de vidrio, que cura con admiración. Ello es mucha verdad, y me consta por haberlo visto y experimentado" (Soriano, *Libro de experimentos médicos*, [1599] fol. 18r).

41. "Yo he curado en las Indias, y en Toro, más de dozientos y todos están buenos y sanos, y no le ha vuelto a nadie y entre los que he curado" (Arias de Benavides, *Secretos de chirurgía* fol. 58v).

42. "Lo mismo hize yo en esta ciudad de Teruel, después de las evacuaciones universales, en uno llamado Juan de la Bastida calcetero. . . . Fue Dios servido curasse contra opinión de cinco médicos doctíssimos, y començasse yo de allí a cobrar crédito, en el año de .1564." (Soriano, *Libro de experimentos médicos* fol. 20v).

43. "Yo vide en México abrir a un niño, hijo de un muy honrado hombre que se dezía Villaseñor, y no abía cinco años, y le sacaron una piedra casi tamaña como un huevo" (Méndez, *Libro de ejercicio*, ed. Alvarez del Palacio 348–49).

44. ". . . haremos relación de un triste acaecimiento desto que en nuestros días avino en la persona de Don Martín de Ayala, doctíssimo y vigilatíssimo pastor y Arçobispo de Valencia, en al año 1566" (Gómez Miedes, *Enchiridión* fol. 95r).

45. "Ansí mismo el año de 1513, viniendo yo de camino para España, vi en Tolosa un caballero con un apostema duro en la ingle, el qual después de muchos emplastros molificativos que los cirujanos le habían puesto paresciendo que no rescebía beneficio, por mi consejo se abrió la dureza con un cauterio de fuego, y salió della una pelota de plomo, y entonces se averiguó que había dos años que le habían dado a aquel caballero un golpe de escopeta por la sien y que nunca se había podido hallar la pelota de lo qual había estado muy malo por espacio de un año con gran dolor de cabeça, y había otro año que esta ya bueno y cerrada la llaga" (Montaña de Monserrate, *Libro de anathomía del hombre* fol. 90v).

46. See Siraisi, "Girolamo Cardano and the Art of Medical Narrative," 587–90; For a detailed overview of the *Consilia*, see Agrimi and Crisciani, *Les consilia médicaux*.

47. "Un religioso del orden del seraphico padre san Francisco me dixo que un provincial de su orden había sido muy molestado de almorranas, y que le aconsejaron hiziesse este ungüento que se sigue, y que curó muy bien, y quantos lo han usado" (Soriano, *Libro de experimentos médicos* fol. 63v).

48. "Y en el tiempo que yo residía en el siendo proveedor un gran capellán del serenissimo rey don Manuel que se dezía Gonçalo de Miranda: eran tantos los dolientes

que salían curados deste mal, que muchas vezes iba el dicho proveedor e yo con él en busca de los enfermos por las puertas de las iglesias e de los monesterios para los traher e curar a este famoso hospital. Lo qual no pienso que se hazen en ningún hospital de la Europa. . . . [Y]o pienso haber sumptuosos hospitales e ricos, pero pienso que en ninguno dellos salgan a buscar los enfermos fuera" (Díaz de Ysla, *Tractado llamado fructo de todos los auctos* fol. 74r).

49. "Puesto desta causa en mucho cuidado con la mayor diligencia que yo pude revolvían el caso las escrituras, ansí de antiguos como modernos, y no hallé en ninguno que espresamente hablasse particularizando esta passión" (Alvarez Chanca, *Tratado nuevo* fol. 3r).

50. ". . . otro ningún médico no ha venido antes que yo porque es gente que no qui[e]ren dexar la buena vida y riquezas que allá tienen" (Arias de Benavides, *Secretos de chirurgía* fols. 54v–55r).

51. "La primera vez que le vi, parescióme la cura ser impossible, con todo dixe al enfermo que yo volvería allá en la mañana, y luego anduve buscando algunos autores, ansí como Juanes de Vigo y Guido, y nunca pude hallar ni la cura, ni semejante cosa, y ansí recorrí mi juyzio, y parescióme que con la forma siguiente se podía curar, y no con otra" (Arias de Benavides, *Secretos de chirurgía* fol. 112r).

52. "Y esto o la mayor parte dellos (discreto Lector) hallarás de mi invención, y con mi sudor tratado, donde también verás los cáusticos calcinados, y con mucha curiosidad corregidos. Verás assí mismo una cosa, de que yo soy el primero en hazello, que es la última intención, que de los que han escrito ninguno lo a soñado, que es el encorecer, cosa tan necessaria para essa cura, y fin la qual no se puede conseguir perfectamente el fin, y lo que se debe de estimar es, que estén los cáusticos en punto que quemen, y gasten la carne sin dolor" (Díaz, *Tratado nuevamente impresso de todas las enfermedades de los riñones, vexiga, y carnosidades de la verga* fol. 4r).

53. "Yo, pues, he sido el primero que para más suavidad, memoria, y doctrina de las cosas que pertenecen a la conservación del individuo, he caminado por este nuevo atajo, en el qual aunque corto y áspero, descubrirá el lector todo lo sustancial que los árabes y griegos, maestros de la racional medicina, dixeron; dexando lo superfluo para quien quisiere caminar por el largo y ancho camino que ellos inventaron" (Sorapán de Rieros, *Medicina española contenida en proverbios vulgares* "Prólogo al lector").

54. "Yo he curado más de veinte mil personas y que se han sanado más de otras veynte mil" (Díaz de Ysla, *Tractado llamado fructo de todos los auctos* fol. 63v).

55. ". . . en particular he gastado, y puesto todas mis vigilias y trabajos en aclarar y desmarañar esta antiquíssima confusión y oscura enigma de la cura de la gota, que parece la fábula de la Hidra, que cortada una cabeça, recobraba siete, y vive y revuelve, y torna a renacer, y va siempre cobrando fuerças, y nuevos bríos, tanto, que si el subjeto que maltrata fuere un robustíssimo Ercules, al fin de la lucha o gran batalla, sin remedio ni reparo, lo ha de acabar y vencer" (Cornejo, *Discurso particular preservativo de la gota*, fol. 3r).

56. "Y assí se tiene por cierto, que Philipo, médico de Alexandro, no menos venció a Dario en la lid, que el proprio Alexandro, al qual poco antes de la vitoria le había restituído la salud y las fuerças perdidas de una muy grave enfermedad, sin la qual salud, no venciera el Magno Alexandro" (Sorapán de Rieros, *Medicina española contenida en proverbios vulgares* fol. 3v).

57. "E desque yo lo tracté en rromançe con mas largos avisamientos que ellos lo dixieron, por ende es e será más público a todos según avino a las leyes del derecho por el rromançe de *Las siete partidas*, que non dubdo que pesó a algunos sabios del derecho por ser divulgada la sçiençia de los sabios. E si soy culpado, non soy en al salvo en rromançar e declarar alguna parte de las maldades e engaños e inorançias que manifiesto se vee que se fazen con el título de medeçina, de lo qual non me rrepiento por que es pro de la rrepublica" (Chirino, *Espejo de medicina* fol. 19v).

58. For an overview of ontological versus physiological notions of disease over the centuries, see Temkin, "An Historical Analysis of the Concept of Infection." On the rise of contagion theory in late medieval and Renaissance Europe, see Nutton, "The Seeds of Disease."

59. By "subaltern healers," I refer to any participant in the healing arts whose status is deemed illegitimate or suspect by the prevailing legal authorities. These include women healers (often prohibited from practicing medicine), non-Christian practitioners (frequently considered suspect), and other healers who had not been university-trained and licensed. In the case of women healers, Montserrat Cabré argues that the "caring meanings ascribed to the words women, mothers, midwives, and nurses in the Iberian mother tongues conflate and describe a *continuum* of practice whose origin is the household, from where it expands to the community" ("Women or Healers?" 18). In this respect, a subaltern healer is one who operates from the domestic setting, often with a degree of indifference or an ambiguous professional status in relation to the university-trained and licensed practitioner.

60. "Llamen luego médico, y no qualquiera, sino doctíssimo, a quien encomienden su salud, y vida. No curen de médicos muy amigos de cordiales, de minorativos, ni ventoseros, quales cada día veo" (Soriano, *Libro de experimentos médicos* [1599] fol. 11r).

61. "E conviene que los çurgianos que sean letrados e non idiotas. Ca los idiotas con sus esperimentos fazen obras por que caen en errores. Ca apenas algunt çilurgiano non aprendará el arte de çilurgia si non sopiera leer. E recuenta en el Almançor que la mayor parte son idiotas e de gruesos entendimientos, e locos, e por la su locura enfermedades se engendran en los omnes malamente por razón que non obran con çierta sçiençia nin con razón así matan los omnes" (Teodorico, *Cirugía*, 1v).

62. "E yo sané un salernitano que había llaga en el espinazo que pasaba adentro. E eran pasados ocho meses que era ferido. E era fecha fistola que pasaba adentro del qual salía podredura muy fonda. E aun quando tosíe, echaba semejante podredura. E los médicos de Salerna, todos lo habían judgado por tísico, e por enpico, e por eptico, e que nunca podrá guaresçer. Enpico es el que escupe sangre que sale de la Canal del pulmon

y de la diaflama. E eptico es en el qual se consume el humor radicar. E aquel omne vino de Salerna a mi, e usando de mío consejo, fue sano en breve tienpo e bien grueso, así que los médicos de Salerna se maravillavan mucho" (Teodorico, *Cirugia*, fol. 62r).

63. For a more general discussion on the relation between narrative and medical practice, see Mattingly (*Healing Dramas and Clinical Plots*) and Mattingly and Garro, eds. (*Narrative and the Cultural Construction of Illness and Healing*).

64. "Y eso me hizo escribir estos Discursos, por que ya, que yo no puedo curar ni dizir la verdad en todas partes, lo hagan ellos" (Méndez, *Discursos medicinales*, ed. Ser Quijano and Rodríguez-San Pedro 54).

65. "Yo entendiendo que era mal hecho no publicar remedios de tanta utilidad y provecho a los próximos, lo començé a divulgar en España y a donde quiera que e residido por cuyo benefiçio yo, con los demás médicos que dél an usado sin me lo agradecer, avemos remediado más de veinte mil enfermos que padeçian grandes tormentos y miserias, de lo que estoy muy contento, y no acabo de dar a Dios o ellos infinitas graçias" (Méndez, *Discursos medicinales*, ed. Ser Quijano and Rodríguez-San Pedro 65).

66. Among the rules of caution for physicians found in Gabriele Zaerbi's fifteenth-century *De cautelis medicorum*, we read "The physician should above all not take on the burden of long-standing and difficult diseases because he hopes for some sort of gain. For if such diseases are later left unhealed by God, they give him a bad reputation" (quoted in Linden 25).

67. Even a relatively successful physician such as Luis Lobera de Avila, at one time head medical examiner and personal physician for Carlos V, found himself traveling over the course of his career to Germany, Flanders, England, Holland, Saxony, Vienna, Hungary, Bohemia, Corinth, France, Lombardia, and Africa, treating patients in cities such as Nice, Milan, Genoa, Venice, Naples, Rome, Sicily, and Tunisia (Hernández Briz, "Introducción" 9–14).

68. "Avicena quando dixo, que con el buen regimiento se curan las enfermedades, allí entendió las cosas no naturales, que son alegría, temor, tristeza, y otras más, y entre estas se debe poner la confiança, que el médico ha ganado para con sus enfermos. Y assí el mismo Avicena affirma, que más vale al enfermo la buena confiança, que tiene de su médico, que todas quantas medicinas le puede aplicar; y la razón desto es porque la confiança grande y efficax que se tiene haze las acciones eficaces y vehementes, como Avicena y Algacer authores árabes escribieron. Y assí como las cosas no naturales, que llaman los médicos, y la comida y bebida alteran el cuerpo, assí la confiança le altera" (*Retrato del perfecto médico* 199–200). Enríquez is quoting "the Conciliator" Peter of Abano.

Chapter 3. Fictions and Pharmaceuticals

1. "Infinitas vezes suele venir en las tetas dolor, calor, y hinchazón: y no viene sino por abundancia de leche o por ser gorda o muy espessa o por quajarse en las tetas" (Carbón, *Libro del arte de las comadres* [1541] fol. 43r).

2. For sources and a complete description of the correspondence between Elionor and Mata, see Cabré, "From a Master to a Laywoman."

3. The bibliography on the history of pharmaceuticals and the pharmaceutical profession is extensive; see Jean-Pierre Bénézet's highly detailed analysis of late medieval and Renaissance apothecaries, *Pharmacie et médicament en Méditerranée occidentale*; and Jerry Stannard's compendious works, *Herbs and Herbalism in the Middle Ages and Renaissance* and *Pristina medicamenta: Ancient and Medieval Medical Botany*.

4. For a general overview of the collection and dissemination of medical recipes from antiquity through the Middle Ages, see Hunt, *Popular Medicine* 1–6.

5. On the so-called "Recetario de Enrique IV" and the *Recetario de Alba*, two fifteenth-century examples of recipes written for a specific patient, see García-Ballester's discussion in *La búsqueda de la salud* 585–84.

6. To my knowledge, scholars have yet to undertake an extensive study of the vernacular recipe in late medieval and early modern Spain. My personal database contains more than three thousand recipes extracted from a mere ten late fifteenth- and sixteenth-century vernacular medical works, among which are included Fernando Alvarez's *Regimiento contra la peste* (1501), the anonymous *Tesoro de la medicina* (or *Tesoro de los remedios*), Juan de Aviñón's *Sevillana medicina* (1545), Alfonso Chirino's *Menor daño de la medicina* (Biblioteca Nacional MS 3384), and Jerónimo Soriano's *Libro de experimentos médicos, faciles y verdaderos* (1599).

7. Medieval and early modern authors inspired by Galen distinguished between pharmaceuticals and mere foods by arguing that medicaments alter the patient's basic nature while foods maintain or augment the patient's normal substance: "Medicamento se llama todo aquello que puede alterar nuestra naturaleza, a diferencia del mantenimiento, el qual puede aumentar nuestra sustancia. Alteran los medicamentos nuestra naturaleza con una o dos calidades, calentando, enfriando, humedeciendo, o dessecando, o con toda su sustancia. Los que con una o dos calidades tan solamente sin hazer otro daño nos alteran, se llaman absolutamente medicamentos: mas los que assí alterando, de tal manera padecen, que son vencidos, y de todo punto hechos semejantes a nosotros, tienen nombre de medicamentos y mantenimientos juntamente" (Luis de Oviedo, *Methodo de la colección y reposición de las medicinas simples* [1595] fol. 1r).

8. The terms *experiments* and *secrets* have strong empirical connotations, and in the case of secrets point to the dissemination of popular how-to books, such as Alessio Piemontese's *Secreti* (1555; translated into Spanish and published in 1570, 1640, and 1647), that circulated throughout Europe in the sixteenth and seventeenth centuries. See Eamon's *Science and the Secrets of Nature* for extensive discussion of these works.

9. "Recepta para la melancolía: sen y epitimo, de cada uno, una onça; açucar de cantueso dos onças; toma cada día una cuchara" (Aviñón, *Sevillana medicina*, fol. 80r).

10. "Item, dize Mazer que la yerba que es dicha *milifoliun odorada* y llegada a las narizes rrestraña la sangre. Y si pusieres el çumo desta yerba en las narizes, fázela más salir. Cosa probada" (Gilberto, *Libro de recetas*, fol. 14r).

11. "son puestas por orden de las letras del a.b.c. por quel que algo obiere menester más ayna, lo pueda fallar" (*Macer herbolario* fol. 1r). On the vernacular versions of the *Macer Floridus*, see Thomas Capuano, "Medieval Iberian Vernacular Versions of the Herbal Called *Macer Floridus*."

12. "Asensio es una yerba que es de caliente natura y fuerte y amarga, esta es la primera virtud della. Et dize Maçer que si es cocha con agua de lluvia, después quel agua fuere esfriada al sereno, aquel que la bebiere si obiere lonbrizes, matárgelas ha. Et fazérgelas [h]a muchas vezes salir. Et si [h]a dolor en el vientre, quitárgelo ha. [H]a otra virtud que faze bien mear. Et faze a la muger venir su flor. Et ha otra virtud que si la pisan con sal e con pimienta, et con fojas de rruda aprovecha al vientre. A otra virtud que si es mezclada con miel e se unte el omne los ojos, fázelos claros. Et el bafo della, quando es cocha, es muy aprovechoso a las orejas que son llenas de çera que non puede omne oír. Et ha otra virtud que si es pisada et puesta sobre la llaga de la cabeça, móndargela ha. Et si es cocha con agua, el agua es muy buena para aquellos que han comezón. Et ha otra virtud al que entrare en la mar y la beba con vino non [h]abrá fastidio nin embargo. Et [h]a otra virtud si es pisada e con paño atada sobre los coraçones que son finchados, fazen los atorrnar en su estado. Et ha otra virtud que si es puesto debaxo del cabeçal que lo non sepa el enfermo, fazer le ha bien dormir. Et si el omne tuviere la lengua finchada et pones esta yerba desuso de la lengua, desfinchársele ha. Et si la mezclas con la tinta y con el vino, y la carta será escripta con esta tinta, y non se desfará nin fará gusanos" (*Macer herbolario* fol. 1r).

13. "La salvia provecha a la flaqueza de nervios usando della en qualquier manera puesta en el agua para bañar y echándola a remojar en el vino etcetera" (Chirino, *Menor daño de la medicina*, Escorial MS b.IV.34, fol. 192v); "Huevos de gallinas cozidos y yema dura molido con açafrán y azeyte rosado para ençima del ojo que duele" (fol. 197r–v); "Rubia molida y masada con vinagre para tirar las manchas blancas del cuerpo" (fol. 201r–v).

14. "[Delos sándalos] aprovechan (principalmente) el amarillo o cetrino, y blanco, contra los dolores de cabeça, de causa caliente. Y a los delirantes, y que están aparejados a caer en frenesís, aplicándolos sobre la frente y sienes, molidos y mezclados con agua rosada y vinagre, templan el grande ardor del estomago. Tomándolos por la boca refrescan y dan vigor en las fiebres ardientes. Aplicándolos con agua rosada sobre el coraçon, hígado, y pulsos, alegran y resucitan los vitales espíritus, mezclados con las medicinas cordiales" (Acosta, *Tractado de las drogas, y medicinas de las Indias Orientales* 171).

15. Monardes's *Dialogo de las grandezas del hierro, y de sus virtudes medicinales* and his *Libro que trata de la nieva y de sus propriedades* appear in the 1574 version and subsequent editions of the author's *Primera y segunda y tercera partes de la historia medicinal*.

16. "Toma la manteca de las ovejas, y toma otro al tanto de poleo; sécalo y muélelo, y ciérnelo, y amásalo con la manteca fasta que sea bien incorporado en uno. Et toma desto

en ayuno un bocado y otro en la noche. Et non comas nin bebas sobre ello. Et sanará de la tos" (*Tesoro de la medicina* fol. 30v).

17. "Para homne que non puede dormir. Toma las cimas verdes y los tallos del sahuco; pisalos bien y saca el çumo. Et mételos en así que sea atapada del un cabo con su nudo mismo, y del otro cabo átele la boca enderedor con un filo que non quiebre. Et después, atápalo bien con estopas de guisa que non entre agua dentro. Et estos canutos serán quantos quisieren y obieres mester. Et sean puestos en olla o en caldera en buen agua fierva tanto fasta que mengue el terçio o mas. Et después, seca los canutos y quebrántalos. Et fallar lo as dentro ungüento fecho. Et con este ungüento unta las sienes a vuelta con la fruentre y los pulsos. Et desí, toma leche de pepitas de las calabazas, et unta el çelebro de parte detrás, y cúbrelo bien. Et échalo a dormir en logar do nol fagan roído, y dormir sea luego. Et nol despiertes" (*Tesoro de la medicina* fol. 27r–v).

18. "[Dolor y torzon y rompimiento de los estentinos] Iten, dize Gilbertus, toma estiércol del hombre y del buey y de gallinas y de palomas y de aves de caça y de cabras y cal viva; sea fecho todo polvos por igual peso y sean destemplados y amasados con çumo de cogombros amargos; y sea freído o escalentado en la sartén con açeite o con unto de puerco; y caliente sea emplastrado todo el vientre delante y detrás lo más caliente que podiere sofrir. Esto es cosa probada" (Gilberto, *Libro de recetas* fol. 22r).

19. Examples of mother's milk used in medical recipes to treat ailments include the following: gout (Chirino, *Menor daño de la medicina*, Biblioteca Nacional MS 3384, fols. 175r–76v); eye inflammation (Farfán, *Tractado breve de medicina* 176v–77r); general eye ailments (Hispanus, *Libro de medicina llamado thesoro de pobres* [1596], fol. 11v); earaches (Bernard of Gordon, *Lilio de medicina*, Biblioteca Nacional MS I-315, fol. 183r), headaches (fol. 182v), fevers (fol. 8r); water in the ear (Córdoba, *Suma de la flor de cirugía* fol. 150v); frenzy (Gilberto, *Libro de recetas* fol. 5r); burns (*Tesoro de la medicina* fol. 26v); insomnia (Enríquez, *Secretos de la medicina* fols. 3v–4r).

20. "Otrosí, oí dezir que si pusiesen estas palabras escritas en una cartilla puesta al cuello que luego la echaría. E es ésta la oraçion: 'leçio ljbri job cancaris cancaris cancaris tartani tartani tartani'" (Córdoba, *Suma de la flor de cirugía* fol. 157v). For the use of charms, prayers, and verbal remedies in works of medical writers such as Gilbertus Anglicus, John Gaddesden, and John Arderne see Olsam ("Charms and Prayers"). Olsam refutes claims that such therapies were limited to folk practitioners who resort to magical cures.

21. "El de la Ruda es bueno / para todo dolor manifiesto de frio" (Chirino, *Menor daño de la medicina* fol. 6v).

22. ". . . iten, toma tres partes del çummo de los puerros, una de miel, y échalo por las narizes destellando. Tira el gran dolor de la cabeça. Mazer" (Gilberto, *Libro de recetas* fol. 5v).

23. "En las llagas viejas, es cosa maravillosa las obras y grandes efetos que esta yerba haze: porque las cura y sana maravillosamente, limpiándolas, y mundificándolas, de todo lo superfluo y podrido que tienen, y criando les carne, y reduziéndolas a perfeta

sanidad, lo qual es ya tan común en esta ciudad, que lo saben todos. Y yo la he administrado en muchas gentes, assí hombres como mugeres, en mucho número dellos, que de diez y veinte años han sanado de llagas podridas antiguas en piernas, y otras partes del cuerpo con solo este remedio con gran admiración de todos" (Monardes, *Primera y segunda y tercera partes de la historia medicinal* [1580] fol. 42v).

24. "Celidonia es una yerba ansí como dize Prinis que esclaresçe la vista de los ojos. Et que esto crea que es verdat, pruébalo en esta guisa: que fue un tiempo quando los golondrinos crían sus fijos, un moço tomó de los golondrinos pequeños y quebrantó les los ojos, y después torrnólos al nido; y vino la madre con esta yerba çelidonia y pusógela en los ojos, y perdieron la çeguedat, et cobraron la vista por esto. Y probó Prinis que esto es verdat" (Macer, *Macer herbolario* fol. 5v).

25. "Tiene este azeite grandes virtudes, como se ha visto por el uso dél, assí en las Indias como en nuestras partes, y todo lo que diré es con muy grande experiencia, y mucho uso dél en diversas personas" (Monardes, *Primera y segunda y tercera partes de la historia medicinal* [1580] fol. 12v).

26. "Tiene ansí mismo esta yerba virtud contra la yerba de Ballestero que usan nuestros caçadores para matar las fieras, que es veneno potentíssimo que mata sin remedio. Lo qual queriendo averiguar su Magestad, mandó se hiziesse la experiencia, y hirieron a un perro pequeño en la garganta, y pusiéronle luego en la herida yerba de Ballestero; y desde a un poco le pusieron en la misma herida que habían untado con la yerba de Ballestero, buena cantidad del çumo del tabaco y el borujo encima, y atáronlo. El perro escapó, no sin grande admiración de todos los que lo vieron" (Monardes, *Primera y segunda y tercera partes de la historia medicinal* [1580] fol. 42r). *Hierba ballestero* is a poison created from *helleborus*.

27. "De lo qual el muy excelente médico de cámara de su Magestad, el doctor Bernardo, en la margen deste libro que vio por mandado de su Magestad, dize estas palabras: yo hize esta experiencia por mandado de su Magestad; yo herí al perro con un cuchillo, con yerba, y después metí más yerba de Ballestero en la herida, y la yerba era escogida; el perro estuvo tomado de la yerba, y puesto el tabaco y su çumo en la herida, escapó el perro, y quedó muy sano" (Monardes, *Primera y segunda y tercera partes de la historia medicinal* [1580] fol. 42r).

28. *Macer herbolario* explains that "muchas y son de las yerbas sus virtudes encubiertas para los menges que las han menester para fazer sus melezinas. Et todo omne sabio debe saber que Dios puso sus virtudes en yerbas y en las piedras y en palabras" (fol. 1r).

29. "Orina de niño" or "orina de un niño pequeño" was called for in remedies used to alleviate earaches and to remove worms and fluid from the ears (Córdoba, *Suma de la flor de cirugía* fol. 151r–v), and to cure weak eyesight (Soriano, *Libro de experimentos médicos* [1599] fols. 27v–28r).

30. "Pollos grandes vivos, y quitadas las plumas del lugar por donde purgan el vientre, y arrimándolos mucho a la seca, hasta que se mueran, y en muriéndose poner otro"

(Zamudio de Alfaro, *Orden para la cura y preservación de las secas y carbuncos* fols. 15v–16r).

31. "Dize Giraldo que tomes el estiércol del hombre y quémalo y hazlo polvos y échalo en los ojos y alimpiará qual quier mal que aya en ellos" (Hispanus, *Libro de medicina llamado thesoro de pobres* [1596] fol. 15v).

32. "De experimentos contra melancholía. Parecer es de Arnaldo de Villanova (aunque no lo creo) pero por haber sido gravíssimo varón y excellentíssimo astrólogo, lo pongo aquí. Dize assí: toma algunos garuanços, y pon los al sereno en creciente de luna, untados con azeite; y remójalos en agua por espacio de tres horas; después cuézelos y déselos a comer al melanchólico. Que no sólo le quitarás los pensamientos tristes, pero todo género de melancholía" (Soriano, *Libro de los experimentos médicos* [1599] fol. 25r–v).

33. "Iten, los pelos de la liebre mojados en agua batida con vinagre y puestos estancará la sangre. Cosa probada" (Gilberto, *Libro de recetas* fol. 14v).

34. "Dos maneras de colirios o aguas pongo aquí y otros remedios para deshazer las nubes. Vayan probándolos, y con él que más provecho sintieren, se acaben de curar" (Farfán, *Tractado brebe de medicina* [1592] fol. 178r).

35. I am very grateful to Michael Cornett for drawing my attention to this article and providing me with the citation.

36. "En esta segunda impresión, soy más breve y llevo otro modo de curar las llagas diferente del primero, como se verá. No es invención mía, sino volver a uso y práctica lo que los antiguos escribieron, habiéndolo ellos esperimentado largos años con mucho estudio y trabajo suyo. Este nuevo modo de curar las llagas he yo es perimentado muchas vezes no me harto de dar gracias a nuestro buen Dios de ver con quanta facilidad y brevedad sanan las heridas y llagas. Y viendo y esperimentando esto que digo, determiné tomar el trabajo de ponerlo aquí para que todos se aprovechen y consigan tan grande beneficio" (Farfán, *Tractado brebe de medicina* [1592] fol. 285r–v).

37. ". . . procurando emplear los ratos de mi estudio en escribir un pequeño tractado de theriaca, en nuestro vulgar lenguaje, por que los no acostumbrados paladares a gustar de la lengua Griega y Latina, en su común estilo se aprovechen de los delicados ingenios passados, y de mi tengan algún nuevo fructo, con que olvidar los celebrados errores" (Pérez, *Libro de theriaca* 2).

38. "Finalmente diremos que este antídoto es excelentísimo para todo mal que no aya podido sanar con otros remedios; a causa que por gravísimo que sea, y casi sin esperanza de sanar, acontecido muchas vezes haber sido increíblemente sanado con el ayuda de la theriaca" (Pérez, *Libro de theriaca* 19).

39. "Por donde concluimos que si por haber descubierto muchos males y enfermedades de que se libra el cuerpo humano con la presente hubiéssemos de referir los muchíssimos bienes y saludes que les acarrea la mesma; son tantos que sería menester hazer nuevo tratado para solos ellos, pero bastara por agora apuntar algunos de los mas essenciales, quales con la experiencia hemos observado, y se descubren por señales

externos de prospera salud en los que usan esta medicina" (Gómez Miedes, *Enchiridión* fols. 105r–106v). '

40. "Y pues en tierras nuevas hay nuevas curas" (Arias de Benavides, *Secretos de chirurgía* fol. 63v).

41. "Anduvo por varias tierras y regiones, como él mesmo escribe en sus obras, lo que no es de poca importancia para ser uno perfeto médico. Lo que también hizo Galeno, como él mesmo cuenta en diversos lugares de sus libros (In lib. Hipp. derat. vict. In morb. acutis. comen. 3 sect. 8. libr. 3 de comp. in 5.g.cap. 2.li.9.5.in facul. etc libr 6. sanit. tuend). Pues estuvo dos vezes en Roma, navegó toda Lycia, estuvo en Tracia, Cypro, Macedonia, Syria, Alexandría, Cilicia, Fenicia, Palestina, Cyro, Creta, Italia, Bitinia, y Egipto, y otras muchas que buscó. Y anduvo por conocer simples yervas, y varios géneros de medicamentos y diversas especies de enfermedades que suele haver en cada una dellas, como él mesmo también escribe (In I.lib. Hippocrat. de morb. vulg. in proemio), diziendo que Hippócrates enseñó en el libro de los ayres, aguas y regiones, las enfermedades regionales, que suelen engendrarse en cada tierra diferentes. Y también ay algunos que escriven, que por esto se pinta Hippócrates cubierta la cabeça, en señal de que era amigo de peregrinar y ver tierras" (Amato Lusitano, *Diálogo en el cual se trata de las heridas de cabeça*, ed. Gandia, "A los platicantes de cirurgía," fol. 6r–v).

42. "Dize maestre Arnaldo de Villanova que él andando por el mundo a buscar las sciencias filosófales que hubo de llegar a la çibdad de Babilonia. Y dize que ende halló un moro muy grande filósofo. Y era maestro en medecina en la çibdad y era muy grande estrólogo que se trabajó por haber con él conversación de mucha amistança. Y esto hazía por sacar del moro algunos secretos filosófales. Y estando assí en su amistança, díxole con grand diligencia, rogándole que por bondad le quisiesse dezir y enseñar las virtudes que el romero había y ha que enfermedades aprovechaba; y esso mesmo que lo enseñasse a sacar el olio de la flor y para que enfermedades aprovechaba. E el moro le respondió que uno de los grandes secretos de la medecina quél tenía eran las virtudes del romero y de su flor. Lo qual sopiesse de çierto que jamás a ninguno había revelado nin enseñado tales cosas. Empero pues, quél le rogaba y con muy grand diligencia de saber los muchos y grandes secretos encerrados y escondidos de las virtudes del romero:; quería saber que él con mucho amor gelo quería enseñar y declarar. Lo que nunca hasta hoy había hecho a criatura ninguna" (Maestre Gil, *Libro de medicina llamado Macer* [1518] fol. 29v).

43. For useful overview of New World materia medica, its reception and practical impact in Spain and Europe, see Teresa Huguet-Termes's thoughtful article, "New World Materia Medica in Spanish Renaissance Medicine."

44. "Allende destas riquezas tan grandes, nos envían nuestras Indias Occidentales muchos árboles, plantas, yerbas, raíces, çumos, gomas, frutos, simientes, licores, piedras que tienen grandes virtudes medicinales, en las quales se han hallado, y hallan muy grandes efetos que exceden mucho en valor y precio. . . . Y esto no es de maravillar, que así sea, como dize el philosopho; no todas las tierras dan iguales plantas, y frutos, porque una región, o tierra lleva tales árboles, plantas y frutos, que otra no los lleva. Vemos que

en Creta solamente nasce el diptamo y el encienso en sola la región de Saba; y el alma-ciga, en sola la Insula de Chio; y la canela y clavo y pimienta, y otras especias sólo en las Islas de Maluco; y otras muchas cosas hay en diversas partes del mundo que no han sido conoscidas hasta nuestros tiempos. . . . Y ansí, como se han descubierto nuevas regiones y nuevos reinos y nuevas provincias por nuestros españoles, ellos nos han traído nuevas medicinas y nuevos remedios con que se curan y sanan muchas enfermedades que si caresciéramos dellas, fueran incurables y sin ningún remedio" (Monardes, *Primera y segunda y tercera partes de la historia medicinal* [1580] fol. 8v).

45. The title of the 1596 edition of Frampton's translation is *Joyfull newes out of the new-found worlde. Wherein are declared, the rare and singuler vertues of divers herbs, trees, plantes, oyles y stones, with their applications, as well to the use of phisicke as of chirurgery.* . . .

46. "Y Marco Emperador Romano trabajó y puso tanta diligencia en saber las natu-ralezas y propiedades de los animales, quanto más se debe tener cuidado en alcanzar el conocimiento de las yerbas de las quales proviene y mana una abundantíssima copia de remedios, una creación tan grande que no hay otra que se le iguale. Quien será él que no se holgara de saber las virtudes dellas y los secretos tan excesivos que en ellas están encerrados?" (Jarava, *Historia de las yeruas* fol. 1r).

47. "Puede lo hazer, juntamente con la experiencia y uso dellas de cuarenta años que ha que curo en esta ciudad, do me he informado de los que de aquellas partes las han traído con mucho cuidado, y las he experimentado en muchas y diversas personas, con toda diligencia, y miramiento posible, con felicísimos sucesos" (Monardes, *Primera y segunda y tercera partes dela historia medicinal* [1580] fol. 2r).

48. For a detailed overview of the history, mythology, and use of balsam in the mid-dle ages see Marcus Milwright, "The Balsam of Matariyya."

49. "Nota que para subtiliar y quitar las cicatrizes untando las con bálsamo/ no ay cosa tan sublime, mas es en gran precio, ni lo tienen sino los poderosos y grandes seño-res, porque en el mundo no ay sino una viña de aquellos árboles: la qual viña es del gran soldan de los moros" (*Compendio de los boticarios* 14r).

50. For example, in the *Tesoros de remedios* we read that agua ardiente was "as va-luable for embalming cadavers as balsam": "Et esta agua vale al tanto como si se untaren con balssamo" (2v). Soriano describes a remedy for treating wounds that is "like bal-samo" (como balsamo) (*Libro de experimentos médicos* 1599, 93r).

51. Huguet-Termes speculates that New World medicines, especially the new bal-sam, were "distributed outside the enviornment of the learned élite, in 'an underground way'" for patients who prefered to self-medicate themselves (372), whereas Latinate sur-geons tended to ingore or resist these new drugs (369).

52. "Quando lo traxeron a España la primera vez, fue tenido en tanto quanto era razón, porque le vieron hazer maravillosas obras, valía una onça diez, y veynte ducados: y agora vale una arroba tres, o quatro ducados. La primera vez que lo llevaron a Roma, vino a valer una onça cien ducados: después como han traydo tanto, y en tanta cantidad,

no sólo no tiene precio, pero se da dado. Esto tiene la abundancia de las cosas, o la rareza dellas, que quando valía muy caro, todos se aprovechaban de sus virtudes: y después como vino a valer tan vil precio, no lo tienen en nada, siendo el mismo Bálsamo, el que era entonces, quando valía cien ducados la onça, que el de agora que no tiene precio. Cierto aunque no se descubrieran las Indias, sino para efeto de embiarnos este licor maravilloso, era bien empleado el trabajo que tomaron los nuestros Españoles. Porque el Bálsamo que solía aver en Egypto, a muchos años que pereció, porque se secó la viña, de adonde se sacaba, por do ya no lo ay en el mundo. Tuvo nuestro Señor por bien en su lugar darnos este Bálsamo, de nueva España, el qual a mi juyzio, en virtudes medicinales, no es menos que aquello de Egypto, según vemos sus grandes efetos, y lo mucho que aprovecha" (Sevilla 1580, 15r)

53. "conserva la juventud. Yo conoscí una persona de mucha calidad que lo usaba, y con

ser de mucha edad, parecía moço, y vivía sin achaques después que lo usaba" (15v).

54. "Monardes haze ventaja al Egypcio, o Siriaco, en cuyo lugar se puede poner muy bien todas las vezes que se pidiere para alguna medicina" (*Examen de boticarios* 110).

55. "Todos los doctores de medicina mandan fazer a cada dolencia su melezina cierta, y non escribieron una melezina para todas las dolencias que hayan menester purgación. Y síguese que non puede ser que purguemos con una melezina muchas dolencias" (Juan de Aviñón, *Sevillana medicina* fol. 82r).

56. "E en todo me remito al físico que estoviere presente, al qual conviene moderar según la edad complexión y costumbre del subjecto quese la encomendare" (Alvarez, *Regimiento contra la peste* [1501] fol. 5r).

57. "Muy maravillosa reçebta de las virtudes del romero en especial de la flor del qual se ha de hazer azeite con el qual obrarás y curarás infinitas passiones de enfermedades. Primeramente este conforta mucho el coraçón y da fortaleza a los miembros enflaquecidos y cura a los que tiemblan la cabeça y las manos; y quita las manzillas de la cara y conserva a la persona que se untare el rostro en juventud; y si pusiere una gota en los ojos que tovieren telas enellos o manzilla o lágrima que empache la vista, todo lo deshaze y sana; y ponlo por tres vezes. Otrosí, aprovecha mucho a aquellos o aquellas que tovieren en los miembros algún mal y se untaren con este azeite serán sanos. Otrosí aprovechan a todos los dolores de frialdad o de humor descendientes coyunturas. Otrosí, aprovechan a los pacientes de la passión de cólica, y aprovechan a las enfermedades de las mugeres de tañimiento de la madre. Otrosí, aprovechan a qualesquier enfermos de postemas" (Maestre Gil, *Libro de medicina llamado Macer* [1518] fol. 29r).

58. "El dicromático de buena invención es de grandíssima virtud para todas enfermedades intrínsecas y extrínsecas . . . hazen otros infinitos buenos destos que dexo aquí de referir. Y se podrán ver y cada uno examinar esta verdad con la esperiencia que deste singularíssimo remedio se puede ver en toda suerte de enfermedades y calidad de personas" (Martínez de Leyva, *Remedios preservativos y curativos para en tiempo de peste* fols. 157v–158r).

59. "Habiendo escrito el presente *Regimento de la peste*, en el qual es escrito el modo de hazer algunos remedios notables e importantísimos para usar en la dicha peste, no quiero dexar de traer a la memoria el modo de usar de los dichos remedios en muchas otras especies de enfermedades de condición que este libro sea bueno y de provecho en todo tiempo y ocasión, y que cada uno se pueda servir de la toda su voluntad, quando fuere necesario; porque los dichos remedios son de tanta virtud y eficacia que sirven y aprovechan casi a todas las enfermedades que padecen los cuerpos humanos, tan intrínsecas como extrínsecas" (Martínez de Leyva, *Remedios preservativos y curativos para en tiempo de peste* fol. 162v).

Conclusions: Fictions of Ill-Being

Epigraph: "Entre las cosas de mayor admiración que ay en la facultad de medicina, es ver la multitud y variedad de enfermedades, que con quantas los esplendidos Griegos, y los elegantes Latinos, y los curiosos Arabes escribieron, se ofrecen muchas nuevamente cada día" (Francisco Díaz, *Tratado de todas las enfermedades de los riñones, vexiga y carnosidades de la verga y orina y de su cura*, "Prólogo al lector").

1. Illustrative is the case of Melissa Woyechowsky, a woman who spent four hours a day on the Internet, believing she had developed the early stages of multiple sclerosis, and later, Lou Gehrig's disease. See the newspaper accounts by Valley and Seligman.

2. "E veemos que el omne sano que teme de enfermar, enferma" (*Visita* 63r).

3. Monardes: "Yo vi un hombre que tenia unas llagas antiguas en las narizes por do echaba mucha materia, y se le iban comiendo, y aconsejele que tomasse por las narizes el çumo del Tabaco, y hizolo, y a la segunda vez echo mas de veynte gusanos chiquitos, y después otros pocos, hasta que quedo sin ningunos, y usando la assí algunos días, sano de las llagas que tenía en lo interior de las narizes, aunque no de lo que se le había roydo y caydo dellas; que si más tardara creo que no le quedaran narizes, que todas se le comieran, como acontesce a muchos" (*Primera Y segunda y tercera partes de la historia medicinal*, Sevilla 1574: 46v–47r). Arias de Benavides: "Un curtidor de la Ciudad de México, hora de andar en el agua, de alguna corrupción de humores o de lo que Dios fue servido—que yo no pude saber de lo que le había sucedido—hiziéronsele unas fístulas en el nacimiento de la verga, tres agugeros por donde orinaba, y por el orificio de la dicha verga ninguna gota, antes por la continua abituación se le cerró el orificio della, de tal suerte que no tenía más manera de agugero que si nunca hubiera orinado por el caño. El mancebo se determinó a que le curassen o morir, y no passar aquella pena, que como estaban los orificios tan a rayz del nacimiento de el miembro, todo lo que orinaba se le caya por las ingles y se veya el triste todo escozido y ulzerado de aquellos orines" (*Secretos de chirurgia* 111r–112r).

4. "Vos quiero dezir de la epilepsia que yo tuve en mi cura muchos mancebos, y viejos, pobres y ricos, y varones, y mugeres, y de todas especies de epilepsia, pero por mi nin por otro nunca vi alguno ser curado . . . E esto vos digo por que si algunos enfermos

vinieren a vosotros, non vos querades desonrrar con vanos y falsos prometimientos en la cura de la epilensia" (*Lilio de medicina* ms I-315. Biblioteca Nacional, Madrid 65r).

5. "Como uno por sanar de la gota, murió del mal de orina. . . . Haremos relación de un triste acaecimiento desto que en nuestros días avino en la persona de Don Martín de Ayala, doctíssimo y vigilatíssimo pastor y Arçobispo de Valencia, en el año 1566… Como estando el dicho Arçobispo aquexadíssimo de la gota, le aconsejó un empírico morisco, dizen de Granada, permitiese que le cortassen, o quemassen ciertas venillas tenuíssimas y casi imperceptibles que son collaterales a las emulgentes, donde se haze el receptáculo, y como arcaduze de la orina para de allí passar junta a los reñones, y por consiguiente a la bexiga. Y que cerradas dichas venillas, divertirían el humor frío de la gota, y sanaría della. Plugó al Arçobispo el discurso, y con el desseo de su salud, se fue luego a poner en execución el experimento en unos baños, no lexos de Granada. Lo qual hecho, sintió luego total alivio de la gota, y volviéndose a Valencia muy alegre y contento de su cura, a medio camino le faltó la orina, y sintió notable impedimento y cessación della, a lo qual acudieron médicos. Y como no hallaron que el impedimento se causaba en la bexiga, ni mas adelante, començaron con baños y otros muchos remedios a entender en la cura, pero como no aprovechasse cosa, y el orín se aumentasse, y hallando cerrado el passo para los reñones, poco a poco regurgitase pecho arriba para la garganta; llego a tanto, que echo por la boca la orina, y ahogó" (*Enchiridión*, 95r–96r).

6. For example: "para el dolor de qualquier miembro" (5v); "dolor de vientre" (5v); "para dolor de las costillas" (5v); "para todo dolor manifiesto de frío" (5v); "para dolor de cólica" (15r); "dolor de cabeça (16r); "Si oviere grant dolor en la cabeça" (28r); "dolor en las espaldas" (41v); "dolores en qualquier miembro" (41r); "dolor de la cabeça" (43v); "para dolores de las conjunturas" (52); "E si sintiere que va el dolor a lo profundo del cuerpo" (64v).

7. "Estas por la mayor parte vienen por comunicación de tener acesso con mugeres, que no estén limpias. Ay más contagiosidad en tiempo caliente que no en frío, a causa de la relaxación de los poros, y la calor grande, y el sudor que se recibe en el acto, pegase mas brevemente, en tiempo frío es al contrario por la clausura de los poros, naturaleza está más fuerte a resistir y deffender, y la virtud espulsiva a expeler lo malo, no embargante que se pega más presto y con menos causa a unos que a otros, y también esta enfermedad se paga de beber por una vasija que aya bebido el que tuviere la dicha enfermedad, o dormir con quien la tuviere, y ansí mismo digo que fuera de todas las causas dichas, puede tener esta enfermedad qualquiera persona sin contagiossidad ninguna, si no por corrupción de humores que se le corrompan y derramen por el cuerpo. Ejemplo: el primer hombre que en el mundo tuvo las bubas, ¿quién se las pudo apegar? Pues de la misma manera que a este se le engendraron, también se les puede engendrar a otra qualquiera persona. Como yo he visto muchas monjas, donde jamás se había visto esta enfermedad, y entrar en la orden y después tener muchas bubas. Y ansí lo he visto en religiosos" (fol. 71v–72r).

BIBLIOGRAPHY

Vernacular Medical Works 1305–1650

Note: Bibliographic entries for modern editions and facsimiles appear below each primary text. Anonymous works appear alphabetically under the title of the treatise or manuscript. Recipes and recipe collections have been placed under the general rubric "Recipes."

Abreu, Alexo de
Tratado de las siete enfermedades, de la inflammación universal del higado, zirbo, pyloron, y riñones, y de la obstrución, de la satiriasi, de la terciana y febre maligna, y passión hipocondriaca. Lleva otros tres tratados, del mal de loanda, del guzano, y de las fuentes y sedales. . . . Lisboa: Pedro Craesbeeck, 1623. [Colophon 1622].

Abulcasis. See Rodríguez de Tudela, Alonso

Acebedo, Pedro de
Alivio de pestilencia e otros males. Sevilla, 1570.
Recreación del alma y defensa del evangelio. Contra la supersticiosa astrología. Sevilla, 1570.
Remedios contra pestilencia. Zaragoza: Pedro Puig, 1589.

Acosta, Cristóbal
Tractado de las drogas, y medicinas de las Indias Orientales, con sus plantas debuxadas al vivo. En el qual se verifica mucho de lo que escribió el Doctor García de Orta. Burgos: Martín de Victoria, 1578.
Facsimiles
Fernández Ares, José Carlos, ed. *Cristóbal Acosta. Tratado de las drogas y medicinas de las Indias Orientales: edición facsímil del ejemplar rarísimo de la biblioteca Universitaria de Salamanca.* León: Universidad de León, 1995.
Rodríguez Nozal, Raúl, and Antonio González Bueno, eds. *Tractado de las drogas y medicinas de las Indias Orientales: con sus plantas debuxadas al biuo por Christoual Acosta.* Madrid: Cultura Hispánica, 1995.
Tractado de las drogas y medicinas de las Indias Orientales: con sus plantas debuxadas al bivo. Valencia: Vicent García, 1996.
Tractado de las drogas, y medicinas de la Indias Orientales, con sus plantas debuxadas

al biuo por Cristobal Acosta. En el qual se verifica mucho de lo que escriuio el doctor Garcia de Orta. Madrid: Agencia Española de Cooperación Internacional, 2000.

Edition

López Piñero, José María, ed. *Tractado de las drogas y medicinas de las indias orientales, con sus plantas debuxadas al vivo (1578), de Cristóbal de Acosta.* Valencia: Vicent García, 2002.

Agramont, Jacme d'. See Jacme d'Agramont

Aguilera, Antonio de
Exposición sobre las preparaciones de Mesue. Alcalá, 1569.

Alcanyís, Lluis
Regiment preservatiu e curatiu de la pestilència. Valencia: Nicolás Spindeler, 1490.

Facsimile

Regiment preservatiu e curatiu dela [sic] *pestilencia.* Valencia: Vicent García, 1992.

Editions

Ferrando i Francés, Antoni, ed. *Lluís Alcayis. Regiment preservatiu e curatiu de la pestilència.* Valencia: Universitat de Valencia, 1999.

Tarazona, Paco, ed. *Regiment preservatiu i curatiu de la pestilència*: Prosa. Valencia: L'Oronella, 2007.

Alfaro, Andrés. See Zamudio de Alfaro, Andrés

Alonso de Burgos
Méthodo curativo y uso de la nieve en que se declara y prueba la obligación que tienen los médicos de dar a los purgados agua de nieve . . . Córdoba: Andrés Carrillo, 1640.

Alfonso de Miranda. See Miranda, Alfonso de

Alvarez, Fernando
Regimiento contra la peste. 1501.

Editions

Sancho de San Román, Rafael. *Tres escritos sobre pestilencia del Renacimiento español.* Salamanca: Real Academia de Medicina de Salamanca, 1979.

Zabía, María Purificación, ed. *Fernando Alvarez. Regimiento contra la peste (1501).* Textos y concordancias electrónicos del corpus médico español CD-ROM, ed. María Teresa Herrera and María Estela González de Fauve. Madison, Wis.: Hispanic Seminar of Medieval Studies, 1997.

Regimiento contra la peste . . . Salamanca: Hans Gysser, 1507.

Regimiento contra la peste . . . Valladolid: Arnao Guillén de Brocar, 1518.

Alvarez Chanca, Diego
Libro del ojo. Sevilla: Brun, 1499.

Tratado nuevo, no menos útil que necessario, en que se declara de que manera se ha de curar el mal de costado pestilencial . . . Sevilla: Jacobo Cromberger, 1506.

Editions

Sancho de San Román, Rafael. *Tres escritos sobre pestilencia del Renacimiento español.* Salamanca: Real Academia de Medicina de Salamanca, 1979.

Zabía, María Purificación. *Diego Alvarez Chanca. Tratado nuevo, no menos útil que necessario, en que se declara de que manera se ha de curar el mal de costado pestilencial.* Sevilla: Jacobo Cromberger, 1506. Textos y concordancias electrónicos del corpus médico español CD-ROM, ed. María Teresa Herrera and María Estela González de Fauve. Madison, Wis.: Hispanic Seminar of Medieval Studies, 1997.

Alvarez de Miravall, Blas

Libro intitulado la conservación de la salud del cuerpo y del alma, para el buen regimiento de la salud. Medina del Campo: Santiago del Canto, 1597.

Libro intitulado la conservación de la salud del cuerpo y del alma. Salamanca: Diego Cussio, 1599.

Libro intitulado la conservación de la salud del cuerpo y del alma, para el buen regimiento de la salud. Salamanca: Andrés Renau, 1601.

Alvarez y Carcía de Salcedo, Tomás

Recopilaçao das coisas que conuem guardarse no modo de perseruar a cidade de Lixboa. E os sanos et curar-os que esteuerem enfermos de peste. Lisboa, 1569.

Amato Lusitano

Dialogo en el qual se trata de las heridas de la cabeza con el casco descubierto . . . Traduzido del latín en romance castellano por Geronimo de Virues. Valencia: Compañia de Libreros, 1588.

Edition

Gandia, Imma. ed. *Diálogo de las heridas de la cabeça, escrit per Amato Lusitano, traduït del llatí al castellà per Gerónimo de Virués (1588).* Lemir (anexos), 6 (2002). http://parnaseo.uv.es/Lemir/Textos/Amato/Index.html

Anglicus, Bartholomaeus. See Bartholomaeus Anglicus

Arias de Benavides, Pedro

Secretos de chiruríia, especial de las enfermedades de morbo galico y lamparones y mirrarchia, y assí mismo la manera como se curan los Indios de llagas y heridas y otras passiones en las Indias, muy útil y provechoso para en España y otros muchos secretos de chirurgía hasta agora no escriptos. Valladolid: Francisco Fernández de Córdova, 1567.

Edition

Arismendi, Andrea L. *Pedro Arias de Benavides. Secretos de chirurgia.* Textos y concordancias electrónicos del corpus médico español CD-ROM, ed. María Teresa Herrera and María Estela González de Fauve. Madison, Wis.: Hispanic Seminary of Medieval Studies, 1997

Arnau de Vilanova

Lo regiment de sanitat / lo qual l'onrat maestre de Vilanova ha ordonat al molt alt senyor

rey d'Aragon. Trans. Berenguer Sariera Furgia. MS. 10078. Biblioteca Nacional, Madrid.

Edition

Batllori, Miquel. "Arnau de Vilanova. Regiment de sanitat. [Trans. Berenguer Sarriera (Ça Rierra)]." *Obres Catalanes: Escrits médics,* vol. 2. Barcelona: Barcino, 1947. 99–200.

Regiment de sanitat. Barberini lat. 311. Biblioteca Vaticana, Vatican.

Regimento de sanidad. Thesaurus Pauperum. Burgos, 1524.

Regimiento de sanidad. Thesaurus Pauperum. Sevilla, 1609.

Aviñón, Juan de. See Juan de Aviñón

Barba, Alonso
Libro de la verdadera preservación y curación de la peste. 1569.

Barba, Pedro
Breve, y clara resumpta, y tratado de la essencia, causas, prognostico, preservación, y curación de la peste. Madrid: Alonso de Paredes, 1648.

Bartholomaeus Anglicus
De proprietatibus rerum [Spanish]. Toulouse: Henricus Mayer, 1494.

Edition

Liber de proprietatibus rerum; Propiedades de las cosas. Trans. Vicente de Burgos, ed. García Toledano, María Jesús and Galiano Sierra, Isabel María. Toulouse: Enrique Meyer, 1494. ADMYTE Archivo Digital de manuscritos y textos españoles. Madrid: Micrones, 1992.

Libro de proprietatibus rerum en romance. Tolosa: Gaspar de Auila, 1494.

Libro de proprietatibus rerum en romance. Toledo: Gaspar de Auila, 1529.

Bernard of Gordon (Bernardo de Gordonio)
Lilio de medicina. ms I-315. Biblioteca Nacional, Madrid.

Edition

Cull, John, and Cynthia M. Wasick. *Text and concordance of Lilio de medicina I-315, Biblioteca Nacional de Madrid.* Microfiche. Madison, Wis.: Hispanic Seminary of Medieval Studies, 1989.

Lilio de medicina. Sevilla: Meynardo, 1495.

Edition

Cull, John, and Brian Dutton, eds. *Lilio de medicina: un manual básico de medicina medieval [Sevilla 1495].* Madison, Wis.: Hispanic Seminary of Medieval Studies, 1991.

Lilio de medicina. Toledo: Juan Villaquiran, 1513.

Bernardino de Laredo. See Laredo, Bernardino de

Bocangelino, Nicolás
Libro de las enfermedades malignas y pestilentes, causas, pronósticos, curación y preservación. Madrid: Luis Sánchez, 1600.

Bustos, Hernando de
Tratado de peste. Granada, 1600.

Calvo, Juan
Primera y segunda parte de la cirugía universal y particular del cuerpo humano. Sevilla, 1580.

Libro muy útil y provechoso de medicina, y crigurgia, que trata de las cosas naturales, no naturales y preternaturales, de las indicaciones, humores, y apostemas assí en general como en particular. Barcelona: Iayme Cenda, 1591.

Libro de medicina y cirurgía que trata de las llagas en general y en particular: y assi mesmo del Morbo Gallico, de la curación de el, y de cada uno de sus accidentes. Barcelona: Jayme Cendrat, 1592.

Tratado de los simples. Valencia: Pedro Patricio, 1596.

Segunda parte de la medicina y cirugía, que trata de las ulceras y del antidotario. Valencia: Juan Chrysostomo Garriz, 1599.

Primera y segunda parte de la cirugía universal, y particular del cuerpo humano, quae trata de las cosas naturales, no naturales. y del antidotario, en el qual se trata de la facultad de todos los medicamentos. Valencia: Los herederos de Chrysostomo Garriz, por Bernardo Noguès, 1647.

Carbón, Damián
Libro del arte de las comadres o madrinas y del regimiento de las preñadas y paridas y de los niños. Mallorca, 1541.

Facsimile
Libro del arte de las comadres [Ed. facs. Mallorca 1541]. Valencia: Vicent García, 2000.

Editions
Piñeyrua, Alejandra. *Damian Carbón. Libro del arte de las comadres o madrinas y del regimiento de las preñadas y paridas y de los niños [Mallorca 1541]*. Textos y concordancias electrónicos del corpus médico español CD-ROM, ed. María Teresa Herrera and María Estela González de Fauve. Madison, Wis.: Hispanic Seminary of Medieval Studies, 1997.

Susarte Molina, Francisco, ed. *Libro del arte de las comadres o madrinas, del regimiento de las preñadas y paridas y de los niños [de] Damían Carbón*. Alicante: Universidad de Alicante, 1995.

Cardoso, Fernando
Utilidades del agua i de la nieve del beber frío i caliente. Madrid: Buidad de Alonso Martín, 1637.

Cartagena, Pedro de
Sermón en medicina para precaverse en tiempo dañado. Alcalá, 1522.

Carvajal, Juan de
Breve comisión de doctores antiguos para saber de pestilencia, sus señales, y remedios. Con la qual se satisfaze a otra que Sevilla juntó. Sevilla: Rodrigo Cabrera, 1600.

Utilidades de la nieve, deducidas de buena medicina. Sevilla: Simón Faxardo, 1622.

Castell, Antonio

Theórica y practica de boticarios, en que se trata de la arte y forma como se han de componer las confectiones ansi interiores como exteriores. Barcelona: Sebastián de Cormellas, 1592.

Castrillo, Martinez de. See Martinez de Castrillo

Chauliac, Guido de (Guy de Chauliac). See Guido de Chauliac

Chirino, Alfonso

Menor daño de la medicina. MS. b.IV.34. Escorial, El Escorial.

Menor daño de la medicina. MS. 2262 Biblioteca de la Universidad de Salamanca, Salamanca.

Menor daño de la medicina. MS 1478 Olim Biblioteca Nacional, Madrid.

Editions

> González Palencia, Angel. *Chirino, Alonso. Menor daño de la medicina y Espejo de medicina.* Biblioteca Clásica de la Medicina Española, vol. 14. Madrid: Cosano, 1944.

> Herrera, María Teresa. *Menor daño de la medicina de Aflonso de Chirino.* Acta Salmanticensia. Filosofia y letras, vol. 75. Salamanca: Universidad de Salamanca, 1973.

> Ardemagni, Enrica J., et al. *Alfonso Chirino. The text and concordances of Escorial manuscript b. IV, 34 menor daño de la medicina.* Textos y concordancias electrónicos del corpus médico español CD-ROM, ed. María Teresa Herrera and María Estela González de Fauve. Madison, Wis.: Hispanic Seminary of Medieval Studies, 1997.

Menor daño de medicina. Toledo, 1505.

Tractado llamado Menor daño de medicina. Sevilla: Jacobo Cromberger, 1506.

Tratado llamado menor daño de medicina. Sevilla: Jacobo Cromberger, 1511.

Tratado llamado menor daño de medicina. Toledo: Iuan de Villaquiran, 1513.

Tratado llamado menor daño de medicina. Sevilla: Jacobo Cromberger, 1515.

Tratado llamado menor daño de medicina. Sevilla: Jacobo Cronberger, 1519.

Tratado llamado menor daño de medicina. Toledo: Roman de Petras, 1526.

Menor daño de medicina. Sevilla: Dominico de Robertis, 1536.

Tractado llamado Menor daño de medicina. Sevilla: Juan Cromberger, 1538.

Tractado llamado menor daño de medicina. Sevilla: Juan Cromberger, 1542.

Tractado llamado menor daño de medicina. Sevilla: Jacobo Cromberger, 1547.

Tractado llamado menor daño de medicina. Sevilla: Jacobo Cromberger, 1550.

Tractado llamado menor daño de medicina. Sevilla, 1551.

Replicación al espejo de medicina. 3384. Madrid Biblioteca Nacional, Madrid.

Editions

> González Palencia, Angel. *Chirino, Alonso. Menor daño de la medicina y Espejo de medicina.* Biblioteca Clásica de la Medicina Española, vol. 14. Madrid: Cosano, 1944.

Ardemagni, Enrica J. et al., eds. *Alfonso Chirino. Replicación al espejo de Medicina. Text and Concordance of Biblioteca Nacional de Madrid, MS. 3384* [microfiche]. Madison, Wis.: Hispanic Seminary of Medieval Studies, 1988. Textos y concordancias electrónicos del corpus médico español CD-ROM, ed. María Teresa Herrera and María Estela González de Fauve. Madison, Wis.: Hispanic Seminary of Medieval Studies, 1997.

Congregación de Bernardino de Obregón
Instrucción de enfermeros y consuelo a los afligidos: y verdadera practica de como se han de aplicar los remedios que ordenan los médicos: muy necessaria para que los enfermos sean bien curados y provechosa a los practicantes [sic] de Medicina y vista por muchos Médicos desta Corte / compuesta por los Hermanos de la Congregación del Hermano Bernardino de Obregón. Madrid: la Imprenta Real, 1617.

Conjurs per a guarir diverses malàlties
Conjurs per a guarir diverses malàlties. MS. 1276. Biblioteca de Catalunya, Barcelona.

Córdoba, Fernando de
Suma de la flor de cirugía. MS. 3383. Biblioteca Nacional, Madrid.
Edition
Villar, María Carmen, ed. *Fernando de Córdoba. The text and concordance of the Suma de la flor de cirugia, Biblioteca Nacional, Madrid, 3383.* Madison, Wis.: Hispanic Seminary of Medieval Studies, 1987

Cornejo, Juan
Discurso particular preservativo de la gota. Madrid, 1594.
Edition
Bau, Andrea María. *Juan Cornejo. Discurso y despertador preservativo de enfermedades [Madrid 1594].* Textos y concordancias electrónicos del corpus médico español, CD-ROM, ed. María Teresa Herrera and María Estela González de Fauve. Madrid: Hispanic Seminary of Medieval Studies, 1997.

Cortés, Jerónimo
Tratado del computo por la mano, muy breve y necessario para los eclesiásticos. Valencia: Herederos de Ioan Navarro, 1591.
Libro de phisonomía natural y varios efetos de naturaleza, el qual contiene cinco tratados de materias diferentes, no menos curiosas que provechosas. Alcalá de Henares: Iuan Gracian, 1607.
Phisonomía y varios secretos de naturaleza: contiene cinco tratados de materias diferentes, todos revistos y mejorados en esta quarta impresión, a la qual se han añadido muchas cosas notables y de mucho provecho. Barcelona: Geronymo Margarit and Miguel Menescal, 1614.

Cortés de Vargas, Juan
Discurso apológico y excelencias de la medicina en que se responde a algunas objeciones, que suelen ponderar contra este noble exercicio. Madrid: la viuda de Iuan Gonçalez, 1638.

Phisonomía y varios secretos de naturaleza. Contiene cinco tratados. Barcelona: Lorenço Déu, 1629.

Cremona, Gerardus (Gerardus Cremonensis). See Gerardus Cremona

Cuando reinan los cuatro humores, anónimo. MS. 2262. Biblioteca Universitaria, Salamanca.

Daza Chacón, Dionisio

Pratica y theórica de cirugía en romance y latín. Valladolid: Bernardino de Sancto Domingo, 1582.

Prática y theorica de cirugía en romance y latín. Valladolid: Bernardino de Sancto Domingo, 1584.

Práctica y teórica de cirugía en romance y en latín compuesta por el licenciado Dionysio Daça Chacon. Valladolid: Ana Velez, 1609.

Prática y teórica de cirugía en romance y en latín / compuesta por el licenciado Dionisio Daça Chacon. Madrid: viuda de Alonso Martín, 1626.

Prática, y teórica de cirugía en romance y en latín / compuesto por . . . Dionisio Daça Chacon . . . ; va enmendada en esta ultima impresión de los yerros que tenían las passadas. Valencia: Francisco Cipres, 1673.

Segunda parte de la práctica y theorica de Cirugía en romance y en latín, que trata de todas las heridas en general y en particular. Valladolid: Herederos de Bernardino de Sancto Domingo, 1595.

Segunda parte de la prática y teórica de cirugía en romance y en latín, que trata de todas las heridas en general, y en particular. Madrid: Viuda de Alonso Martín, 1626.

De las melecinas.

De las melecinas. MS. 1734. Biblioteca Universitaria, Salamanca.

Edition

Sylvia Fernández, ed. *Texto y concordancias de* De las melecinas [microform]: *MS. 1743, Biblioteca Universitaria de Salamanca.* Madison, Wis.: Hispanic Seminary of Medieval Studies, 1989.

De les orines

De les ventoses. MS. 10162. Biblioteca Nacional, Madrid.*De les ventoses.* MS. 10162. Biblioteca Nacional, Madrid.

De los pesos de las medicinas

De los pesos de las medicinas. MS. 2262. Universitaria, Salamanca

De los sueños

De los sueños. MS. 2262. Universitaria, Salamanca.

Declaración de algunos vocablos de las especias de la medicina y de otros materiales

Declaración de algunos vocablos de las especias de la medicina y de otros materiales, anónimo. MS. 2262. Universitaria, Salamanca.

Díaz, Francisco

Compendio de chirugía con otros breves tratados de las cuatro enfermedades compuesto por coloquios. Madrid: Pedro Cosin, 1575.

Tratado nuevamente impresso de todas las enfermedades de los riñones, vexiga, y carnosidades de la verga. Madrid: Francisco Sánchez, 1588.

Facsimile

Tratado nuevamente impresso, de todas las enfermedades de los riñones, vexiga. [Madrid 1588]. Facsimile edition. Barcelona: Eco, D.L., 1968.

Edition

Mollá y Rodrigo, Rafael, ed. *Tratado de todas las enfermedades de los rinones, vejiga y carnosidades de la verga, y urina / del Dr. Francisco Díaz.* Cosano, 1923.

Tratado de todas las enfermedades de los riñones, vexiga y carnosidades de la verga y orina y de su cura. Bound with Juan Fragoso, *Cirugía uniuersal.* Madrid: La viuda de Alonso Martín, 1627.

Tratado nuevamente impresso, de todas las enfermedades de los riñones, vexiga, y carnosidades de la verga, y urina, y de su cura. Madrid: Carlos Sánchez, 1643.

Díaz de Ysla, Ruy

Tractado co[n]tra el mal serpentino que vulgarmente en España es llamado bubas q[ue] fue ordenado en el ospital de Todos los Santos d[e] Lisboa / fecho por Ruy Diaz de Ysla. Sevilla: Dominico de Robertis, 1539.

Tractado llamado fructo de todos los auctos: contra el mal serpentino. Venido de la ysla Española. Hecho y ordenado en el grande y famoso hospital de todos los Sanctos de la insigne e muy nombrada ciudad de Lisboa. Sevilla: Andrés de Burgos, 1542.

Edition

Gubitosi, Patricia, ed. *Ruy Díaz de la Isla. Tractado llamado fructo de todos los auctos: contra el mal serpentino. Venido de la ysla Española. Hecho y ordenado en el grande y famoso hospital de todos los Sanctos de la insigne e muy nombrada ciudad de Lisboa [Sevilla 1542].* Textos y concordancias electrónicos del corpus médico español CD-ROM, ed. María Teresa Herrera and María Estela González de Fauve. Madrid: Hispanic Seminary of Medieval Studies, 1997.

Diego el Covo

Cirugía rimada [Segundo tractado, de las apostemas]. MS. 2153. Biblioteca Nacional, Madrid.

Editions

Herrera, María Teresa, ed. *Tratado de las apostemas de Diego el Cobo.* Salamanca: Universidad de Salamanca, 1983.

García-Serrano, Victoria, and Michael R. Solomon, eds. *Cirugía Rimada [text and concordance]: Biblioteca Nacional MS 2153.* 2 microfiches. Madison, Wis.: Hispanic Seminary of Medieval Studies, 1987.

Dies de Calatayud, Manuel
Flos de medicines, o, Receptes de beautat. Spanish y Catalan Flor del tesoro de la belleza.
1450c.
Editions
Teresa Ma. Vinyoles, ed. *Dies de Calatayud, Manuel Flores del tesoro de la belleza :*
tratado de muchas medicinas o curiosidades de las mujeres: manuscrito no. 68 de
la Bib. Un. de Barcelona, Folios 151 a 170. Palma de Mallorca: Lunas, D.L. 1993.

Díez Daza, Alonso
Avisos y documentos para la preservación y cura de la Peste. Sevilla: Clemente Hidalgo,
1599.
Libro de los provechos y damnos que provienen con la sola bebida del agua. Y como se deba
escoger la mejor. Y retificar la que no es tal, y de como se a de beber frió en tiempo de
calor sin que haga daño. Sevilla: Alonso de Barrera, 1578.

Dioscorides. See Laguna, Andrés de

Enríquez, Enrique Jorge
Retrato del perfecto médico. Salamanca, 1595.
Facsimile
Retrato del perfecto médico. Salamanca: Real Academia de la Medicina, 1981.
Edition
McInnis, Meghan, ed. *Enrique Jorge Enríquez: Retrato del perfecto médico* (in
preparation).

Enríquez, Juan
Secretos de la medicina. MS. 3063. Biblioteca de Palacio, Madrid.
Edition
Enrique Jiménez Rios, ed. *Juan Enríquez. Secretos de la medicina.* Madison, Wis.:
Hispanic Seminary of Medieval Studies, 1997. Textos y concordancias electróni-
cos del corpus médico español CD-ROM, ed. María Teresa Herrera and María
Estela González de Fauve. Madrid: Hispanic Seminary of Medieval Studies,
1997.

Escobar, Manuel de
Tratado de la essencia, causas, y curación de los bubones y carbuncos pestilentes. Alcalá,
1600.

Espina, Alonso
Tratado contra toda pestilencia e ayre corrupto preservativo y parte curativo. Valladolid:
Arnao Guillen de Brocar, 1518.

Estéfano de Sevilla
Libro de visitaçione e conssiliaçione medicorum. MS. 18052. Biblioteca Nacional, Madrid.
Edition
Ardemagni, Enrica J. et al., eds. *Estéfano. Text and concordance of Biblioteca Nacional*

MS 18052, Visita y consejo de médicos. Microform. Madison, Wis.: Hispanic Seminary of Medieval Studies, 1988.

Exposition paraphrástica: sobre los quatro canones universales de Mesue. Nuevamente compuesta y publicada con la qual muy fácilmente se puede entender la letra y sentido de Mesue. Muy útil y necessario a todos los apothecarios, por lo que en el primero o segundo canon se contiene en tercero y quarto canon. Barcelona: Pedro Montpezat, 1541.

Fabra, Lluis
Discurs sobre la peste explicant la esferencia della causes, senyals, pronóstic y curació. Perpinyà: Sampsó Abus, 1581.

Farfán, Agustín
Tractado breve de anathomía y chirugía, y de algunas enfermedades, que más comunmente suelen haber en esta nueva España. Mexico: Antonio Ricardo, 1579.
Tractado breve de medicina y de todas las enfermedades. Mexico: Pedro Ocharte, 1592.
Edition
Piñeyrua, Alejandra, ed. *Texto y concordancias del Tratado breve de medicina de Agustin Farfan.* Madison, Wis.: Hispanic Seminary of Medieval Studies, 2001.
Tratado breve de medicina y de todas las enfermedades. Mexico: Geronymo Balli, 1610.

Ferrer, Jaime
Libro en el qual se trata del verdadero conocimiento de la peste y sus remedios. Valencia: Rovella, por Juan Chrysostomo Garriz, 1600.

Ficino, Marsilio
Tratado de la peste. Libro compuesto por Marsilio Ficino Florentino: en el qual se contienen grandes advisos, y secretos maravillosos, assí de medicina, como de çirugía, para curar y preservar los hombres de pestilencia con otros mucho tratados muy necessarios de diversos Autores esperimentados en esta enfermedad. Çaragoça: Pedro Bernuz, 1564.
Libro compuesto por Marsilio Ficino Florentino: en el qual se contienen grandes advisos, y secretos maravillosos, assí de medicina, como de çirugía, para curar y preservar los hombres de pestilencia con otros mucho tratados muy necessarios de diversos autores esperimentados en esta enfermedad. Pamplona: Mathias Mares, 1598.
Edition
Campagne, Fabián Alejandro. *Marsilio Ficino. Libro compuesto por Marsilio Ficino Florentino: en el qual se contienen grandes advisos, y secretos maravillosos, assi de medicina, como de çirugia, para curar y preservar los hombres de pestilencia con otros mucho tratados muy necessarios de diversos autores esperimentados en esta enfermedad. [Pamplona 1598].* Textos y concordancias electrónicos del corpus médico español CD-ROM, ed. María Teresa Herrera and María Estela González de Fauve. Madison, Wis.: Hispanic Seminary of Medieval Studies, 1997.

Figueroa, Francisco de
Tratado de las causas, curas y preservación de la peste. Sevilla: Rodrigo de Cabrera, 1598.

Forés, El Licenciado

Tratado útil. Salamanca: Maestre Hans Gysser, 1507.

Edition

Zabía, María Purificación. *Licenciado Forés. Tratado útil (Salamanca 1507).* Textos y concordancias electrónicos del corpus médico español CD-ROM, ed. María Teresa Herrera and María Estela González de Fauve. Madison, Wis.: Hispanic Seminary of Medieval Studies, 1997.

Tratado muy útil y muy provechoso contra toda pestilencia y ayre corrupto . . . Logroño: Maestre Arnao Guillem de Brocar, 1507.

Edition

Sánchez, María Nieves. "Tratado útil y muy provechoso contra toda la pestilencia y aire corrupto." *Tratados de la peste.* Ed. María Nieves Sánchez. Madrid: Arco Libros, 1993.

Fragoso, Juan

Chirurgía universal. Madrid: Buida de Alonso Gomez, 1581.

Chirurgía universal. Aora de nuevo revista, emendada y añadida. Madrid: viuda de Alonso Gomez, 1586.

Chirurgía universal. Aora nuevamente emedada y añadida. Alcalá: Juan Gracián, 1592.

Cirugía universal. Madrid, 1596.

Cirugía uniuersal. Madrid: Alonso Martín, 1627.

Discurso de las cosas aromaticas, arboles y frutales, y de otras muchas medicinas simples que se traen de la India oriental, y sirven al uso de la medicina. Madrid: Francisco Sanchez, 1572.

Erotemas quirúrgicos, en los cuales se enseña lo más necesario del arte de cirugía. Madrid: Pierres Cosin, 1570.

Franco, Francisco

Libro de las enfermedades contagiosas y de la preseruación dellas. Sevilla: Alonso de la Barrera, 1569.

Tratado de la nieve y uso de ella. Sevilla: Alonso de la Barrera, 1569.

Edition and Facsimile

Santonja, Gonzalo, ed. *Tractado de la nieve y del uso della / Francisco Franco.* Madrid: Visor, 1984.

Freilas, Alonso de

Conocimiento, curación y preservación de la peste. Jaén, 1605.

Conocimiento, curación, y preservación de la peste. Va añadido un tratado nuevo del arte de descontagiar las ropas de seda, telas de oro, y plata, tapicerías. Con un discurso al fin, Si los melancólicos pueden saber lo que está por venir: con la fuerça de su ingenio, ò soñando. Jaén: Fernando Díaz de Montoya, 1606.

García, Marcos

Honor de la medicina, y aplauso de la cirugía castellana. Madrid: Carlos Sánchez, 1638.

Gerardus Cremona (Gerardus Cremonensis)
De la coneixença de les orines. MS. esp. 508. Bibliothèque Nationale, Paris.
Llibre d'Almassor. MS. esp. 212. Bibliotèque Nationale, Paris.
Llibre d'Almassor. MS. esp. 508. Bibliothèque Nationale, Paris.
Tractat de les viandes. MS. esp 508. Bibliothèque Nationale, Paris.

Gil y de Pina, Jerónimo
Tratado breve de la curación del garrotillo: dividido en cinco enarraciones médicas muy útiles provechosas para todos los que exercitan el arte de medicina y cirugía. Zaragoça: Iuan de Lanaja y Quartanet, 1636.

Gilberto
El libro de recetas. MS. 3063. Biblioteca de Palacio, Madrid.
Editions
Zurrón, Isabel, ed. *Text and concordance of MS 3063 de la Biblioteca del Palacio Real, El libro de recetas de Gilberto de recetas de Gilberto [15th Century].* Madison, Wis.: Hispanic Semin ary of Medieval Studies, 1988.
———. "Gilbertus (Gilberto). *Libro de recetas* (MS. 3063. Biblioteca de Palacio, Madrid)." Textos y concordancias electrónicos del corpus médico español CD-ROM, ed. María Teresa Herrera and María Estela González de Fauve. Madison, Wis.: Hispanic Seminary of Medieval Studies, 1997.

Girualt, Antonio
Utilissim, promte y fecil remey e memorial per preservarse y curar de la peste. Perpinyà: Samsó Abus, 1587.

Gómez Miedes, Bernardino
Enchiridión, o manual instrumento de salud, contra el morbo articular, que llaman gota, y las demás enfermedades que por catarro y destilación de la cabeça se engendran en la persona. Zaragoza: Lorenço y Diego de Robles, 1589.
Edition
Incarnato, Cecilia Estela. *Bernardino Gómez Miedes. Enchiridion, o manual instrumento de salud, contra el morbo articular, que llaman gota, y las demas enfermedades que por catarro y destilacion de la cabeça se engendran en la persona [Zaragoza 1589].* Textos y concordancias electrónicos del corpus médico español CD-ROM, ed. María Teresa Herrera and María Estela González de Fauve. Madison, Wis.: Hispanic Seminary of Medieval Studies, 1997.

Gómez de Salamanca
Propiedades del romero. MS. 2262. Biblioteca Universitaria, Salamanca.
Edition
López, Marcela, ed. *Gomez de Salamanca. Propiedades del romero [MS. 2262. Biblioteca Universitaria, Salamanca].* Textos y concordancias electrónicos del corpus médico español CD-ROM, ed. María Teresa Herrera and María Estela González de Fauve. Madison, Wis.: Hispanic Seminary of Medieval Studies, 1997.

Compendio de Medicina. MS. 2262. Universidad de Salamanca, Salamanca.

Guido de Chauliac (Guy de Chauliac)

Cirugía de Guido de Cauliaco con la Glosa de Falco, nuevamente corregida y enmendada, muy añadida con un tratado de los simples por Juan Calvo. Valencia: Pedro Patricio, 1596.

Guido en romance. Sevilla: Menardo Ungut, 1493.

Guido en romance. Sevilla: Menardo Ungut, 1498.

Inventario o colectario en la parte cirurgical de la medicina. Sevilla: Jacobo Cromberger, 1518.

Inventario o collectorio en cirurgia, compuesto por Guido Cauliaco con la glosa de Joan Falco. Trans. Joan Laurenço Carnicer. Zaragoza: Jorge Coci, 1533.

Inventario o colectorio en cirugía: compuesto por Guido de Cauliaco. con la glosa del maestre Joan Falcó. Çaragoça: Pedro Bernuz, 1555.

Inventario o colectorio en cirugía. Con la glosa del maestre Juan Falcó. Alcalá de Henares: Juan Gracian, 1574.

Prática o reportori utilissim de cirurgia. ensemps ab algunes addicions doctorals e scientiffiques e trauida de lati en lengua vulgar catalana per en Narcis Sola. Barcelona: Johan Rosembach e Carles Amoros, 1508.

Guillelmus Thomas

Recepta de G. Thomas contra dolor de ronyons e de pedra e de colica passi e es prouat en la persona del rey en Johan. MS. 10162. Biblioteca Nacional, Madrid.

Gutiérrez de Godoy, Ivan

Para probar que están obligadas a criar sus hijos a sus pechos todas las madres quando tienen buena salud, fuerças, y buen temperamento, buena leche, y suficiente para alimentarlos. Jaén: Pedro de la Cuesta, 1629.

Gutiérrez de Toledo, Julian

Cura de la piedra y dolor de la ijada y cólica renal. Toledo: Pedro Hagenbach, 1498.

Hernández, Francisco

Quatro libros De la naturaleza, y virtudes de las plantas, y animales que están recebidos en el uso de medicina en la Nueva España, y la méthodo, y corrección, y preparación, que para administrallas se requiere con lo que el Doctor Francisco Hernández escribió en lengua Latina. / traduzido y aumentados muchos simples, y compuestos y otros muchos secretos curativos, por Fr. Francisco Ximenez. México: la viuda de Diego López Dávalos, 1615.

Hidalgo de Agüero, Bartolomé

Tesoro de la verdadera cirugía y vía particular contra la común opinión. Sevilla, 1604.

Tesoro de la verdadera cirugía y vía particular contra la común. Barcelona, 1624.

Tesoro de la verdadera cirugía y vía particular contra la común opinión. Valencia: Claudio Macè, 1654.

Hispanus, Petrus (Pope Johannes XXI)

Tresor de pobres; Llibre de medicina. MS. 864. Biblioteca de Catalunya, Barcelona.

Thesoro de los pobres en medicina y cirugía. Granada: Andrés de Burgos, 1519.

Libro de medicina llamado Tesor de los Pobres: con un regimiento de sanidad. Sevilla: Juan Cromberger, 1535.

Libro de medicina llamado tessoro de los pobres. Sevilla: Juan Cromberger, 1540.

Libro de medicina llamado Tesoro de los Pobres . . . con un regimiento de sanidad. Sevilla: Juan Cromberger, 1543.

Libro de medicina llamado Tesoro delos Pobres: con un regimiento de sanidad. Sevilla: J. Cromberger, 1547.

Libro de medicina llamado Tesoro delos Pobres: con un regimiento de sanidad. Sevilla: Dominico de Robertis, 1548.

Libro llamado Tesoro delos Pobres. En romance con el tractado o regimiento de sanidad, hecho por A. de Villa nova. Agora nuevamente corregido. Burgos: Juan de Junta, 1551.

Libro llamado Tesoro delos Pobres. En romance con el tractado o regimiento de sanidad, hecho por A. de Villa nova. Agora nuevamente corregido. Burgos: Alonso de Melgar, 1554.

Regimen sanitatis ad regem Aragonum [Spanish]. Libro de medicina llamado Thesoro de los pobres, con un regimiento de sanidad. Agora nuevamente impresso y emendado . . . Sevilla: Trugillo, 1562.

Libro llamado Tesoro delos Pobres. En romance con el tractado o regimiento de sanidad, hecho por A. de Villa nova. Agora nuevamente corregido. Burgos: Phelippe de Junta, 1564.

Libro llamado Tesoro delos Pobres. En romance con el tractado o regimiento de sanidad, hecho por A. de Villa nova. Agora nuevamente corregido. Alcalá de Henares: Sebastian Martinez, 1584.

Libro de medicina llamado thesoro de pobres con un Regimiento de Sanidad. Barcelona: Gabriel Graells, 1596.

Libro de medicina, llamado Thesoro de pobres. Con un regimiento de sanidad. Agora nuevamente corregido y emendado. Valencia: Alvaro Franco, 1598.

Libro de medicina llamado Thesoro de pobres. Con un Regimiento de sanidad. Agora nuevamente corregido y emendado, por Arnaldo de Villanova. Barcelona: Francisco Dotil, 1611.

Libro de medicina, llamado Tesoro de pobres. Con un regimiento de sanidad [hecho por Arnaldo de Villanova] Aoro nuevamente corregido y enmendado . . . Zaragoza: Diego Dormer, 1643.

Libro de medicina llamado Tesoro de pobres. En que se hallaran remedios muy aprobados para la sanidad de diversas enfermedades. Con un Regimiento de sanidad . . . por el Maestro Julián . . . Aora nuevamente corregido, y enmendado por Arnaldo de Villanova. Madrid: D.D. de la Carrera, 1644.

Huarte de San Juan, Juan

Examen de ingenios, para las sciencias. Baeça: Juan Baptista de Montoya, 1575.

Examen de ingenios para las sciencias. Pamplona: Thomas Porralis, 1578.

Examen de ingenios para las sciencias. Valenica: Pedro de Huete, 1580.

Examen de ingenios para las sciencias. Bilbao: Mathias Mares, 1580.

Examen de ingenios para las sciencias. Huesca: Ioan Pérez de Valdivielso, 1581.

Examen de ingenios para las sciencias. Leyda: Iuan Pats, 1591.

Examen de ingenios para las sciencias. Amberes: Francisco Raselengio, 1593.

Examen de ingenio. Baeça: Iuan Baptista de Montoya, 1594.

Ibn al-Khatib

Tratado de patología general

Edition

Herrera, María Teresa, ed. *The Text and Concordance of the Tratado de patologia general, Biblioteca Nacional, Madrid, 10.051.* Madison, Wis.: Hispanic Seminar of Medieval Studies, 1987.

Ibn Wafid

Libre de les medicines particulars

Edition

Kitab al-Adwiya al-Mufrada. El "libre de les medicines particulars": versión catalana trescentista del texto árabe del tratado de los medicamentos simples de Ibn Wáfid, autor médico toledano del siglo XI. Ed. Luis Faraudo de Saint-Germain. Barcelona: Real Academia de Buenas Letras de Barcelona, 1943.

Israeli, Ischaq (Isaac Israeli)

Tratado de las fiebres. MS. M.I.28. Escorial, El Escorial.

Editions

Llamas, R. P. J., ed. *Ishaq Israeli. Tratado de las fiebres.* Madrid: Instituto "Arias Montano" de Estudios Hebraicos y Oriente Proximo, 1945.

Richards, Ruth, ed. *Text and concordance of Isaac Israeli's Tratado de las fiebres* [microform]. Madison, Wis.: Hispanic Seminary of Medieval Studies, 1982.

Jacme d'Agramont (Jaume d'Agramunt)

Regiment de preservació de pestilència. MS. 107, Arxiu Parroquial de Verdú.

Edition

Veny i Clar, Joan, ed. *Regiment de preservació de pestilència de Jacme d'Agramont (S.Xiv).* Tarragona: Diputación de Tarragona, 1971.

Ardeiu, Enrich, and Joseph M. Roca. *Jaume d'Agramunt. Regiment de preservació a epidèmia o pestilència e mortaldats.* 2000. Biblioteca Virtual Joan Lluís Vives. http://www.lluisvives.com/servlet/SirveObras/jlv/12920522027817162321435/index.htm. [Edició digital basada en l'edició de Lleyda, Estampa de Joseph A. Pagés, 1910]

Jacobi, Johannes, and Luis de Raz

Regimento proueytoso contra ha pestenença. Lisboa: Valentim Fernandes de Moravia, 1476.

Jarava, Juan de (translator)
Leonhard Fuchs. *Historia de las yerbas y plantas, sacada de Dioscorides de Anarzabeo, con los nombres griegos, latinos, y españoles; con sus virtudes y propiedades, y el uso de ellas, juntamente con sus figuras.* Anvers: Arnaldo Byrckman, 1557.
Facsimile
Garcia, Vicent, ed. *Historia de yerbas y plantas realizada por Leonard Fuchs y traducida al castellano por Juan de Jarava [facsimile edition].* Rafelbuñol (Valencia): Vicent Garcia Editores, D.L, 1995.
Editions
López Piñero, José María, José Pardo Tomás, and María Luz López Terrada, eds. *Juan de Jarava. Historia de yervas y plantas: un tratado renacentista de materia médica [Anvers 1557].* Barcelona: Edicions Juan de Serrallonga, 1998.
Mancho, Mª Jesús, ed. *Historia de las yervas y plantas / [Leonhart Fuchs]; [traducido por] Juan Jarava Salamanca.* Salamanca: Ediciones Universidad de Salamanca, 2005.

Jiménez Savariego, Juan
Tratado de peste, donde se contienen las causas, preservación y cura. Antequera: Claudio Bolan, 1601.

Johan, Micer
Llibre de reseptes. Barcelona, 1466.

Juan de Aviñón
Sevillana medicina. Sevilla: Andres de Burgos, 1545.
Editions
Naylor, Eric W., ed. *The text and concordance of the Sevillana medicina, Burgos. 1545.* Madison, Wis.: Hispanic Seminary of Medieval Studies, 1987.
Mondéjar Cumpián, José, ed. *Juan de Aviñón. Sevillana medicina.* Madrid: Arco, 2000.

Ketham, Johannes de
Compendio de la salud humana. Zaragoza: Paulus Hurus, 1494.
Editions
María Teresa Herrera, ed. Ketham, Johannes de. *Compendio de la humana salud.* Madrid: Arco/Libros, 1990.
Epílogo de medicina y cirugía conveniente a la salud. Burgos: Juan de Burgos, 1495.
Epílogo en medicina y cirugía o Compendio de la salud humana. Pamplona: Arnaldo Guillen de Brocar, 1495.
Libro de medicina llamado compendio de la salud humana. El tratado de la peste de maestre Valesco de Taranta de la phisonomía. Sevilla: Jacobo Cromberge, 1517.

Laguna, Andrés de
Discurso breve, sobre la cura y preservación de la pestilencia. Amberes: Christobal Plantin, 1556.

Discurso breve sobre la cura y preservación de la pestilencia. Salamanca: Mathias Gast, 1566.

Discurso de como se ha de preservar y curar de pestilencia. Dirigido a los jurados de la ciudad de Valencia. Valencia: Petrus Ioannes Assensius, 1600.

Pedacio Dioscorides Anazarbeo, Acerca de la materia medicinal y de los venenos mortíferos / traduzido de lengua griega en la vulgar castellana e illustrado con claras y substantiales annotationes por Andrés de Laguna. Anuers: Juan Latio, 1555.

Pedacio Dioscorides Anazarbeo, Acerca de la materia medicinal y de los venenos mortíferos / traduzido de lengua griega en la vulgar castellana e illustrado con claras y substantiales annotationes. Salamanca: Mathias Gast, 1563.

Pedacio Dioscorides Anazarbeo, Acerca de la materia medicinal y de los venenos mortiferosedacio Dioscorides Anazarbeo, Acerca de la materia medicinal y de los venenos mortiferos. Salamanca: Mathias Gast, 1566.

Pedacio Dioscorides Anazarbeo, Acerca de la materia medicinal y de los venenos mortiferosedacio Dioscorides Anazarbeo, Acerca de la materia medicinal y de los venenos mortíferos. Salamanca: Mathias Gast, 1570.

Lanfranco de Milan, Guido

Cirugía mayor. MS. 2147. Biblioteca Nacional. Madrid.

Laredo, Bernardino de

Metaphora medicine: con .dc. autoridades declaradas sin contar.cxciii. aphorismos.... Hyspali: Joannis Varelae, 1522.

Metaphora medicine y chirurgie nuevamente copilada.... Sevilla: Juan Varla de Salamanca, 1536.

Modus faciendi cum ordine medicandi. A médicos y boticarios muy común y necesario. Sevilla, 1521.

Modus faciendi cum ordine medicandi. A médicos y boticarios muy común y necesario. Madrid, 1527.

Modus faciendi cum ordine medicandi. A médicos y boticarios muy común y necesario. Sevilla, Jacobo Cromberger 1527.

Sobre el Mesue y Nicolao. Modus faciendi. Sevilla: Juan Cromberger, 1542

　　Edition

　　Laín, Milagro and Doris Ruiz Otín. *Modus faciendi cum ordine medicandi: 1527 / edición con estudio introductorio, transcripción y glosarios.* Madrid: Fundación Ciencias de la Salud, D.L. 2001.

León, Andrés de

Libro primero, de annathomia. Recopilaciones, y examen general de evacuaciones, annathomia y compostura del cuerpo humano, differencias y virtudes del ánima, diffiniciones de medicina, con muchas cosas curiosas y provechosas de philosophia, y astrología. Repartidos en quatro libros, en los quales últimamente se rematan dos tratados de avisos para sangrar, y purgar: en todo respectando los signos y planetas. Baeça: Juan Baptista de Montoya, 1590.

Practico de morbo gallico: en el qual se contiene el origen y conocimiento de esta enfermedad, y el mejor modo de curarla por el doctor Andrés de León. Valladolid: Luis Sánchez, 1605.

Tratados de medicina, cirugía y anatomía. Valladolid: Luis Sánchez, 1605.

Libro de los olios

Libro de los olios. MS. 2262. Biblioteca Universitaria, Salamanca.

Edition

Marcela López Hernández, ed. Texto and [sic] concordancias cel Libro de los olios, MS. 2262, Salamanca, Universitaria. Madison, Wis.: Hispanic Seminary of Medieval Studies, 1989.

Llibre de coneixences d'espécies i de drogues

Llibre de coneixences d'espécies i de drogues. MS. 4. Biblioteca Universitària, Barcelona.

Llibre de totes maneres de confits

Llibre de totes maneres de confits. MS. 68. Biblioteca Universitària, Barcelona.

Lobera de Avila, Luis

Banquete de nobles caballeros e modo de vivir desde que se levantan hasta que se acuestan . . . Augsburg: Henricum Stainerum, 1530.

Vergel de sanidad que por otro nombre se llamaba Banquete de caballeros, y orden de vivir: ansi en tiempo de sanidad como de enfermedad: y habla copiosamente de cada manjar que complexión y popriedad tenga: y. Alcalá de Henares: Joan de Brocar, 1542.

Editions

López Piñero, José, ed. *El vanquete de nobles cavalleros (1530), de Luis de Lobera de Avila y la higiene individual del siglo XVI.* Madrid: Ministerio de Sanidad y Consumo, 1991.

Mora Sádaba, Francisco, ed. *Luis Lobera de Avila. Banquete de Nobles Caballeros, El.* San Sebastián: R y B Ediciones, 1996.

Libro de experiencias de medicina y muy aprobado por sus effectos, ansi en esta nuestra España como fuera della. Toledo: Juan de Ayala, 1544.

Libro de las quatro enfermedades. Toledo, 1543.

Libro de las quatro enfermedades cortesanas que son catarro, gota arthética, sciatica, mal de piedra y de otras cosas utilissimas. Toledo: Juan de Ayala, 1544.

Libro de pestilencia curativo y preseruatio y de fiebres pestilenciales, con la cura de todos los accidentes dellas, y de las otras fiebres, y habla de phlebotomía, ventosas, sanguisuelas: y de las diez y nueve enfermedades subitas que son utilissimas. Y ciertas preguntas muy útiles en medicina en romance Castellano y Latín: y otras cosas muy necessarias en medicina y cirugía. Alcalá: Brocar, 1542.

Libro del regimiento de la salud, y de la esterilidad de los hombres y mugeres, y de las efermedades de los niños y otras cosas utilissimas. Valladolid: Sebastian Martínez, 1551.

Edition

Hernández Briz, Baltasar, ed. *Libro del régimen de la salud, y de la esterilidad de los*

hombres y mujeres, y de las enfermedades de los niños, y otras cosas utilísimas del
Dr. Avila de Lobera. Vol. 5. Madrid: Cosano, 1923.

Remedio de cuerpos humanos y silva de experiencias y otras cosas utilíssimas. Alcalá: Joan
de Brocar, 1542.

Lope de Saavedra

Regimiento preseruativo en romançe. Sevilla, 1522.

López de Corella, Alfonso

Secretos de filosophia y medicina collegidos por el Bachiller Alonso López de Corella pues-
tos a manera de perque por que mejor se encomienden a la memoria. Salamanca,
1539.

Secretos de philosophia y astrología y medicina y de las quatro mathemáticas sciencias:
collegidos de muchos y diversos autores. Çaragoça: George Coci, 1547.

Trescientas preguntas. Con sus repuestas. Alcalá, 1546.

Trezientas preguntas de cosas naturales. En diferentes materias. Con lus [sic] respuestas
y alegaciones d'auctores, las ques fueron antes preguntadas a manera de perque. Valladolid: Francisco Fernández de Córdova, 1546.

López de Hinojosos, Alonso

Suma y recopilación de cirugía con un arte para sangrar muy útil y provechosa. México:
Pedro Balli, 1578.

Suma y recopilación de cirugía, con un arte para sangrar, y examen de barberos. México:
Pedro Balli, 1595.

Edition

López de Hinojosos, Alonso. *Suma y recopilación de cirugía con un arte para sangrar*
muy útil y provechosa. México: Academia Nacional de Medicina, 1977.

López de Villalobos, Francisco

Sumario de la medicina con un tratado sobre las pestíferas bubas. Salamanca: Antonio
Nebrija, 1498.

Editions

García del Real, Eduardo, ed. *Francisco López de Villalobos. El sumario de la me-*
dicina, con un tratado sobre las pestíferas bubas. Madrid: Cosano, 1948.

Herrera, María Teresa, ed. *Francisco López de Villalobos. El sumario de la medicina*
con un tratado de las pestíferas bubas. Salamanca: Universidad de Salamanca,
1973.

Sánchez, Mª Nieves, ed. *The text and concordance of the Sumario de la medicina,*
I-1169, Biblioteca Nacional, Madrid. Madison, Wis.: Hispanic Seminary of Medieval Studies, 1987.

Libro intitulado Los problemas de Villalobos; que tracta de cuerpos naturales y morales.
Y dos diálogos de medicina. Y el tractado de los tres grandes. Zamora: Juan Picardo,
1543.

Libro intitulado Los problemas de Villalobos, que trata de cuerpos naturales y morales y dos diálogos d[e] medicina y el tractado de las tres gra[n]des y una canción y la comedia de Amphytrion. Çaragoça: George Coci, 1544.

Libro intitulado Los problemas de Villalobos; que tracta de cuerpos naturales y morales. Y dos diálogos de medicina. Y el tractado de los tres grandes. Sevilla: Cristobal Alvarez, 1550.

Libro intitulado Los problemas de Villalobos; que tracta de cuerpos naturales y morales. Y dos diálogos de medicina. Y el tractado de los tres grandes. Sevilla: Hernando Díaz, 1574.

Luis de Toro

Discursos o consyderaciones sobre la materia de enfriar la bebida en que se tracta de las differentias de enfriar y del uso y propiedad de cada una. Salamanca, 1569.

Edition and facsimile

Sanz Herminda, Jacobo, ed. *Luis de Toro. Discursos o consyderaciones sobre la materia de enfriar la bevida en que se tracta de las differentias de enfriar y del uso y propiedad de cada una (1569).* Salamanca: Universidad de Salamanca, 1991. [Introduction, facsimile and transcription.]

Macer (also see Maestre Gil)

Macer herbolario. Colombina. MS. 7-6-27 (fifteenth century).

Edition

Ardemagni, Enrica J., and Ruth M. Richards, eds. *Macer. Macer herbolario.* [Colombina. MS. 7-6-27 (fifteenth century)]. Madison, Wis.: Hispanic Seminary of Medieval Studies, 1997.

Maestre Gil

Libro de medicina llamado Macer. Granada: Andrés de Burgos, 1518.

Edition

Capuano, Thomas. *Maestre Gil. Libro de medicina llamado Macer [Granada 1518].* Textos y concordancias electrónicos del corpus médico español CD-ROM, ed. María Teresa Herrera and María Estela González de Fauve. Madison, Wis.: Hispanic Seminary of Medieval Studies, 1997.

Libro de medicina llamado Macer. Granada: Andrés de Burgos, 1519.

Libro de medicina llamado Macer que trata delos mantenimientos. Valladolid: Miguel de Eguía, 1527.

Manfredi, Girolamo

Libro llamado el Porque, provechosissimo para la conservación de la salud. Çaragoça: Iuan Millán, 1567.

Libro llamado el Porque, provechosissimo para la conservación de la salud. Madrid: Guillermo Drouy, 1579.

El Porque libro de problemas en que se da razones naturales de muchas cosas prouechosissimo para conservación de la salud, con las virtudes calidades de algunas yerbas / agora nuevamente corregido y enmendado, y en muchos lugares añadido; traducido de Toscazo en lengua Castellana por Pedro de Ribas. Madrid: Francisco Sánchez, 1581.

Libro llamado el Porque, provechosissimo para la conservación de la salud. Alcalá: J. Iñiguez de Leguerica, 1587.

Libro llamado el Porque, provechosissimo para la conservación de la salud. Alcalá de Henares: Hernan Ramírez, 1589.

Libro llamado el Porque, provechosissimo para la conservación de la salud. Madrid: Pedro Madrigal, 1598.

Martínez de Castrillo

Coloquio breve y compendioso sobre la materia de la dentadura y maravillosa obra de la boca: con muchos remedios y avisos necessarios y la orden de curar y adreçar los dientes . . . Valladolid: Sebastian Martínez, 1557.

Tratado breve y compendioso sobre la maravillosa obra de la boca y dentadura. Madrid: Alonso Gómez, 1570.

Edition

Forteza, Patricia de, ed. *Martínez de Castrillo. Tratado breve y compendioso sobre la maravillosa obra de la boca y dentadura.* Textos y concordancias electrónicos del corpus médico español CD-ROM, ed. María Teresa Herrera and María Estela. González de Fauve. Madison, Wis.: Hispanic Seminary of Medieval Stuides, 1997.

Martínez de Leyva, Miguel

Remedios preservativos y curativos para en tiempo de peste. Madrid: Juan Flamenco, 1597.

Mas, Bernat

Orde breu y regiment molt útil y profitós per a preservar y curar de peste. Barcelona: Esteve Liberós, 1625.

Méndez, Cristóbal

Libro del ejercicio corporal y de sus provechos, por el qual cada uno podrá entender que exercicio le sea necessario para c seruar su salud . . . Sevilla: Gregorio de la Torre, 1553.

Editions

Alvarez del Palacio, Eduardo, ed. *Cristóbal Méndez: Libro del ejercicio corporal y de sus provechos.* León: Universidad de León, 1996.

Vitoria Ortíz, Manuel, ed. *Cristóbal Méndez. Libro del ejercicio corporal y de sus provechos [1953].* Madrid: Comunidad, Consejería de Educación y Cultura, 1998.

Translation

Guerra, Francisco, trans. *Cristóbal Méndez. Book of bodily excercise.* New Haven, Conn.: Licht, 1960.

Méndez, Gregorio

Regimiento de salud: Arte para conservar el dinero en la bolsa con el qual en gran manera se remedia lo mucho que se gasta con el orinal. Salamanca: Pedro de Castro, 1562.

Méndez Nieto, Juan
Discursos medicinales. MS. 2208. Universidad de Salamanca, Salamanca.
Edition
Ser Quijano, Gregorio del, and Luis E. Rodríguez-San Pedro, eds. *Discursos medicinales de Juan Méndez Nieto.* Salamanca: University of Salamanca, 1998.

Mercado, Luis
Diálogos de Philosophía natural y moral. Granada: Hugo de Mena y Rene Rabut, 1558.
Diálogos de Philosophía natural y moral. Granada: Hugo de Mena, 1574.
Instituciones para el aprovechamiento y examen de los algebristas. Madrid, 1539.
Edition
Ciapparelli, Lidia, ed. *Luis Mercado. Instituciones para el aprovechamiento y examen de los algebristas (Madrid 1539).* Textos y concordancias electrónicos del corpus médico español CD-ROM, ed. María Teresa Herrera and María Estela González de Fauve. Madison, Wis.: Hispanic Seminary of Medieval Studies, 1997.
Instituciones para el aprovechamiento y examen de los algebristas. Madrid, 1598.
Instituciones para el aprovechamiento y examen de los algebristas. Madrid: Pedro Madrigal, 1599.
Libro en que se trata con claridad la naturaleza, causas providencias, y se declaran la orden y modo de curar la enfermedad vulgar, y peste que en estos años se ha divulgado por toda España. Pamplona, 1599.
Libro en que se trata con claridad la naturaleza, causas, providencia, y verdadera orden y modo de curar la enfermedad vulgar, y peste que en estos anos se ha divulgado por toda España. Madrid: Licenciado Castro, 1599.

Micer Johan
Tròtula [Llibre de receptes de Micer Johan]. MS. 3356. Biblioteca Nacional, Madrid.

Micón, Francisco
Alivio de sedientos en el qual se trata la necessidad que tenemos de beber frío y resrescado con nieve, y las condiciones que para esto son menester, y quales cuerpos lo pueden libremente soportar. Barcelona: Diego Galvan, 1576.

Miranda, Alfonso de
Dialogo da perfeyçam y partes qeu sam necessarias ao bom medico. Lisboa: Ioam Alverez, 1562.
Edition
Mingote Muñiz, Manuel E, ed. *Alfonso de Miranda. Diálogo del perfecto médico.* Madrid: Editora Nacional, 1983.

Moix, Joan Rafael
Libre de la peste dividit en tres tractas. Barcelona: Jaume Cendrat, 1587.
Utilissim prompt y facil remey e memorial para preservarse y curar de la peste [de Girauld de Montpellier]. Perpignan, 1587.

Molina, Rodrigo de
Modo perservativo y curativo de la pestilencia. Granada, 1554.

Monardes, Nicolás
Dialogo de las grandezas del hierro, y de sus virtudes medicinales. Sevilla: Alonso Escrivano, 1574. [Published with *Primera y segunda y tercera partes de la historia medicinal* (fols. 157r–185v).
"Prólogo." Juan de Aviñón. *Sevillana medicina.* Sevilla: Andres de Burgos, 1545. 1v–4v.
Primera y segunda y tercera partes de la historia medicinal de las cosas que se traen de nuestras Indias occidentales que sirven en medicina. Sevilla: Alonso Escrivano, 1574.
Primera y segunda y tercera partes dela historia medicinal. Sevilla: Fernando Díaz, 1580.
Edition
Bau, Andrea María, ed. *Texto y concordancias de primera y segunda y tercera partes de la Historia medicinal de las cosas que se traen de nuestras Indias Occidentales que sirven en medicina de Nicolás Monardes, 1580.* Madison, Wis.: Hispanic Seminar of Medieval Studies, 1998.
Libro que trata de la nieva y de sus propriedades, y del modo que se ha de tener, en el beber enfriado con ella: y de los otros modos que ay de enfriar. Sevilla: Alonso Escriuano, 1574.

Mondino dei Luzi
Tratado de la fisonomía en breve suma contenida. Zaragoza: Pablo Hurus, 1494.

Montaña de Monserrate, Bernardino
Libro de la anathomía del hombre. Valladolid: Sebastian Martínez, 1551.
Edition
Balestra, Mirta Alejandra, and Patricia Gubitosi. *Bernardino Montaña de Monserrate. Libro de la anathomía del hombre. [Valladolid 1551].* Textos y concordancias electrónicos del corpus médico español CD-ROM, ed. María Teresa Herrera and María Estela González de Fauve. Madison, Wis.: Hispanic Seminary of Medieval Studies, 1997.

Muñoz de Castro, Gerónimo
Parecer y discurso tercero del Doctor Geronimo Muñoz medico desta ciudad de Sevilla: contra todos los que no han tenido lo muy bueno del primero que hizo su amigo y señor. 1630.

Murillo, Gerónimo
Interpretación del tratado de la materia de cirugía, compuesto por Jacobo Hollerio Stempano, medico de Paris. Çaragoça: Miguel de Huessa, 1576.
Therapéutica méthodo de Galeno en lo que toca a cirugía. Çaragoça: Vuida de Bartolomé de Nágera, 1572.
Therapéutica méthodo de Galeno en lo que toca de cirugía. Recopilada de varios libros suyos, y adornada con paraphrases en muchos lugares obscuros: nuevamente traducida en romance por Geronymo Murillo. Añadido un tratado de Jacobo Holerio, y

traduzidas las receptas de latín en romance. Valencia: Miguel Sorolla, a costa de Juan Antonio Tavano, 1624.

Murillo y Velarde, Tomás
Aprobación de ingenios y curación de hipocóndricos. Zaragoça: Diego de Ormer, 1672.
Tratado de raras y peregrinas yerbas que se han hallado en esta corte, y sus maravillosas virtudes, y la diferencia que ay entre el antiguo abrótano, y la natural, y legítima planta Buphthalmo. Y unas anotaciones de las yerbas mandrágoras, macho y hembra. Madrid, 1674.

Núñez, Ambrosio
Tratado repartido en cinco partes principales que declaran el mal que significa este nombre peste. Coimbra, 1601.

Nuñez de Acosta, Duarte
Apología necessaria y útil en el exercicio practico de la medicina por la resolución de dos questiones: la primera si en los decúbitos o raptos de humor a la cabeça se debe purgar con medicamento electivo: la segunda si en las perlesías que suceden a las appoplexias se haya de sangrar del lado enfermo. / compuesta por el Doctor Duarte Núñez de Acosta. 1601
Tratado practico del uso de las sangrías assí en las enfermedades particulares, methódico de la cura racional con que Galeno procede, y los demás authores. Xerez: Diego Pérez de Estupiñan, 1653.

Núñez de Coria, Francisco
Libro intitulado del parto humano. Alcalá de Henares: Juan Gracian, 1580.
  Edition
  Bau, Andrea María, and Fabián Alejandro Campagne. *Francisco Núñez de Coria. Libro intitulado del parto humano. [Alcalá 1580].* Textos y concordancias electrónicos del corpus médico español CD-ROM, ed. María Teresa Herrera and María Estela González de Fauve. Madison, Wis.: Hispanic Seminary of Medieval Studies, 1997.
Regimiento y aviso de sanidad: que trata de todos los generos de alimentos y del regimiento della. Medina del Campo: Francisco del Canto, 1586.
Tratado del uso de las mugeres. Madrid: Pierres Cusin, 1572. 289r–320r.
  Edition
  Dangler, Jean. *Francisco Nuñez de Coria. Transcription and critical study of the sixteenth-century medical treatise, Tratado del uso de las mugeres.* L.E.M.I.R., Literatura Española Medieval y del Renacimiento, Universitat de València. http://parnaseo.uv.es/Lemir/Textos/Trat_mugeres/Trat_mugeres.html.
Tractado del uso de las mugeres. Medina del Campo: Francisco del Canto, 1586.
  Edition
  Canavese, Gabriela. *Francisco Núñez de Coria. Tractado del vso de las mugeres [Medina del Campo 1586].* Textos y concordancias electrónicos del corpus médico

español CD-ROM, ed. María Teresa Herrera and María Estela González de Fauve. Madison, Wis.: Hispanic Seminary of Medieval Studies, 1997.

Oviedo, Luis de

Méthodo de la colección y reposición de las medicinas simples, y de su correción y preparación: va añadido el tercer libro, en el qual se trata de los letuarios, xaraues, píldoras, trociscos, y azeytes que están en uso. Madrid: Luis Sánchez, 1595.

Méthodo de la colección y reposición de las medicinas simples, de su corrección y preparación . . . Va añadido en algunos lugares el tercer libro, y todo el quarto libro: en que se trata de la composición de los ungüentos, cerotos, y emplastos, que están en uso, y las recetas. . . . Madrid: Luis Sánchez, 1622.

Méthodo de la colección, y reposición de las medicinas simples, de su corrección, y preparación . . . Va añadido en algunos lugares el tercer libro, y todo el quarto libro, en que se trata de la composición de los ungüentos, cerotos, y emplastos, que estàn en uso, y las recetas. . . . Madrid: Melchor Alvarez, 1692.

Para reducir al enfermo a su propia tierra.
Para reducir al enfermo a su propia tierra. MS. 2262. Universitaria, Salamanca.

Pascual, Miguel Juan. See Vigo, Juan de

Pereira Bracamonte, Domingo

Banquete que Apolo hizo a los embaxadores del rey de Portugal Don Iuan Quarto: en cuyos platos hallaran los señores combidados, mezclada con lo dulce de alguna poezia y política la conservación de la salud humana. Lisboa: Lourenço de Amberes, 1642.

Pérez, Antonio

Breve tratado de peste. Madrid: Luis Sánchez, 1598

Summa y examen de chirurgía y de lo mas necessario que en ella se contiene, con breves exposiciones de algunas sentencias de Hypócrates y Galeno. Madrid: Pierres Cosin, 1568.

Summa y Examen de Chirurgia, y de lo más necessario que en ella se contiene, con breves exposiciones de algunas sentencias de Hypócrates y Galeno. Alcalá de Henares: Sebastián Martínez, 1568.

Suma y examen de chirurgía con breves exposiciones de algunas sentencias de Hypócrates y Galeno. Alcalá: Pierres Cosin, 1575.

Suma y examen de chirurgía con breves exposiciones de algunas sentencias de Hypócrates y Galeno. Aphorismos de chirugia, entresacados de los de medicina de Hypócrates. Traduzidos de lengua latina en nuestro vulgar castellano, por el licenciado Antonio Pérez portugués cirujano. Alcalá, 1591.

Suma y examen de chirurgía con breves exposiciones de algunas sentencias de Hypocrates y Galeno. Aphorismos de chirugia, entresacados de los de medicina de Hypócrates. Traduzidos de lengua latina en nuestro vulgar castellano, por el licenciado Antonio Pérez portugués cirujano. Alcalá, 1604.

Suma y examen de chirurgía con breves exposiciones de algunas sentencias de Hypocrates y Galeno. Aphorismos de chirugia, entresacados de los de medicina de Hypocrates. Traduzidos de lengua latina en nuestro vulgar castellano, por el licenciado Antonio Pérez portugués cirujano. Valencia, 1634.

Pérez, Lorenzo
Libro de theriaca, limpio de los errores hasta nuestros tiempos en ella cometidos, y utilíssimo para preparar y consigir muchos simples y compuestos cada día recebidos en el uso de medicina .... Toledo: Juan de Ayala, 1575.

Perez Merino, Isidro
Breve antipologia a el discurso nuevo de el doctor Miguel Fernández de la Peña: método verdadero de el uso del agua de nieve en día de purga. Jaén: Francisco Pérez de Castilla, 1641.

Pérez Morales, García
Tractado del bálsamo y de sus utilidades para las enfermedades del cuerpo humano. Sevilla: Juan Verla de Salamanca, 1530.

Piemontese, Alessio. See also Ruscelli, Girolamo
Libro de los secretos del reverendo don Alexio Piamontes traduzido de lengua italiana en castellana, añadido y emendado en muchos lugares en esta ultima impressión. Salamanca: Mathias Màres, 1570.
Secretos del reverendo Don Alexo Piamontes traduzidos de lengua italiana en castella, añadidos y emendados en muchos lugares en esta última impresión. Alcalá de Henares: Manuel López, 1640.
Secretos del reverendo Don Alexo Piamontes / traduzidos de lengua italiana en castellana, añadidos y emendados. en esta ultima impressión. Alcalá: Maria Fernández, 1647.

Ponce de Santa Cruz, Antonio
Tratado de las causas y curación de las fiebres con secas pestilenciales que han oprimido a Valladolid y otras ciudades de España. Valladolid: Pedro de Merchán Calderón, 1600.

Porcell, Juan Tomás
Información y curación de la peste de Zaragoza y preservación contra peste en general. Zaragoza, 1565.

Porras, Matías de
Breves advertencias para beber frío con nieve. Lima: Gerónimo Contreras, 1621.

Ramírez de Carrión, Manuel
Maravillas de naturaleza, en que se contienen dos mil secretos de cosas naturales. Recogidos de la lección de diversos autores. Montilla: Juan Batista de Morales, 1629.

Recipes and Recipe Collections
Recipes for Specific Ailments
Para hacer a las mujeres apretadas como si fueran vírgenes. MS. 2262. Salamanca: Biblioteca Universitaria.

Recepta per al cap i la vista. MS. 3066. Madrid: Biblioteca Nacional.

Recepta. Pólvora per al mal de mara. MS. 3356. Madrid: Biblioteca Nacional.

Unguento para la sarna. MS. 7-6-26. Sevilla: Colombina.

Unguent per als mugrons. MS. 3356. Madrid: Biblioteca Nacional.

Various Recipes and Recipe Collections

Llibre de medicina i recetari. MS. 360. Biblioteca de Catalunya, Barcelona

Manual de mugeres en el qual se contienen muchas y diversas reçeutas muy buenas. MS. Parmense 834 (antes HH.V.163). Biblioteca Palatina, Parma (Italy).

Edition

Alicia Martínez Crespo, ed. *Manual de mugeres en el qual se contienen muchas y diversas reçeutas muy buenas*. Salamanca: Universidad, 1995.

Recepta. Confecció de litarge. MS. 864. Catalunya, Barcelona.

Receptari florenti. MS. 1115. Firenze: Nazionale, Firenze.

Receptari. MS. 10162. Biblioteca Nacional, Madrid.

Receptes. MS. lat. 11228. Biblioteque Nationale, Paris.

Receptes. MS. 864. Catalunya, Barcelona.

Receptes. MS. 1920. Biblioteca Universitaria y Provincial, Valencia.

Receptes. MS. 216, Olim 92-4-18. Biblioteca Universitaria y Provincial, Valencia.

Receptes. MS. esp. 57. Bibliothéque Nationale, Paris.

Receptes. MS. 10162. Biblioteca Nacional, Madrid.

Receptes. MS. 864. Catalunya, Barcelona.

Receptes. MS. 1292. Biblioteca Capitular, Zaragoza.

Receptes i medecines. MS. çIII.18. El Escorial, El Escorial.

Receptes i medecines. MS. 3066, Olim L.12. Biblioteca Nacional, Madrid.

Recetas. MS. 2262. Biblioteca Universitaria, Salamanca.

Regles de medicina

Regles de medicina. MS. n.a.1. 1536. Bibliothèque Nationale, Paris.

Remedio de cuerpos humanos y silva de experiencias y otras cosas utilíssimas: nuevamente compuesto. Alcalá de Henares: Juan de Brocar, 1542.

Facsimile

Remedio de cuerpos humanos y silua de exp[er]iencias y otras cosas vtilissimas [facsimile edition Alcalá de Henares (Joan de Brocar), 1542]. Madrid: Ministerio de Sanidad y Consumo, 2001.

Remedios para la pestilencia.

Remedios para la pestilencia. Alcalá: Arnao Guillem de Brocar, 1515.

Respuesta de los médicos

Respuesta de los médicos, a quien el illustrissimo señor Conde del Villar assistente de Sevilla mando, que le averiguassen la causa de averse muerto tantos niños de viruelas. En que se trata la essencia, causas, y señales desta enfermedad con la cura que pide. Sevilla: Alonso de Barrera, 1583.

Ribera, Enrique de
Tractado contra pestilencia. Valladolid: Nicolás Tierry, 1527.

Rioja, Francisco de
Tratado de las causas, cura y preservación de la peste. Sevilla, 1599.

Rodriquez de Tudela, Alonso
Servidor de Albuchasis, trasladado del arábigo en latín por Simón Genoves siendo Abraam judío de Tortona interprete; agora nuevamente trasladado y corregido del latín en la lengua vulgar castellana por Alonso Rodríguez de Tudela. Valladolid: Arnao Guillen de Brocar, 1516.

Romano de Córdoba, Alonso
Recopilación de toda la teórica y práctica de cirugía, muy importante para los praticantes della. Valencia: Iua[n] Chrysóstomo Garriz, 1624.

Ruscelli, Girolamo
Secretos del reverendo Don Alexo Piamontes / traduzidos de lengua italiana en castellana, añadidos y emendados. en esta ultima impressión. Alcalá: Maria Fernández: a costa de Manuel López, 1647.

Saavedra, Juan de
En que prueba que Sevilla gozara de muy buna salud este año, y que no ay que temer peste, ni tercianas, ni otras enfermedades. Sevilla: Juan de Cabrera, 1599.
Parecer en que se dice que el estado de la salud de Sevilla no es la peste. Sevilla: Rodrigo de Cabrera, 1599.

Sabuco, Miguel, and Oliva Sabuco de Nantes
Nueva Filosofía de la naturaleza del hombre: no conocida ni alcançada de los grandes filósofos antiquos: la qual mejora la vida y salud humana. Madrid: P. Madrigal, 1587.
Edition
Martinez Tomé, Atilano, ed. *Nueva filosofía de la naturaleza del hombre y otros escritos.* Madrid: Editora Nacional, D.L. 1981.
Nueva Filosofía De La Naturaleza Del Hombre, No Conocida, Ni Alcançada De Los Grandes Filósofos Antiguos. Braga: Fructuoso Loueço de Basto, 1622. Madrid: P. Madrigal, 1588.
Nueva filosofía de la naturaleza del hombre, no conocida, ni alcançada de los grandes filósofos antiguos. Braga: Fructuoso Loueço de Basto, 1622.

Saladino de Ascoli
Compendio de los boticarios compuesto por el doctor Saladino físico principal del príncipe de Taranto. Traslado del latín en lengua vulgar castellana. Trans. Alonso Rodríguez de Tudela. Valladolid: Arnao Guillen de Brocar, 1515.
Edition
Capuano, Thomas M., ed. *Saladino da Ascoli: Compendio de los boticarios.* Madison, Wis.: Hispanic Seminary of Medieval Studies, 1997.

Salazar, Ambrosio de

Thesoro de diversa lición en el qual ay XXII historias muy verdaderas y otras cosas tocantes a la salud del cuerpo humano, con una forma de gramática muy provechosa para los curiosos. Paris: chez Louys Boullanger, 1637.

Sánchez de Oropesa, Francisco

Discurso para averigurar, que mal de urina sea el que padece Diego Anriquez León su compadre y amigo: en que incidentemente se tratan las cosas, que pareceron dificultosas, i de mas consideración, cera de la essencia, causa, señales, i cura de todos lo males de este genero. Sevilla: Juan de León, 1594.

Proposición a la ciudad de Sevilla sobre la landre, que tantos enfermos causa en la ciudad y perplejidad sobre si es o no contagiosa. Se precisa la necesidad de fundar uno o dos, o más hospitales para que los pobres sean con brevedad socorridos. Sevilla: Clemente Hidalgo, 1599.

Respuesta acerca de una palpitación y tremor que padeció un enfermo en Guatemala. Sevilla, 1594.

Respuesta i parecer a lo que le a sido preguntado por una relación que al principio va copiada. Sevilla: Juan de León, 1593.

Segunda proposición a la ciudad de Sevilla en que se ponen algunas advertencias para la preservación i cura del mal que anda. Sevilla: Clement Hidalgo, 1599.

Tres proposiciones a la ciudad de Sevilla en que se ponen algunas advertencias para la preservación i cura del mal que anda en la ciudad. Sevilla: Clemente Hidalgo, 1599.

Sánchez de Valdes de la Plata, Juan

Crónica y historia general del hombre en que se trata del hombre en común. De la división del hombre en cuerpo y alma. De las figuras monstruosas de los hombres. De las invenciones dellos. Y de la concordia entre Dios, y el hombre. Madrid: Luis Sánchez, 1598.

Santiago, Diego de

Arte separatoria y modo de apartar todos los licores, que se sacan por vía de destilación para que las medicinas obren con mayor virtud y presteza. Con la manera de hazer el instrumento separatorio que invento el autor, que es el mejor y mas fácil que hasta oy se ha visto. 1598.

Preservativos contra la peste. Sevilla, 1599.

Savonarola, Miguel

Regimiento de sanidad de todas las cosas que se comen y beben. Sevilla: Dominco de Robertis, 1541.

Silva de Olivera, Francisco

Discurso de la providencia y curación de las secas y carbunclos por contagio. Granada, 1603.

Sorapán de Rieros, Ivan

Medicina española contenida en proverbios vulgares de nuestra lengua, muy provechosa para todo género de estados, para philosophos y médicos, para théologos y juristas, para el buen regimiento de la salud y más larga vida. Granada: Martín Fernández Zambrano, 1616.

Sobre la veracidad de los sueños
Sobre la veracidad de los sueños. MS. 2262. Universitaria, Salamanca.

Sobre la virtut de la sang
Sobre la virtut de la sang. MS. 10162. Biblioteca Nacional, Madrid.

Sobre los cuatro elementos
Sobre los cuatro elementos. MS. 2262. Universitaria, Salamanca.

Soriano, Jerónimo
Libro de experimentos médicos, fáciles y verdaderos. Zaragoza: Juan Pérez de Valdivieso, 1598.
Libro de experimentos médicos, fáciles y verdaderos. Madrid: Luis Sánchez, 1599.
Edition
Forteza, Patricia de. *Jeronimo Soriano. Libro de experimentos médicos, faciles y ver-daderos [1599].* Textos y concordancias electrónicos del corpus médico español CD-ROM, ed. María Teresa Herrera and María Estela González de Fauve. Madison, Wis.: Hispanic Seminar of Medieval Studies, 1997.
Libro de experimentos médicos fáciles y verdaderos. Çaragoça: Angelo Tauano, 1601.
Libro de experimentos médicos fáciles, y verdaderos. Recopilados de gravíssimos autores, por el Doctor Geronymo Soriano. Barcelona: Geronymo Margarit, 1614.

Soto, Pedro de
Respuesta a la relación de la enfermedad de la Marquesa de Quintana que el doctor Iuan de Biana escribió contra el doctor Tomás del Castillo Ochoa. Málaga: Iuan Serrano de Vargas, 1634.

Soto, Sebastián de
Discurso médico y moral de las enfermedades porque seguramente pueden las religiosas dexar la clausura. Madrid: Iuan Sanchez, 1639.

Speculum al foderi
Speculum al foderi. MS. 3356. Biblioteca Nacional, Madrid.
Editions and translations
Vicens, Teresa, ed. *Speculum al joder: tratado de recetas y consejos sobre el coito.* Barcelona: Hesperus, 1978 [Spanish translation].
Solomon, Michael. *The Mirror of Coitus: A Translation and Edition of the Fifteenth-Century* Speculum al foderi. Medieval Spanish Medical Texts Series, no 29. Madison, Wis.: Hispanic Seminary of Medieval Studies, 1990.
Vallribera Puig, Pere. *Literatura médica medieval catalana. "Speculum al foderi." Transcripció i estudis medics d'un text del segle xv sobre sexologia.* Barcelona: Universidad de Barcelona, 1993.
Gifreu, Patrick, ed. *El Kamasutra català: Mirall del fotre, anónim del segle XIV.* Barcelona: Columna, 1996. [Modernized Catalan edition.]
Anna Alberni, ed. *Speculum al foder.* Bellcaire d'Empordà: Vitel·la, 2007.

Tamayo, Andrés de
Tratados breves de álgebra, y garrotillo. Con una instrucción de los barberos flobotomia-nos. Por Alonso Muñoz. Valencia: Juan Chrysóstomo Garriz, a costa Filipo Pincinali, 1621.

Tárrega, Gabriel de
Traité contra la peste. Burdeos, 1519.

Teodorico dei Borgognoni [Tedrico, Teodoro]
Cirugía. MS. Escorial h.III.17. El Escorial.
Edition
> Herrera, María Teresa. *Teodorico dei Borgognoni. Cirugia. [MS. Escorial h.III.17].* Textos y concordancias electrónicos del corpus médico español CD-ROM, ed. María Teresa Herrera and María Estela González de Fauve. Madison, Wis.: Hispanic Seminary of Medieval Studies, 1997.

Terradas, Francisco
Compendi de la peste y de la precaució y curació de aquella. Mallorca, 1590.

Tesoro de la medicina (Tesoro de los remedios)
Tesoro de la medicina. MS. 5-1-17. Colombina, Sevilla.
Edition
> Zabía, María Purificación. *Tesoro de la medicina [Tesoro de remedios] (MS. 5-1-17. Colombina, Sevilla).* Textos y concordancias electrónicos del corpus médico español CD-ROM, ed. María Teresa Herrera and María Estela González de Fauve. Madison, Wis.: Hispanic Seminary of Medieval Studies, 1997.

Toro, Luis de. See Luis de Toro

Torres, Pedro de
Libro que trata de la enfermedad de las bubas. Madrid: Luis Sanchez, 1600.
Edition
> Bau, Andrea María. *Pedro de Torres. Libro que trata de la enfermedad de las bubas [Madrid 1600].* Textos y concordancias electrónicos del corpus médico español CD-ROM, ed. María Teresa Herrera and María Estela González de Fauve. Madison, Wis.: Hispanic Seminary of Medieval Studies, 1997.

Trasmiera, Juan Remon de
Flores romanas de famosos y doctos varones compuestas para salud y reparo delos cuerpos humanos: gentilezas de hombres de palacio y de criança transladados de lengua ytali-ana en nuestra española. enmendadas con addicion de muchas receptas. 1513.
Probadas flores romanas de famosos y doctos varones compuestas para salud y reparo delos cuerpos humanos: gentilezas de hombres de palacio y de criança transladados de lengua ytaliana en nuestra española. Valencia: 1510.

Tratado de la generación de la criatura
Tratado de la generación de la criatura. MS. I-1335. Biblioteca Nacional, Madrid.

Tratado de las orinas, de los pulsos y de otras señales
Tratado de las orinas, de los pulsos y de otras señales. MS. 2262. Biblioteca Universitaria, Salamanca.

Trotula. See Micer Johan

Valdes, Fernando de
Disputa y averiguaciones de la enfermedad pestilente. Sevilla: Clemente Hidalgo, 1599.
Tratado de la utilidad dela sangría en las viruelas y otras enfermedades de los muchachos. Sevilla: Fernando Díaz, 1583.

Valdivia, Andrés de
Tractado en el cual se explica la esencia y naturaleza de la enfermedad que llaman landres que ha andado en Sevilla. Sevilla, 1609.

Valesco de Taranta
Compendi utilissim contra pestilencia tret de la font de medicina, de lengua latina artificiosa en vulgar trasledat. Barcelona, 1475.
Tratado de la epidemia y pestilencia. Zaragoza, 1494.
Tratado de la peste. Pamplona: Arnaldo Guillen de Brocar, 1495.
Compendi utilissim contra pestilencia tret de la font de medicina. Barcelona: Johan Rosembach Alemany, 1507.
Edition
Compendi ultissim pestilencia tret de la font de la medecina [facsimile edition of *Barcelona, 1507 Catalan edition*]. Biblioteca virtual Joan Lluís Vives. http:// www.lluisvives.com/servlet/SirveObras/jlv/12482175339130413087846/index .htm.
Tratado de la epidemia y pestilencia. Pamplona, 1507.
Editions
Zabía, María Purificatión. *Valesco de Taranta. Tratado de la epidemia y pestilencia* [*Zaragoza 1494*]. Textos y concordancias electrónicos del corpus médico español CD-ROM, ed. María Teresa Herrera and María Estela González de Fauve. Madison, Wis.: Hispanic Seminary of Medieval Studies, 1997.
Sánchez, María Nieves. "Velasco de Taranta. Tratados de la peste." *Tratados de la peste.* Ed. María Nieves Sánchez. Madrid: Arco Libros, 1993.

Valles de Covarrubias, Francisco
Tratado de las aguas destiladas, pesos y medidas. Madrid: Luis Sánchez, 1592.

Valverde de Amusco, Juan
Historia de la composición del cuerpo humano. Roma: Antonio Salamanca y Antonio Lafreri, 1556.

Velazquez, Andres
Libro de la melancholía, en el qual se trata de la naturaleza desta enfermedad assí llamada Melancholía y de sus causas y símptomas. Sevilla: Hernando Díaz, 1585.

Velez de Arciniega, Francisco
Historia de los animales mas recebidos [sic] en el uso de medicina: donde se trata para lo que cada veo entero ò parte del aprovecha y de la manera de su preparación. Madrid: Imp. Real.

Vigo, Juan de
Libro o practica en Cirugía. Valencia, 1537.
Libro o practica en Cirugía. Toledo: Fernando de Sancta Cathalina, 1548.
Libro o practica en cirugía. Trans. Miguel Juan Pascual. Burgos: Phelippe de Iunta, 1564.
Libro o practica en cirugía. Çaragoça: Iuan Soler, 1581.

Vigo, Juan de, and Miguel Juan Pascual (trans).
Teórica y prática [sic] en cirugía del doctor Iuan de Vigo.; hecha de latina castellana, por el doctor Miguel Iuan Pascual. Perpiñan: Luys Roure, 1627.

Vilanova, Arnau de. See Arnau de Vilanova

Villa, Esteban de
Examen de boticarios. Burgos 1632.
Libro de simples incógnitos en la medicina. Burgos: Pedro Gomes de Valdiuieso, 1643.
Ramillete de Planta. Burgos 1646.

Villafranca, Antonio Juan de
Libro de la sangría artificial y como se ha de hazer, útil y provechoso a los médicos y chirugianos. Valentiae: Ioannes Mey, 1559.

Ximénez, Francisco
Quatro libros De la naturaleza, y virtudes de las plantas, y animales que están recebidos en el uso de medicina en la Nueva España, y la méthodo, y corrección, y preparación, que para administrallas se requiere con lo que el Doctor Francisco Hernández escribió en lengua Latina. / traduzido y aumentados muchos simples, y compuestos y otros muchos secretos curativos, por Fr. Francisco Ximenez. México: la viuda de Diego López Dávalos, 1615.

Ximénez de Carmona, Francisco
Tratado breve de la grande excelencia del agua, y de sus maravillosas virtudes, calidad y elección, y del buen uso de enfriar con nieve. Sevilla: Alfonso Rodríguez, 1616.

Ximénez Guillén, Francisco
Respuesta a los pareceres que hasta agora han salido acerca del mal que anda en esta ciudad de Sevilla. Sevilla, 1599.

Zamora, Alonso de
Tratado muy necessario y muy provechoso, en el qual se contiene un regimiento breve para poder conservar la salud enel tiempo de peste. Cuenca, 1537.

Zamudio de Alfaro, Andrés
Orden para la cura y preservación de las viruelas. Madrid: Luis Sánchez, 1579.
Orden para la cura y preservación de las secas y carbuncos. Madrid: Luis Sánchez, 1599.

Edition

González de Fauve, María Estela. *Zamudio de Alfaro, Andrés. Orden para la cura y preservación de las secas y carbuncos [Madrid 1599].* Textos y concordancias electrónicos del corpus médico español CD-ROM, ed. María Teresa Herrera and María Estela González de Fauve. Madison, Wis.: Hispanic Seminary of Medieval Studies, 1997.

Zaragozano y Zapater, Victoriano
Compendiosa y breve cura de la peste, con la cual cada uno se puede curar sin consulta de médico. Zaragoza: Lorenzo de Robles, 1597.

Primary Sources
(excluding medieval and early modern vernacular medical works)

Arnau de Vilanova. "Bedside Manners in the Middle Ages: The Treatise *De cautelis medicorum* Attributed to Arnald of Villanova." Trans. Henry E. Sigerist in Sigerest, *On the History of Medicine.* Ed. Felix Martí-Ibáñez. New York: MD Publications, 1960. 131–40.

———. *Regimen Sanitatis ad Regem Aragonum.* Ed. Pedro Gil-Sotres. Opera Medica Omnia / Arnaldi de Villanova. Vol. 10. Lérida: Pages, 1996.

———. *Repetitio super canonem vita brevis.* Ca. 1300, in Munich CLM 14245.

Cortes, Jeronimo. *Tratado del computo por la mano, muy breve y necessario para los eclesiasticos.* Valencia: Herederos de Ioan Navarro, 1591.

Della Croce, Giovanni Andrea. *Chirurgiae Ioannis Andreae a Cruce . . . Libri Septem.* Venetiis: apud Iordanum Zilettum, 1573.

Frampton, John, trans. Nicolás Monardes. *Ioyfull nevves out of the newe founde worlde: wherein is declared the rare and singuler vertues of diuerse and sundrie hearbes, trees, oyles, plantes, and stones, with their aplications, as well for phisicke as chirurgerie, the saied beyng well applied bryngeth suche present remedie for all deseases, as maie seme altogether incredible.* Imprinted at London: In Poules Churche-yarde by Willyam Norton, 1577.

Johannes de Toleto. *Regiment de sanitat. Liber de conservanda sanitate.* Barberini lat. 311. Biblioteca Vaticana, Vatican City.

Maimonides. *Maimonides "On sexual intercourse." Fi 'l-jima.* Trans. Morris Gorlin. Brooklyn, N.Y.: Rambash, 1961.

———. *Tractatus Rabbi Moysi de regimine sanitatis ad Soldanum Regem.* Augusta Vindelicorum, 1518.

Macer Floridus. Edición, facsímile del herbario medieval de la Real Colegiata de San Isidoro de León. León: Universidad, 1990.

Mexia, Pedro. *Silva de varia leccion.* Ed. Antonio Castro. 2 vols. Madrid: Cátedra, 1989.

Robles, Juan de. *Arte para enseñar muy breve y perfactamente a leer y escrevir.* n.p.: n.p., 1565.

Secondary Sources

Agrimi, Jole, and Chiara Crisciani. *Les consilia médicaux*. Trans. Caroline Viola. Turnhout, Belgium: Brepols, 1994.

Alberni, Anna. "Introducció." In *Speculum al foder*, ed. Anna Alberni. Barcelona: Vitel·la, 2007: 13–44.

Alejo Montes, Javier. *La Universidad de Salamanca bajo Felip II (1575–1598)*. Burgos: Junta de Castilla y León, 1998.

Amasuno Sárraga, Marcelino V. *Alfonso Chirino, un médico de monarcas castellanos*. Salamanca: Junta de Castilla y León, 1993.

———. *La escuela de medicina del estudio salmantino: siglos XIII–XV*. Acta Salmanticensia. Historia de la Universidad 52. Salamanca: Universidad de Salamanca, 1990.

———. "Nomenclatura de los pesos y medidas usados en la medicina medieval española." *Cuadernos de la Historia de la Medicina Española* (1975): 15–40.

———. *La peste de la corona de Castilla durante la segunda mitad del siglo XIV*. Salamanca: Junta de Castilla y León, 1996.

———. *El "Regimiento contra la pestilencia" de Alfonso López de Valladolid: contribución al estudio del fenómeno epidémico en la Castilla de la primera mitad del siglo XV*. Acta Histórico-Vallisoletana 26. Valladolid: Universidad de Valladolid, 1988.

Arrizabalaga, Jon. "La enfermedad y la asistencia hospitalaria." In *Historia de la ciencia y de la técnica en la corona de Castilla*, ed. Luis García-Ballester. Vol. 1. Salamanca: Junta de Castilla y León, 2002. 603–30.

———. "Facing the Black Death: Perceptions and Reactions of the University Medical Practitioners." *Practical Medicine from Salerno to the Black Death*, ed. Luis García Ballester. New York: Cambridge, 1994. 237–88.

———. "The Ideal Medical Practitioner in Counter-Reformation Castile: The Perception of the Converso Physician Henrique Jorge Henriques (c. 1555–1622)." In *Medicine and Medical Ethics in Medieval and Early Modern Spain: An Intercultural Approach*, ed. Samuel S. Kottek and Luis García-Ballester. Jerusalem: Hebrew University Magnes Press, 1996. 61–91.

———. "Lluís Alcanyís y su *Regiment de la pestilència*." *Dynamis* 3 (1983): 29–54.

———. "Poor Relief in Counter-Reformation Castile: An Overview." In *Health Care and Poor Relief in Counter-Reformation Europe*, ed. Ole Peter Grell, Andrew Cunningham, and Jon Arrizabalaga. New York: Routledge, 1999. 151–76.

Arrizabalaga, Jon, Luis García-Ballester, and Joan Veny, eds. *Regiment de preservació de pestilència: Jacme d' Agramont* Electronic version. Barcelona: Biblioteca Virtual Joan Lluís Vives.

Asúa, Miguel de. "Peter of Spain's Handling of Authorities in his Commentary on the *Isagoge* of Johannitius." *Dynamis* 20 (2000): 107–33.

Atkin, Albert, "Peirce's Theory of Signs." In *The Stanford Encyclopedia of Philosophy*, ed. Edward N. Zalta, Spring 2009 ed. http://plato.stanford.edu/archives/spr2009/entries/peirce-semiotics/.

Bajaen Espanol, M. "Sex, Morals and Medicine in Counter-Reformation Spain: An Unpublished Report on Pollution by the Jesuit Miguel Perez (1550–1605)." *Dynamis* 15 (1995): 443–57.

Bar-On, Yaarah. "Neighbours and Gossip in Early Modern Gynaecology." In *Cultural Approaches to the History of Medicine: Mediating Medicine in Early Modern and Modern Europe*, ed. Willem de Blécourt and Cornelie Usborne. Hampshire: Palgrave Macmillan, 2004. 36–55.

Bar-Sela, Ariel, and Hebbel E. Hoff. "Isaac Israeli, *The Book of Admonitions to the Physicians*." In *Legacies in Ethics and Medicine*, ed. Chester R. Burns. New York: Science History Publications, 1977. 150–57.

Barthes, Roland. *Mythologies*. New York: Hill and Wang, 1972.

Bataillon, Marcel. "Riesgo y ventura del 'licenciado' Juan Méndez Nieto." *Hispanic Review* 37 (1969): 23–60.

Batllori, Miquel. "Noticia preliminar: les obres mèdiques catalanes d'Arnau de Vilanova." *Arnau de Vilanova: obres catalanes*. Vol. 2, *Escrits Mèdics*. Ed. Miquel Batllori. Barcelona: Barcino, 1947. 53–91.

Baur, Susan. *Hypochondria: Woeful Imaginings*. Berkeley: University of California Press, 1988.

Beaujouan, Guy. "Manuscrits médicaux du moyen âge conservés en Espagne." *Mélanges de la Casa de Velázquez* 8 (1972): 161–221.

Bénézet, Jean-Pierre. *Pharmacie et médicament en Méditerranée occidentale*. Paris: Champion, 1999.

Blanco Pérez, José Ignacio. *Humanistas médicos en el Renacimiento vallisoletano*. Burgos: Universidad de Burgos, 1999.

Blécourt, Willem de, and Cornelie Usborne, eds. *Cultural Approaches to the History of Medicine: Mediating Medicine in Early Modern and Modern Europe*. Hampshire: Palgrave Macmillan, 2004.

———. "Medicine, Mediation and Meaning." In *Cultural Approaches to the History of Medicine: Mediating Medicine in Early Modern and Modern Europe*, ed. Willem de Blécourt and Cornelie Usborne. Hampshire: Palgrave Macmillan, 2004. 1–10.

The Body: The Complete HIV/AIDS Resource. http://www.thebody.com/index.html.

Bono, James J. *The Word of God and the Languages of Man: Interpreting Nature in Early Modern Science and Medicine*. Madison: University of Wisconsin Press, 1995.

Bos, Gerrit. *Ibn Al-Jazzar on Sexual Diseases and Their Treatment*. London: Kegan Paul, 1997.

Brockliss, Laurence, and Colin Jones. *The Medical World of Early Modern France*. Oxford: Clarendon, 1997.

Brodman, James William. *Charity and Welfare: Hospitals and the Poor in Medieval Catalonia*. Philadelphia: University of Pennsylvania Press, 1998.

Bujosa Homar, F. "El libro de la peste de Don Alonso de Freylas. Difusion de las teorias de Fracastoro en España." In *Actas del IV Congreso Español de Historia de la Medicina*. Granada, 24–26 April 1973. Vol. 1. 135–38.

Burnett, Charles. "Filosofía natural, secretos y magia." In *Historia de la ciencia y de la técnica en la Corona de Castilla*, ed. Luis García-Ballester. Vol. 1. Salamanca: Junta de Castilla León, 2002. 95–146.

Bylebyl, Jerome J. "Galen on the Non-Natural Causes of Variation in the Pulse." *Bulletin of the History of Medicine* 45 (1971): 482–85.

———. "The Medical Meaning of Physica." *Osiris: A Research Journal Devoted to the History of Science and Its Cultural Influences* 6 (1990): 16–41.

Cabré, Montserrat. La cura del cos femení i la medicina medieval de tradició llatina els tractas "De ornatu" i "De decorationibus mulierum" atribuïts a Arnau de Vilanova, "Trótula" de mestre Joan, i "Flos del tresor de beutat", atribuït a Manuel Dieç de Calatayud . Barcelona: Universitat Autónoma de Barcelona, 1994.

———. "From a Master to a Laywoman; A Feminine Manual of Self-Help." *Dynamis* 20 (2000): 371–93.

———. "Women or Healers? Household Practices and the Categories of Health Care in Late Medieval Iberia." *Bulletin of the History of Medicine* 82, 1 (2008): 18–51.

Cabré, Montserrat, and Teresa Ortiz. *Sanadoras, matronas y médicas en Europa, siglos XII–XX*. Barcelona: Icaria, 2001.

Campagne, Fabián Alejandro. "Cultura popular y saber médico en la España de los Austrias." In *Medicina y sociedad: curar y sanar en la España de los siglos XIII al XVI*, ed. María Estela González de Fauve. Buenos Aires: Instituto de Historia de España "Claudio Sánchez-Albornoz." Universidad de Buenos Aires, 1996. 195–240.

———. "Medicina y religión en el discurso antisupersticioso español de los siglos XVI a XVIII: un combate por la hegemonía." *Dynamis* 20 (2000): 417–56.

Capuano, Thomas M. "Medieval Iberian Vernacular Versions of the Herbal called *Macer Floridus*." *Manuscripta* 35, 35 (1991): 182–202.

Carmichael, Ann G. "Contagion Theory and Contagion Practice in Fifteenth-Century Milan." *Renaissance Quarterly* 44, 2 (1991): 213–56.

Carrera de la Red, Abelina. Introducción to Antonio de Nebrija, *Dictionarium medicum: el diccionario médico de Elio Antonio de Nebrija*. Ed. Carrera de la Red. Salamanca: Ediciones Universidad de Salamanca, 2001. 13–23.

———. "El 'problema de la lengua'." In *El humanismo renacentista español*, ed. Abelina Carrera de la Red. Valladolid: n.p., 1988.

Castillo, Antonio. *Escribir y leer en el siglo de Cervantes*. Barcelona: Gedisa, 1999.

Certeau, Michel de. *The Practice of Everyday Life*. Berkeley: University of California Press, 1984.

Chartier, Roger. *The Order of Books: Readers, Authors, and Libraries in Europe Between the Fourteenth and Eighteenth Centuries*. Stanford, Calif.: Stanford University Press, 1994.

Chiarlone, Quintin, and Carlos Mallaina. *Ensayo sobre la historia de la farmacia*. Madrid: Santiago Sunaque, 1847.

Cifuentes i Comamala, Lluís. *La ciència en català a l'Edat Mitjana i el Renaixement.* Barcelona: Universitat de Barcelona, 2001.

———. "Translatar sciència en romans catalanesch. La difusió de la medicina en català a la Baixa Edat Mitjana i el Renaixement." *Llengua y Literatura* 8 (1997): 7–42.

———. "Vernacularization as an Intellectual and Social Bridge: The Catalan Translations of Teodorico's *Chirurgia* and of Arnau de Vilanova's *Regimen Sanitatis.*" *Early Science and Medicine* 4, 2 (1999): 127–48.

Concheff, Beatrice Jorgensen. *Bibliography of Old Catalan Texts.* Madison, Wis.: Hispanic Seminary of Medieval Studies, 1985.

Conejo Mir, José. "Estudio histórico acerca de Juan de Aviñón y su *Sevillana medicina.*" *Trabajos de la Cátedra de Historia Crítica de la Medicina* 1 (1933): 183–89.

Cook, Harold J. "Good Advice and Little Medicine: The Professional Authority of Early Modern English Physicians." *Journal of British Studies* 33, 1 (1994): 1–31.

Crossgrove, William. "The Vernacularization of Science, Medicine, and Technology in Late Medieval Europe: Broadening Our Perspectives." *Early Science and Medicine* 5, 1 (2000): 47–63.

Curtius, Ernst Robert. *European Literature and the Latin Middle Ages.* Princeton, N.J.: Princeton University Press, 1973.

Daly, Walter J. "Medieval Contributions to the Search for Truth in Clinical Medicine." *Perspectives in Biology and Medicine* 43, 4 (2000): 530–40.

Dangler, Jean. *Mediating Fictions: Literature, Women Healers, and the Go-Between in Medieval and Early Modern Iberia.* Lewisburg, Pa.: Bucknell University Press, 2001.

De la Calle Munoz, I., et al. "Spanish Urology in the Renaissance." *Actas Urológicas Españolas* 15, 3 (1991): 253–59.

Demaitre, Luke. "Medical Writing in Transition: Between Ars and Vulgus." *Early Science and Medicine* 3, 2 (1998): 88–102.

Demaitre, Luke E. "The Art and Science of Prognostication in Early University Medicine." *Bulletin of the History of Medicine* 77, 4 (2003): 765–88.

———. "The Relevance of Futility: Jordanus de Turre (fl.1313–1335) on the Treatment of Leprosy." *Bulletin of the History of Medicine* 70, 1 (1996): 25–61.

Dubler, César E. "Juan de Aviñón." *La materia médica de Dioscórides: transmisión medieval y renacentista.* Vol. 5. Barcelona: Emporium, 1954. 70–76.

Eamon, William. *Science and the Secrets of Nature: Books of Secrets in Medieval and Early Modern Culture.* Princeton, N.J.: Princeton University Press, 1994.

Eisenberg, Leon. "Disease and Illness: Distinctions between Professional and Popular Ideas of Sickness." *Culture, Medicine and Psychiatry* 1 (1977): 9–23.

Emch-Dériaz, Antoinette. "The Non-Naturals Made Easy." In *The Popularization of Medicine: 1650–1850,* ed. Roy Porter. London: Routledge, 1992. 134–53.

Engelhardt, H. Tristram, Jr. "Ideology and Etiology." *Journal of Medicine and Philosophy* 1 (1976): 256–68.

Fanger, Claire, ed. *Conjuring Spirits: Texts and Traditions of Medieval Ritual Magic.* University Park: Pennsylvania State University Press, 1998.

Faulhaber, Charles B., et al. Philobiblon: BETA / Bibliografía Española de Textos Antigous. BITAGAP / Bibliografia de Textos Antigos Galegos e Portugueses. BITECA / Bibliografia de Textos Catalans Antics. 2008. http://sunsite.berkeley.edu/Philobiblon/phhm.html.

Ferragut Domingo, Carmel. "Los profesionales de la medicina en la corona de aragón durante la peste negra (1350–1410)." Universidad de Valencia, 2002.

Finke, Heinrich. *Acta Aragonensia.* Vol. 2. Berlin-Leipzig: n.p., 1908.

Finucci, Valeria. "'There's the Rub': Searching for Sexual Remedies in the New World." *Journal of Medieval and Early Modern Studies* 38 (2008): 523–57.

Fissell, Mary E. "Readers, Texts, and Contexts: Vernacular Medical Works in Early Modern England." In *The Popularization of Medicine 1650–1850*, ed. Roy Porter. London: Routledge, 1992. 72–96.

———. *Vernacular Bodies: The Politics of Reproduction in Early Modern England.* Oxford: Oxford University Press, 2004.

Folch Jou, Guillermo. "Las drogas en la obra de Fray Agustín Farfán." *Asclepio* 9 (1957): 165–72.

———. "Medicamentos empleados por los árabes y su posible influencia en la producción de la química en la farmacia." *Asclepio* 30 (1979): 177–86.

———. "Los médicos, la botánica y la materia farmacéutica en España durante la decimosexta centuria." *Asclepio* 18 (1966): 141–55.

Font i Sagué, Norbert. *Història de les ciències naturals a Catalunya, del s. XI al XVIII.* Barcelona: n.p., 1908.

Foucault, Michel. *Discipline and Punish.* Trans. Alan Sheridan. New York: Vintage, 1995.

French, Roger. "Astrology in Medical Practice." In *Practical Medicine from Salerno to the Black Death*, ed. Luis García-Ballester et al. New York: Cambridge University Press, 1994. 30–59.

———. "The Crisis of Theory." *Medicine Before Science: The Rational and Learned Doctor from the Middle Ages and the Enlightenment.* Cambridge: Cambridge University Press, 2003. 157–85.

Fresquet Febrer, José Luis. *La experiencia americana y la terapéutica en los Secretos de chirurgia (1567), de Pedro Arias de Benavides.* Cuadernos Valencianos de Historia de la Medicina y de la Ciencia. Serie A. Monografías. Vol. 41. Valencia: Instituto de Estudios Documentales e Históricos sobre la Ciencia, Universitat de València, 1993.

Friedenwald, Harry. "Francisco López de Villalobos: Spanish Court Physician and Poet." In *The Jews and Medicine: Essays*, vol. 1. Baltimore: Johns Hopkins Press, 1944.

García-Ballester, Luis. "Arnau de Vilanova (c. 1240–1311) y la reforma de los estudios médicos en Montpellier (1309): el Hipócrates latino y la introducción del nuevo Galeno." *Dynamis* 2 (1982): 97–158.

———. *La búsqueda de la salud*. Barcelona: Ediciones Península, 2001.

———. "Changes in the *Regimina sanitatis*: The Role of the Jewish Physician." In *Medicine in a Multicultural Society*, ed. Luis García-Ballester. Variorum Collected Studies Series 5. Aldershot: Ashgate, 2001. 119–31.

———. "Galenismo y enseñanza médica en la Universidad de Salamanca del siglo XV." *Dynamis* 20 (2000): 209–47.

———. *Los moriscos y la medicina: un capítulo de la medicina y la ciencia marginadas en la España del siglo XVI*. Barcelona: Labor, 1984.

———. "On the Origin of the 'Six Non-Natural Things' in Galen." In *Galen und das hellenistische Erbe*, ed. Jutta Kollesch and Diethard Nickel. Stuttgart: Steiner, 1993: 105–15.

García-Ballester, Luis, Michael R. McVaugh, and Agustín Rubio. *Medical Licensing and Learning in Fourteenth-Century Valencia*. Transactions of the American Philosophical Society 79. Philadelphia: American Philosophical Society, 1989.

Getz, Faye Marie. "Charity, Translation, and the Language of Medical Learning in Medieval England." *Bulletin of the History of Medicine* 64 (1990): 1–17.

Gil Fernández, Luis. *Panorama social del humanismo español*. Madrid: Tecnos, 1997.

Gil Sotres, Pedro. "Derivation and Revulsion: The Theory and Practice of Medieval Phlebotomy." In *Practical Medicine from Salerno to the Black Death*, ed. Luis García-Ballester et al. New York: Cambridge University Press, 1994.

———. Introducción. *Regimen sanitatis ad regem aragonum*, ed. Luis García-Ballester and Michael R. McVaugh. Vol. X.1. Arnaldi de Villanova Opera Medica Omnia. Barcelona: Seminarium Historiae Scientiae Barchinone, 1996. 471–835.

Gómez García, Pedro. *El curanderismo entre nosotros*. Monográfica Antropología 238. Granada: Universidad de Granada, 1997.

González de Fauve, María Estela. *Ciencia, poder e ideología: el saber y el hacer en la evolución de la medicina española (siglos XIV–XVIII)*. Buenos Aires: Instituto de Historia de España "Claudio Sánchez-Albornoz," Universidad de Buenos Aires, 2001.

———, ed. *Medicina y sociedad: curar y sanar en la España de los siglos XIII al XVI*. Buenos Aires: Instituto de Historia de España "Claudio Sánchez-Albornoz," Universidad de Buenos Aires, 1996.

González de Fauve, María Estela, and Patricia de Forteza. "Boticarios y materia médica en España (siglos XV y XVI)." In *Medicina y sociedad: curar y sanar en la España de los siglos XIII al XVI.*, ed. María Estela González de Fauve. Buenos Aires: Instituto de Historia de España "Claudio Sánchez-Albornoz," Universidad de Buenos Aires, 1996. 103–36.

———. "Ética médica y mala praxis en Castilla: una visión realista del quehacer profesional (siglos XIV–XVI)." In *Ciencia, poder e ideología: el saber y el hacer en la evolución de la medicina española*, ed. María Estela González de Fauve. Buenos Aires: Instituto de Historia de España "Claudio Sánchez-Albornoz," Universidad de Buenos Aires, 2001. 13–59.

González Duro, Enrique. *Historia de la locura en España. Historia de la España sorpren-dente.* Madrid: Temas de Hoy, 1994.

Gorlin, Morris, ed. *Maimonides "On Sexual Intercourse." Fi 'l-jima.* Brooklyn: Rambash, 1961.

Gottfried, Robert Steven. *The Black Death: Natural and Human Disaster in Medieval Europe.* New York: Collier Macmillan, 1983.

———. *Doctors and Medicine in Medieval England, 1340–1530.* Princeton, N.J.: Princeton University Press, 1986.

Gracia, Jorge E. J., ed. *Com usar bé de beure e menjar: normes morals contingudes en el "Terç del Crestià" per Francesc Eiximenis.* Barcelona: Curial, 1977.

Gracia Guillén, Diego. "Judaism, Medicine, and the Inquisitorial Mind in 16th-Century Spain." In *The Spanish Inquisition and the Inquisitorial Mind,* ed. Ángel Alcalá. Boul-der, Colo.: Social Science Monographs, 1987. 375–400.

Grafton, Anthony, April Shelford, and Nancy G. Siraisi. *New Worlds, Ancient Texts: The Power of Tradition and the Shock of Discovery.* Cambridge: Harvard University Press, 1992.

Grafton, Anthony, and Nancy G. Siraisi. *Natural Particulars: Nature and the Disciplines in Renaissance Europe.* Dibner Institute Studies in the History of Science and Tech-nology. Cambridge, Mass.: MIT Press, 1999.

Granjel, Luis S. *Bibliografía histórica de la medicina española.* Salamanca: Universidad de Salamanca, 1965.

———. *Boticarios en el escenario de la literatura picaresca.* Salamanca: Universidad de Salamanca, 1971.

———. *Los discursos medicinales de Juan Méndez Nieto.* Salamanca: Real Academia de Medicina de Salamanca, 1978.

———. *La doctrina antropológico-médica de Miguel Sabuco.* Salamanca: Universidad de Salamanca, 1956.

———, ed. *E. J. Enríquez, retrato del perfecto médico (1595).* Salamanca: Universidad de Salamanca, 1980.

———. *El ejercicio de la medicina en la sociedad española del siglo XVII. Discurso pronun-ciado en la solemme apertura del curso académico 1971–1972.* Salamanca: Universi-dad de Salamanca, 1971.

———. "La figura del médico en el escenario de la literatura picaresca." In *Capítulos de la medicina española.* Salamanca: Universidad de Salamanca, 1971. 225–55.

———, ed. *Francisco López de Villalobos: sumario de la medicina.* Salamanca: Consejo Social, Universidad de Salamanca, 1998.

———. *Historia política de la medicina española.* Salamanca: Instituto de Historia de la Medicina Española, Universidad de Salamanca; Real Academia de Medicina de Salamanca, 1985.

———. *Historia y medicina en España: homenaje al profesor Luis S. Granjel.* Valladolid: Junta de Castilla y León Consejería de Cultura y Turismo, 1994.

——. "La medicina europea de 1498." In *Francisco López de Villalobos: sumario de la medicina*, ed. Luis S. Granjel. Salamanca: Consejo Social, Universidad de Salamanca, 1998. 13–16.

——. "Traumatología española renacentista." *Luis Mercado: instituciones para el aprouechamiento y examen de los algebristas (1599)*. Salamanca: n.p., 1977.

——. *La vida y obra de López de Villalobos*. Salamanca: Universidad de Salamanca, 1979.

Granjel, Luis S., and María Teresa Santander. *Bibliografía española de historia de la medicina*. Publicaciones del Seminario de Historia de la Medicina de la Universidad de Salamanca. Serie B, Repertorios Biobibliográficos, Vol. 1. Salamanca: Seminario de Historia de la Medicina, 1957.

Granjel, Mercedes. "El licenciado López de Villalobos." In *Francisco López de Villalobos: sumario de la medicina*, ed. Luis S. Granjel. Salamanca: Consejo Social, Universidad de Salamanca, 1998. 17–35.

Green, Monica H. "Books as a Source of Medical Education for Women in the Middle Ages." *Dynamis* 20 (2000): 331–69.

——. "From 'Diseases of Women' to 'Secrets of Women': The Transformation of Gynecological Literature in the Later Middle Ages." *Journal of Medieval and Early Modern Studies* 30, 1 (2000): 5–39.

Grell, Ole Peter, Andrew Cunningham, and Jon Arrizabalaga, eds. *Health Care and Poor Relief in Counter-Reformation Europe*. New York: Routledge, 1999.

Hahn, Robert A. *Sickness and Healing: An Anthropological Perspective*. New Haven, Conn.: Yale University Press, 1995.

Hahn, Robert A., and Arthur Kleinman. "Belief as Pathogen, Belief as Medicine: 'Voodoo Death' and the 'Placebo Phenomenon' in Anthropological Perspective." *Medical Anthropology Quarterly* 14, 4 (1983): 3 ff.

Hall, Thomas S. "Life, Death and the Radical Moisture: A Study of Thematic Pattern in Medieval Medical Theory." *Clio Medica* 6 (1971): 3–23.

Hankinson, Robert James. "The Growth of Medical Empiricism." In *Knowledge and the Scholarly Medical Traditions*, ed. Don Bates. New York: Cambridge University Press, 1995. 60–83.

Hernández Alcántara, Antonio. *Estudio histórico de la obra toco-ginecológica y pediátrica de Damián Carbón*. Salamanca: Universidad de Salamanca, 1957.

Hernández Briz, Baltasar. Introducción. *Libro del régimen de la salud y de la esterilidad de los hombres y mujeres, y de las enfermedades de los niños, y otras cosas utilísimas*. Madrid: Real Academia Nacional de Medicina, 1923. 9–14.

Herrera, María Teresa. *Diccionario español de textos médicos antiguos*. Madrid: Arco, 1996.

——."La lengua del texto." In *Francisco López de Villalobos: sumario de la medicina*, ed. Luis S. Granjel. Salamanca: Consejo Social, Universidad de Salamanca, 1998. 155–62.

Huguet-Termes, Teresa. "Islamic Pharmacology and Pharmacy in the Latin West: An Approach to Early Pharmacopoeias." *European Review* 16, 2 (2008): 229–39.

———. "New World Materia Medica in Spanish Renaissance Medicine: From Scholarly Reception to Practical Impact." *Medical History* 45 (2001): 359–76.

Hunt, Tony. *Popular Medicine in Thirteenth-Century England: Introduction and Texts.* Cambridge, Mass.: D.S. Brewer, 1990.

Iglesias, Marcos A. "Dr. Diego Alvarez Chanca: Physician, Historian, Merchant." *Scalpel & Tongs* 37 (1993): 2–5.

Jacquart, Danielle. *La médecine médiévale dans le cadre parisien.* Paris: Fayard, 1998.

———. «L'oeuvre de Jean de Saint-Amand et les méthodes d'enseignement à la faculté de médecine de Paris á la fin du XIIIe siècle.» In *Manuels, programmes de cours et techniques d'enseignement dans les universités médiévales*, ed. Jacqueline Hamesse. Louvain-la-Neuve: Institut d'Études Médiévales de l'Université Catholique de Louvain, 1994. 257–75.

———. "Le sens donné par Constantin l'Africain à son oeuvre: Les chapitres introductifs en arabe et en latin." In *Constantine the African and Ali Ibn Al-Abbas Al-Magusi: The Pantegni and Related Texts*, ed. Danielle Jacquart and Charles Burnett. Vol. 10. Leiden: Brill, 1994. 71–89.

———. "Theory, Everyday Practice, and Three Fifteenth-Century Physicians." *Osiris* 6 (1990): 140–60.

Jacquart, Danielle, and Claude Alexandre Thomasset. *Sexuality and Medicine in the Middle Ages.* Princeton, N.J.: Princeton University Press, 1988.

Jarcho, Saul. "Galen's Six Non-Naturals: A Bibliographic Note and Translation." *Bulletin of the History of Medicine* 44 (1970): 372–77.

Jones, Claire. "Formula and Formulation: 'Efficacy Phrases' in Medieval English Medical Manuscripts." *Neuphilologische Mitteilungen* (1998): 109–209.

Jones, Peter Murray. "John of Argerne and the Mediterranean Tradition of Scholastic Surgery." In *Practical Medicine from Salerno to the Black Death*, ed. Luis García-Ballester. New York: Cambridge University Press, 1994. 289–321.

Jordan, Mark D. "The Construction of a Philosophical Medicine." *Osiris* 6 (1990): 42–61.

———. "The Disappearance of Galen in Thirteenth-Century Philosophy and Theology." In *Mensch und Natur im Mittelalter*, ed. Albert Zimmermann and Andreas Speer. Berlin: de Gruyter, 1992. 703–13.

Keiser, George R. "Two Medieval Plague Treatises and their Afterlife in Early Modern England." *Journal of the History of Medicine and Allied Sciences* 58, 3 (2003): 292–324.

Kibre, Pearl. "The Faculty of Medicine at Paris, Charlatanism, and Unlicensed Medical Practices in the Later Middle Ages." *Bulletin of the History of Medicine* 27 (1953): 1–20.

Klebs, A. C. "A Catalan Plague Tract of April 24, 1348 by Jacme d'Agramont." In *Rapport du 6e Congrés International d'Histoire de la Médicine*. Anvers: n.p., 1929. 229–32.

———. "Jacme d'Agramont, Johan Jacme metge del rey d'Aragó y Joannes Jacobi de Montpellier (siglo XIV)." *El Siglo Médico* 96, 4259 (1934): 130–31.

Kleinman, Arthur. "Concepts and a Model for the Comparison of Medical Systems as Cultural Systems." *Social Science and Medicine* 12B (1978): 85–93.

———. *The Illness Narratives: Suffering, Healing, and the Human Condition*. New York: Basic Books, 1988.

Kleinman, Arthur, and Lilias H. Sung. "Why Do Indigenous Practitioners Successfully Heal?" *Social Science and Medicine* 13B (1997): 7–26.

Kottek, Samuel S., and Luis García-Ballester. *Medicine and Medical Ethics in Medieval and Early Modern Spain: An Intercultural Approach*. Jerusalem: Hebrew University Magnes Press, 1996.

Lanning, John Tate. *The Royal Protomedicato: The Regulation of the Medical Professions in the Spanish Empire*. Durham, N.C.: Duke University Press, 1985.

Latour, Bruno. *Aramis, or the Love of Technology*. Cambridge, Mass.: Harvard University Press, 1996.

Lewis, Tania. "Seeking Health Information on the Internet: Lifestyle Choice or Bad Attack of Cyberchondria?" *Media, Culture and Society* 28, 4 (2006): 521–39.

Linden, David E. J. "Gabriele Zaerbi's *De cautelis medicorum* and the Tradition of Medical Prudence." *Bulletin of the History of Medicine* 73, 1 (1999): 1937.

López Piñero, José María. *Bibliografía médica hispánica (1475–1950)*. Vol. 1, *1475–1660, libros folletos*. Valencia: n.p., 1987.

———. "La disección y el saber anatómico en la España de la primera mitad del siglo XVI." *Cuadernos de la Historia de la Medicina Española* (1974): 51–110.

———. *Los impresos científicos españoles de los siglos XV y XVI (inventario, bibliometría y thesaurus)*. 4 vols. Valencia: Universidad de Valencia, 1981[–1986].

López Piñero, José María, and María Luz López Terrada. *La influencia española en la introducción en Europa de las plantas americanas (1493–1623)*. Cuadernos Valencianos de Historia de la Medicina y de la Ciencia. Serie A. Monografías. Vol. 53. Valencia: Instituto de Estudios Documentales e Históricos sobre la Ciencia, Universitat de València C.S.I.C, 1997.

López Terrada, María Luz. "Health Care and Poor Relief in the Crown of Aragon." In *Health Care and Poor Relief in Counter-Reformation Europe*, ed. Ole Peter Grell, Andrew Cunningham and Jon Arrizabalaga. New York: Routledge, 1999. 177–200.

López-Ríos Fernández, Fernando. In *Historia médica de las navegaciones colombinas: 1492–1504*. Acta Histórico-Médica Vallisoletana 41. Monografías. Valladolid: Secretariado de Publicaciones, Universidad de Valladolid, 1993.

Machor, James. "The Object of Interpretation and Interpretive Change." *Modern Language Notes* 113, 5 (1998): 1126–50.

Machor, James L., and Philip Goldstein. *Reception Study: From Literary Theory to Cultural Studies*. New York: Routledge, 2001.

———. "Theoretical Accounts of Reception." In *Reception Study: From Literary Theory to Cultural Studies*, ed. James L. Machor and Philip Goldstein. New York: Routledge, 2001. 1–6.

Maclean, Ian. *Logic, Signs and Nature in the Renaissance*. Cambridge: Cambridge University Press, 2002.

Maroto, M. R. "Oral Ulcers of Infants in 16th-Century Spanish Medical Texts." *Journal of the History of Dentistry* 44, 2 (1996): 61–62.

Marquilhas, Rita. "Orientación mágica del texto escrito." In *Escribir y leer en el siglo de Cervantes*, ed. Antonio Castillo. Barcelona: Gedisa, 1999. 111–28.

Marshall, Louise. "Manipulating the Sacred: Image and Plague in Renaissance Italy." *Renaissance Quarterly* 47, 3 (1994): 485–532.

Mattingly, Cheryl. *Healing Dramas and Clinical Plots: The Narrative Structure of Experience*. Cambridge: Cambridge University Press, 1998.

Mattingly, Cheryl, and Linda C. Garro, eds. *Narrative and the Cultural Construction of Illness and Healing*. Berkeley: University of California Press, 2000.

Martín Ferreira, Ana Isabel. *El humanismo médico en la Universidad de Alcalá (siglo XVI)*. Alcalá: Universidad de Alcalá, 1995.

McConchie, R. W. *Lexicography and Physicke: The Record of Sixteenth-Century English Medical Terminology*. Oxford Studies in Lexicography and Lexicology. New York: Clarendon; Oxford University Press, 1997.

McVaugh, Michael R. "Arnald of Villanova's *Regimen almarie (Regimen castra sequentium)* and Medieval Military Medicine." *Viator* 23 (1992): 201–13.

———. "Bedside Manners in the Middle Ages." *Bulletin of the History of Medicine* 72, 2 (1997): 201–23.

———. "The Development of Medieval Pharmaceutical Theory." *Arnaldi de Villanova Opera Medica Omnia: Aphoismi de Gradibus*. Ed. Michael R. McVaugh. Vol. 2. Granada-Barcelona: Seminarium Historiae Medicae Granatensis, 1975. 1–136.

———. Introduction. *Tractatus de intentione medicorum*. Ed. Michael R. McVaugh. Vol. V.1. Arnaldi de Villanova Opera Medica Omnia. Barcelona: Seminarium Historiae Scientiae Cantabricense, 2000. 129–206.

———. *Medicine Before the Plague: Practitioners and Their Patients in the Crown of Aragon, 1285–1345*. Cambridge History of Medicine. Cambridge: Cambridge University Press, 1993.

———. "The Nature and Limits of Medical Certitude at Early 14th-Century Montpellier." *Osiris: A Research Journal Devoted to the History of Science and Its Cultural Influences* 6 (1990): 62–84.

———. "Royal Surgeons and the Value of Medical Learning: The Crown of Aragon, 1300–1350." In *Practical Medicine from Salerno to the Black Death*, ed. Luis García-Ballester. New York: Cambridge University Press, 1994. 211–36.

———. "Surgical Education in the Middle Ages." *Dynamis* 20 (2000): 283–304.

Melchor Galán, Antonio Marcelina. "Estudio crítico y analítico sobre la obra urologíca de Julián Gutiérrez de Toledo, x. XV–XVI." Madrid: Universidad Complutense de Madrid, 2001.

Mendes Drumond Braga, Isabel M. R. "Poor Relief in Counter-Reformation Portugal: The Case of the Misericórdias." In *Health Care and Poor Relief in Counter-Reformation Europe*, ed. Ole Peter Grell, Andrew Cunningham, and Jon Arrizabalaga. New York: Routledge, 1999. 201–14.

Milwright, Marcus. "The Balsam of Matariyya: An Exploration of a Medieval Panacea." *Bulletin of the School of Oriental and African Studies* 66, 2 (2003): 193–209.

Moliné y Brasés, Ernest. "Receptari de Micer Johan." *Boletín de la Real Academia de Buenas Letras de Barcelona* 7 (1913): 321–36.

Montero Cartelle, E. "El humanismo médico en el Renacimiento castellano (s. XVI)." In *Ciencia, medicina, y sociedad en el Renacimiento castellano*. Valladolid: Universidad de Valladolid, 1989. 19–49.

———. "Sobre el origen árabe del *Speculum al foderi* catalán y su relación con el *Liber minor de coito* salernitano." *Anuari de Filologia* 14 (1991): 71–80.

Moral de Calatrava, Paloma. "El arte de las comadres en los tratados médicos bajomedievales (ss. XIII–XVI)." Universidad de Murcia, 2003.

Niebyl, Peter H. "The Non-Naturals." *Bulletin of the History of Medicine* 45 (1971): 486–92.

Numbers, Ronald L. *Medicine in the New World: New Spain, New France, and New England*. Knoxville: University of Tennessee Press, 1987.

Nutton, Vivian. "The Seeds of Disease: An Explanation of Contagion and Infection from the Greeks to the Renaissance." *Medical History* 27 (1983): 1–34.

O'Boyle, Cornelius. *The Art of Medicine: Medical Teaching at the University of Paris, 1250–1400*. Leiden: Brill, 1998.

———. "Gesturing in the Early Universities." *Dynamis* 20 (2000): 249–81.

———. "Learning Medieval Medicine: The Boundaries of University Teaching." *Dynamis* 20 (2000): 17–30.

Olsam, Lea T. "Charms and Prayers in Medieval Medical Theory and Practice." *Social History of Medicine* 16, 3 (2003): 343–66.

Owens, Joseph. "Aristotelian Ethics, Medicine, and the Changing Nature of Man." In *Philosophical Medical Ethics: Its Nature and Significance, Proceedings*, ed. Stuart F Spicker and H. Tristram Engelhardt. Boston: D. Reide, 1977. 127–42.

Pagel, J. L. *Die Chirurgie des Heinrich von Mondeville*. Berlin, [n.p.], 1892.

Pahta, Pèaivi, and Irma Taavitsainen. «Vernacularisation of Scientific and Medical Writing in Its Sociohistorical Context.» In *Medical and Scientific Writing in Late Medieval English*, ed. Irma Taavitsainen and Pèaivi Pahta. Cambridge: Cambridge University Press, 2004. 1–22.

Palmero J. R. "Nephrology from the Middle Ages to Humanism: The Italian Influence in Spain (12th–16th Centuries)." *American Journal of Nephrology* 14, 4–6: 290–94.

Paniagua, J. A., and Luis García-Ballester. "El regimen santitatis ad regem Aragonum regimen sanitatis ad regem Aragonum." In *El regimen santitatis ad regem Aragonum regimen sanitatis ad regem Aragonum*, ed. Luis García-Ballester and Michael R. McVaugh. Arnaldi de Villanova Opera Medica Omnia. Barcelona: Seminarium Historiae Scientiae Barchinone, 1996. 863–85.

Park, Katharine. "The Criminal and the Saintly Body: Autopsy and Dissection in Renaissance Italy." *Renaissance Quarterly* 4, 1 (1994): 1–33.

Pastor Frechoso, Félix Francisco. *Boticas, boticarios y materia médica en Valladolid (siglos XVI y SVII)*. Salamanca: Junta de Castilla y León, 1993.

Pérez Ibáñez, María Jesus. *El humanismo médico del siglo XVI en la Universidad de Salamanca*. Valladolid: Universidad de Valladolid, 1998.

Pollock, Donald. "Physician Autobiography: Narrative and the Social History of Medicine." In *Narrative and the Cultural Construction of Illness and Healing*, ed. Cheryl Mattingly and Linda C. Garro. Berkeley: University of California Press, 2000. 108–27.

Pormann, Peter E. "The Physician and the Other: Images of the Charlatan in Medieval Islam." *Bulletin of the History of Medicine* 79, 2 (2005): 189–227.

Puerto, Javier. *La leyenda verde: naturaleza, sanidad y ciencia en la corte de Felipe II (1527–1598)*. Salamanca: Junta de Castilla y León, 2003.

Rather, L. J. "The 'Six Things Non-Natural': A Note on the Origins and Fate of a Doctrine and a Phrase." *Clio Medica* 3 (1968): 337–47.

Redondo, Augustin, ed. *Le corps comme métaphore dans l'Espagne des XVI et XVII siècles: du corps métaphorique aux métaphores corporelles*. Paris: Sorbonne, 1992.

Rey Bueno, María del Mar, and María Esther Alegre Pérez. «La ordenación normativa de la asistencia sanitaria en la corte de los Habsburgos españoles (1515–1700)." *Dynamis* 18 (1998): 341–75.

Riera Palmero, Juan. *Historia y medicina en España: homenaje al Profesor Luis S. Granjel*. Estudios de Historia de la Ciencia y de la Técnica 10. Valladolid: Junta de Castilla y León, Consejería de Cultura y Turismo, 1994.

———. "Juan de Aviñón y su *Sevillana medicina*." *Archivo Iberoamericano de Historia de la Medicina* 14 (1962): 253–60.

———, ed. *La medicina en el descubrimiento*. Valladolid: Universidad de Valladolid, 1991.

———. "La medicina precolombina." In *La medicina en el descubrimiento*, ed. Juan Riera Palmero. Valladolid: Universidad de Valladolid, 1991. 11–28.

———. *Vida y obra de Luis Mercado*. Salamanca: Universidad de Salamanca, 1968.

Rojo Vega, Anastasio. *Ciencia y cultura en Valladolid. Estudio de las bibliotecas privadas de los siglos XVI y XVII*. Valladolid: Universidad de Valladolid, 1985.

———. *Enfermos y sanadores en la Castilla del siglo XVI*. Serie Historia y Sociedad 34. Valladolid: Secretariado de Publicaciones, Universidad de Valladolid, 1993.

Rosner, Fred. *Sex Ethics in the Writings of Moses Maimonides*. New York: Bloch, 1974.

Salmón, Fernando. *Medical Classroom Practice: Petrus Hispanus' Questions of "Isagoge, tegni, regimen acutorum" and "Prognostica" (c. 1245–50).* Cambridge: Cambridge Wellcome Unit for the History of Medicine; CSIC, Department of History of Science, 1998.

———. "La medicina y las traducciones toledanas del siglo XII." In *Historia de la ciencia y de la técnica en la Corona de Castilla,* ed. Luis García-Ballester. Vol. 1. Salamanca: Junta de Castilla y León, 2002. 631–46.

———. "Technologies of Authority in the Medical Classroom in the Thirteenth and Fourteenth Centuries." *Dynamis* 20 (2000): 135–57.

Sánchez Capelot, Francisco. *La obra quirúrgica de Francisco Díaz.* Salamanca: Universidad de Salamanca, 1959.

Schleiner, Winfried. *Medical Ethics in the Renaissance.* Washington, D.C.: Georgetown University Press, 1995.

Schmitt, C. B. "Aristotle Among the Physicians." In *Medical Renaissance of the Sixteenth Century,* ed. Andres Wear, Roger French, and I. M. Lonie. Cambridge: Cambridge University Press, 1985. 1–15.

Segura, Jack. "Some Thoughts on the Spanish Language in Medicine." In *Translation and Medicine,* ed. Henry Fischbach. Amsterdam: Benjamins, 1998. 37–48.

Seijo Alonso, Francisco G. *Curanderismo y medicina popular en el País Valenciano.* Publicaciones de Ediciones Biblioteca Alicantina III, Etnografía y Folklore 9. Alicante: Biblioteca Alicantina, 1974.

Seligman, Katherine. "Imaginary Maladies Online: Internet Spreads 'Cyberchondria.'" *San Francisco Chronicle,* February 15, 2004: E-1.

Ser Quijano, Gregorio del, and Luis E. Rodríguez-San Pedro, eds. *Discursos medicinales de Juan Méndez Nieto.* Salamanca: Universidad de Salamanca, 1989.

Settipane, Guy A. *Columbus and the New World: Medical Implications.* Providence, R.I.: OceanSide Publications, 1995.

Sigerist, Henry. "Bedside Manners in the Middle Ages: The Treatise *De cautelis medicorum* Attributed to Arnald of Villanova." In *Henry E. Sigerist on the History of Medicine.* Ed. Felix Martí-Ibáñez. New York: MD Publications, 1960. 131–40.

Siraisi, Nancy G. *Avicenna in Renaissance Italy: The Canon and Medical Teaching in Italian Universities After 1500.* Princeton, N.J.: Princeton University Press, 1987.

———. "The Changing Fortunes of a Traditional Text: Goals and Strategies in Sixteenth-Century Latin Editions of the *Canon* of Avicenna." In *The Medical Renaissance of the Sixteenth Century,* ed. Andres Wear, Roger French, and I. M. Lonie. Cambridge: Cambridge University Press, 1985. 16–41.

———. "Girolamo Cardano and the Art of Medical Narrative." *Journal of the History of Ideas* 52, 4 (1991): 581–602.

———. "How to Write a Latin Book on Surgery: Organizing Principles and Authorial Devices in Guglielmo da Saliceto and Dino del Garbo." In *Practical Medicine from Salerno to the Black Death,* ed. Luis García-Ballester, Roger French, Jon

Arrizabalaga, andAndrew Cunningham. New York: Cambridge University Press, 1994. 88–109.

———. "Medicine and the Renaissance World of Learning." *Bulletin of the History of Medicine* 78 (2004): 1–36.

———. *Medieval and Early Renaissance Medicine: An Introduction to Knowledge and Practice*. Chicago: University of Chicago Press, 1990.

———. "Oratory and Rhetoric in Renaissance Medicine." *Journal of the History of Ideas* 65, 2 (2004): 191–211.

———. "Some Current Trends in the Study of Renaissance Medicine." *Renaissance Quarterly* 37, 4 (1984): 585–600.

———. "Taddeo Alderotti and Bartolomeo da Varignana on the Nature of Medical Learning." *Isis* 68, 1 (1977): 27–39.

Solomon, Michael. "Fictions of Infection: Diseasing the Sexual Other in Francesc Eiximenis's *Lo Llibre de les Dones*." In *Queer Iberia: Sexualities, Cultures, and Crossings from the Middle Ages to the Renaissance*, ed. Josiah Blackmore and Gregory S. Hutcheson. Durham, N.C.: Duke University Press, 1999. 277–90.

———. *The Literature of Misogyny in Medieval Spain: The "Arcipreste de Talavera" and the "Spill"*. Cambridge Studies in Latin American and Iberian Literature 10. Cambridge: Cambridge University Press, 1997.

———. "The Sickly Reader and the Vernacular Text in Late Medieval and Early Modern Spain." In *Two Generations: A Tribute to Lloyd A. Kasten*, ed. Francisco Gago Jover. New York: Hispanic Seminary of Medieval Studies, 2002. 217–29.

———. "Spectacles of Erudition: Physicians and Vernacular Medical Writing in Early Modern Spain," *Digital Proceedings of the Lawrence J. Schoenberg Symposium on Manuscript Studies in the Digital Age*: Vol. 1: Iss. 1, Article 6. http://repository.upenn.edu/ljsproceedings/vol1/iss1/6

———. "Towards a Definition of the Popular Medical Treatise in Late Medieval and Early Modern Spain." *Textos medievales y renacentistas: jornadas del Seminario Internacional en Homenaje a la Profesora María Teresa Herrera*, ed. María Teresa Navarro et al. New York: Hispanic Seminary of Medieval Studies, 2002. 183–93.

———. "Women Healers and the Power to Disease in Late Medieval Spain." In *Women Healers and Physicians: Climbing a Long Hill*, ed. Lillian R. Furst. Lexington: University Press of Kentucky, 1997. 79–92.

Sowadsky, Rick. *Are You a "Worried Well" Person?* 1999. http://www.thebody.com/sowadsky/worried.html.

Stannard, Jerry. *Herbs and Herbalism in the Middle Ages and Renaissance*. Ed. Katherine E. Stannard and Richard Kay. Aldershot: Ashgate Variorum, 1999.

———. *Pristina medicamenta: Ancient and Medieval Medical Botany*. Ed. Katherine E. Stannard and Richard Kay. Aldershot: Ashgate Variorum, 1999.

Struever, Nancy. "Petrarch's Invective *Contra medicum*: An Early Confrontation of Rhetoric and Medicine." *MLN* 108, 4 (1993): 659–79.

Taavitsainen, Irma, and Pèaivi Pahta. *Medical and Scientific Writing in Late Medieval English.* Studies in English Language. Cambridge: Cambridge University Press, 2004.

Taussig, Michael. "Reification and the Consciousness of the Patient." *Social Science and Medicine* 14B (1980): 3–13.

Temkin, Owsei. "An Historical Analysis of the Concept of Infection." In *The Double Face of Janus and Other Essays in the History of Medicine.* Baltimore: Johns Hopkins University Press, 1977. 456–71.

Torres, Esteban. *Sobre lengua y literatura en el pensamiento científico español de la segunda mitad del siglo XVI.* Sevilla: Servicio de Publicaciones de la Universidad, 1984.

Torres-Gómez, J. M. "Dr. Diego Alvarez Chanca, Introducer of Universal Medicine in America." *Boletín Asociación Médica de Puerto Rico* 84, 1 (1992): 2–3.

Trias Teixidor, Ana. "Sobre un pretendido *Segon libre del Regiment de Sanitat,* atribuido a Arnau de Vilanova." *Dynamis* 3 (1983): 281–87.

Valley, Paul. "New Disorder, Cyberchondria, Sweeps the Internet." *New Zealand Herald,* April 28, 2001, sec. Technology. http://www.nzherald.co.nz/category/story.cfm?c_id=55&objectid=185422.

van der Geest, Sjaak, and Susan Reynolds Whyte. «The Charm of Medicines: Metaphors and Metonyms.» *Medical Anthropology Quarterly* 3, 4 (1989): 345–67.

van der Geest, Sjaak, Susan Reynolds Whyte, and Anita Hardon. "The Anthropology of Pharmaceuticals: A Biographical Approach." *Annual Review of Anthropology* 25 (1996): 153–78.

Vázquez Medina, Antonio José. "Sevillana cirugía (1550–1650): escuelas quirúrgicas en Sevilla siglo XVI." Universidad de Sevilla, 2001.

Vernet, André. "Les traductions latines d'oeuvres en langues vernaculaires au moyen âge." In *Traduction et traducteurs au moyen âge: Actes du Colloque International du CNRS,* ed. Geneviève Contamine. Paris: Institut de Recherche et d'Histoire des Textes, 1989. 225–2412.

Vinyoles, Teresa María. Prólogo. *Flor del tesoro de la belleza de Manuel Dies de Calatayud.* Ed. José J. Olañeta. Barcelona: Archivo Tradiciones Populares, 1981. 3–11.

Viñao Frago, Antonio. "Alfabetización y primeras letras (siglos XVI–XVII)." In *Escribir y leer en el siglo de Cervantes,* ed. Antonio Castillo. Barcelona: Gedisa, 1999. 39–84.

Virseda Rodríguez, J. A. "Julian Gutierrez de Toledo and His Book *Cure of the Stone and Pain in the Loin and/or Renal Colic* in 1498." *Actas Urológicas Españolas* 18, 3 (1994): 165–77.

Voigts, Linda Ehrsarn. "What's the Word? Bilingualism in Late-Medieval England." *Speculum* 71, 4 (1996): 813–26.

Wallis, Faith. "The Experience of the Book: Manuscripts, Texts, and the Role of Epistemology in Early Medieval Medicine." In *Knowledge and the Scholarly Medical Traditions,* ed. Don Bates. New York: Cambridge University Press, 1995. 101–26.

————. "Inventing Diagnosis: Theophilus' *De urinis* in the Classrom." *Dynamis* 20 (2000): 31–73.

Wear, Andrew. "Epistemology and Learned Medicine in Early Modern England." In *Knowledge and the Scholarly Medical Traditions*, ed. Don Bates. New York: Cambridge University Press, 1995. 151–74.

————. *Knowledge and Practice in English Medicine, 1550–1680*. Cambridge: Cambridge University Press, 2000.

"Worried Well Hell Is No Place to Be." The Body: Ask the Experts About Safe Sex and HIV Prevention, 2006. http://www.thebody.com/Forums/AIDS/SafeSex/Archive/Thanks/Q178358.html

Ziegler, Joseph. *Medicine and Religion c. 1300: The Case of Arnau de Vilanova*. Oxford: Clarendon, 1998.

————. "Ut Dicunt Medici: Medical Knowledge and Theological Debates in the Second Half of the Thirteenth Century." *Bulletin of the History of Medicine* 73, 2 (1999): 208–37.

INDEX

ACKNOWLEDGMENTS

Medieval physicians and medical theorists suspected that writing could prove pathological and could be treated with diet, drugs, and following the advice of competent and learned healers. While researching and writing this book, I have depended greatly on the wisdom, kindness, and generosity of many highly knowledgeable professionals. My manuscript would have never made it into print without Marina and Kevin Brownlee's ongoing and enthusiastic support. I owe an extraordinary debt to María Teresa Herrera for her encouragement and for generously making her sizable personal library available to me, thus allowing me to consult difficult to find editions and facsimiles of vernacular medical treatises. I thank Jean Dangler for her friendship and for her reading of an early draft of this manuscript. Scott Williams and David Rue Johnson, physicians and public health specialists, helped me sort out the possible physiological and anatomical basis for medieval and early modern ideas about the body and its functions. A special word of thanks is in order for John Nitti, the former director of the Hispanic Seminary of Medieval Studies, and John O'Neill, the current director, for their longstanding willingness to publish electronic editions of medieval and early modern vernacular medical works. I owe a debt to Jerry Singerman, senior humanities editor at the University of Pennsylvania Press, for his patience, guidance, and productive critical intervention. Likewise, I thank Luke Demaitre and Meg Greer, readers for Penn Press, who generously offered many valuable suggestions for improving the book. There are many medievalist and early modern specialists, who—whether they are aware of it or not—have helped me in this endeavor. I thank Wolfram Aichinger, Enrica Ardemagni, Catherine Brown, Montserrat Cabré, Ivy Corfis, John Dagenais, Friederike Hassauer, Mary Jane Kelly, Luce López Baralt, Nancy Marino, María Rosa Menocal, Nieves Sánchez, and Dayle Seidenspinner-Núñez. I am also grateful for the extraordinary community of medieval scholars at the University of Pennsylvania, including Ann Matter, Rita Copeland, Robert Maxwell, Emma Dillon, Victoria Kirkham, and David Wallace.

Unfortunately, I have found no medieval or early modern cures for the treatment of dyslexia. I have, therefore, depended greatly on the editorial eyes of Jennifer van Frank, Rachel Burk, Tania Gentic, Michael Cornett, and Linda Grabner. Sixteenth-century medical writers often pointed to good health and good friends as the two most important ingredients for a happy life. I have been blessed over the years with wonderful colleagues who have not only endured my enthusiasm for the modern applicability of medieval non-natural hygiene, but who also have helped me through many difficult moments in my career. I thank Carlos Alonso, José Luis Boigues, Román de la Campa, Toni Esposito, Hazel Gold, Barbara Fuchs, Reinaldo Laddaga, Yolanda Martínez de San Miguel, Sara Nadal, Dierdra Reber, José Regueiro, Karen Stolley, and Don Tuten. Finally, I thank Juan Carlos Temprano, my longstanding mentor and friend.